AF412550

Community Power and Empowerment

BRIAN D. CHRISTENS

OXFORD
UNIVERSITY PRESS

OXFORD

UNIVERSITY PRESS

Oxford University Press is a department of the University of Oxford. It furthers
the University's objective of excellence in research, scholarship, and education
by publishing worldwide. Oxford is a registered trade mark of Oxford University
Press in the UK and certain other countries.

Published in the United States of America by Oxford University Press
198 Madison Avenue, New York, NY 10016, United States of America.

© Oxford University Press 2019

CIP data is on file at the Library of Congress
ISBN 978–0–19–060558–2

1 3 5 7 9 8 6 4 2

Printed by Webcom Inc., Canada

CONTENTS

SERIES FOREWORD

The Society for Community Research and Action (SCRA), Division 27 of the American Psychological Association, is an international and interdisciplinary organization that supports the development of theory, research, and social action. Members share a common interest in promoting empowerment, health, and well-being, with special attention to multiple levels of analysis, including the individual, group, organizational, community, cultural, and societal levels. Division members focus on an array of pressing social issues within national and global contexts (such as violence, mental health, HIV/AIDS, poverty, racism) and have developed, using a continuum of approaches from prevention to intervention to social change, effective social interventions to address seemingly intractable issues. These approaches to change involve diverse strategies, including, for example, advocacy, citizen participation, collaboration, community organizing, economic development, prevention education, self-help/mutual help, sociopolitical development, social movements, and policy change. These change strategies typically share the goal of challenging and altering underlying power structures in the pursuit of social justice and community and individual well-being.

This book series, Advances in Community Psychology, is sponsored by the SCRA and aims to aid in the dissemination of theory, research, and social action as developed by SCRA members as well as nonmembers working in allied disciplines. The overarching mission of the series is to create a publication venue that (a) highlights the contributions of the fields of community psychology and, more generally, community action, research, and practice; (b) integrates current knowledge regarding pressing topics and priorities for the field; and (c) offers the foundations for future directions.

This volume in the series, *Community Power and Empowerment*, provides a comprehensive and in-depth examination of empowerment. Brian Christens addresses both conceptual and methodological issues, leaving the reader with an appreciation for the complexity of power and empowerment—in research and in action.

Christens begins with power and the pursuit of social justice. In doing so, Christens anchors the investigation of empowerment in the realities of structural power and the value of empowering processes to fundamentally change power structures. He begins with a historical overview of the study of power and empowerment, orienting the reader to the constructs and their interplay. Consistent with the growing body of literature on empowerment, Christens takes an ecological approach explicating empowerment as a multilevel construct and giving each level of analysis ample attention and review: psychological, organizational, and community. Importantly, Christens not only reviews the vast literature on empowerment, but also provides new directions for research and action in this volume.

With attention to community power, Christens offers a new integrative framework for thinking about empowering processes as they manifest at multiple levels. As an extension of this framework, Christens also articulates the multiple pathways by which empowering processes contribute to health and well-being, including participant, ecological, and pluralist pathways. These articulated pathways set an agenda to inform action (i.e., how to think about structuring empowering processes) and also research given that some pathways (i.e., participant) are more intensively studied than others. Finally, Christens directs researchers and practitioners to address critical aspects of design when pursuing empowering processes that increase the chances that empowering processes will actually foster structural change and fundamentally address issues of power. Everyone engaged in community-based research and action, or employing empowerment-based approaches to change, should consider this book required reading.

Nicole E. Allen
Bradley Olson
Series Co-Editors

Community Power and Empowerment is a major contribution to one of the most pressing questions of the day: how to understand, generate, sustain, and use social power to promote social justice. If you are passionate about this goal, I highly recommend this book, but if you are impatient, do not expect quick answers. Instead, be ready for a thoughtful analysis, which is what we need to move fairness forward.

The hallmark of scholarly work is rigor. Rigor cannot be attained without a thorough understanding of the subject matter or without attention to conceptual and methodological detail. Christens excels at both. He demonstrates erudition in the field of empowerment, and he makes sense of the literature in clear interpretive frameworks. He goes beyond a review to offer a fresh view—a view that is integrative, comprehensive, contextual, and practical.

The book helps elucidate the virtues and vices associated with community power and empowerment as *values, processes,* and *outcomes.* The virtue of empowerment as a *value* is that it fosters self-determination, autonomy, and control over one's life. These are necessary but insufficient values, for they address mainly individual well-being. To thrive as individuals, we need to exercise freedom over our environment and over our lives. But, the exclusive pursuit of control leads to a diminished existence, one focused on personal freedom above all else. Human beings cannot flourish without relational and communal values as well. You find relational health in pretty much every list of essential elements of well-being. Communal values such as solidarity, equality, and social justice are not equally popular but nonetheless essential for fulfillment as human beings.

The virtue of empowerment as a value is that it strengthens one pillar of well-being, the individual one. The vice of empowerment is that a single focus on personal control can occlude the value of relational and communal values. The exclusive pursuit of any one value threatens the balance among personal, interpersonal, and collective goods required for the good life and the good society. The French

Revolution espoused values commensurate with this tripartite model: liberty, fraternity, and equality, corresponding to personal, relational, and communal goods, respectively. Too much liberty comes at the expense of equality and fraternity, as recently demonstrated in the tax bill passed by the Trump administration. The legislation extols individual liberty of citizens and corporations at the expense of solidarity and justice. The bill is very empowering for a small segment of the population that admires freedom and ignores fairness.

Christens is careful to pair empowerment with justice, but this is not always the case in the literature. This is one of the reasons why empowerment as a concept has been co-opted by so many corporations and elites. Unless we couple the pursuit of empowerment with the pursuit of fairness, a descent into self-preoccupation is so much more likely, not only for individuals, but also for entire groups. Empowerment risks being misused, as with identity politics, which has the virtue of claiming rights for marginalized groups but can have the vice of ignoring the plight of other groups. We should remember that the pursuit of liberation for all is not a sequential but rather a parallel process. The assumption that we should achieve liberation for my group before I join others in their struggle for emancipation is short-sighted and fragmenting. The struggle for freedom must be inclusive and must blend emancipation with communitarianism. In this book, Christens argues for the intended aims of empowerment to advance liberty, fraternity, and equality.

As a *process*, when properly managed, empowerment builds self-efficacy and engenders a virtuous cycle of action and satisfaction. Moreover, it can lead to buy-in, ownership, and participation. But, this process is not without risks. At times, the health of the process comes at the expense of some healthy outcomes. For example, a process where consensus building is a precondition for action can threaten positive changes. As director of the community psychology program at Wilfrid Laurier University several lifetimes ago, we engaged the graduate students in a process of curriculum revision. The group was so intent on reaching consensus that the process became a talkfest, and people dropped out of it. Process fatigue won the day. The curricular revision did not get done.

Another challenge for empowering processes is sustainability. Some people described the Occupy Movement as having run out of steam. Christens explores the relational dynamics that can lead to ongoing bonds of solidarity and engagement, which leads us to community power. Power is dynamic and must be frequently exercised in order to be sustained.

The *value* of community power is that it furthers democracy. People must exercise voice and choice. But, like empowerment, community power without the tempering value of social justice can lead to nationalism and xenophobia. Many of the people who voted for Trump in the recent election felt tremendous momentum—that their voices would finally be heard. In particular, the "forgotten" white, working class men were engaged through identity politics to help put Trump in office. This emphasized power in the absence of fairness or concerns for social justice.

The *process* of acquiring power can show a group of people what they are capable of, thereby enhancing collective self-efficacy. If the process is inclusive and fair, most participants gain from it. However, if the process becomes just a means to an end, certain groups are bound to suffer. In the 1960s, for instance, many women engaged in active resistance against being relegated to stereotypically feminine roles in the civil rights movement. Empowerment processes should work to prefigure and reinforce the kinds of social relations that participants wish to bring about in their broader societies.

Whereas empowerment runs the risk of descending into individualism, community power threatens individual freedom. This is a most undesirable *outcome*. There are communities where services for women's health are curtailed because the majority think that women should not have the right to decide what is good for them. This is power without fairness.

The virtues and vices of empowerment and community power must be put in the current psychosocial context. People vote primarily based on their emotions, and many people, especially white, working class men, felt threatened during the last election. They did not feel valued in the national discourse, and they felt that they could not add value, either to themselves or to others. In short, they felt like they did not matter, and the allure of power, embodied in a strong leader like Trump, gave expression to their most vengeful feelings. For many, it was their chance to feel power by associating politically with a xenophobic bigot that legitimized their most primitive instincts.

The challenge for advocates of social justice is to make people feel like they matter, not as a means to power, which is what Trump did, but as ends in themselves. The process of gaining power must foreshadow how we want to live together as a community. It should not treat people as means to an end. Social movements of community power for social justice should attend to personal, interpersonal, and communal spaces at the same time. This brilliant book by Christens discusses best practices in light of empirical research and field experience. I can think of nothing better to read now to prepare for the struggle of pairing power with fairness.

Isaac Prilleltensky
University of Miami

Community Power and Empowerment

‖ 1 ‖

Introduction

As societal challenges mount—from environmental degradation to increasing inequality to mass incarceration and concentrations of corporate power—so do the calls for more people to get more deeply engaged in and committed to efforts to make changes at the local, national, and global levels. But, which forms of civic involvement and collective action are most likely to be effective? On the one hand, those who care about social issues and the well-being of their community are exhorted to maintain hope and are often coaxed toward greater involvement with platitudes such as the following: "Never doubt that a small group of thoughtful, committed citizens can change the world; indeed, it's the only thing that ever has."[1] On the other hand, most efforts to change systems are slow, difficult, and full of setbacks, if not outright failures. This reality creates a kind of dissonance that was satirically captured in *The Onion*'s (1999) headline: "Small, Dedicated Group of Concerned Citizens Fails to Change World."

Several branches of social science have sought to generate greater understanding of the ways that people work together to build power and exercise greater control over issues of concern to them. This book examines this existing interdisciplinary work and seeks to simultaneously integrate and advance it. Perhaps the most notable difference between the perspectives put forward in this book and much of the work that has preceded it is the attention to relationships between collective action processes and community power structures. In much of what follows, however, I simply draw together insights generated by others that have either not yet been presented together or have not been presented in as much detail as is included here.

The book therefore aims toward both a contribution to the scholarship of community power and empowerment and the creation of a resource useful for not only students and researchers, but also community leaders, organizers, activists, and practitioners pursuing systemic changes. For more efforts to succeed in making meaningful changes, what is needed is not only more people to become more involved in change efforts, but also continual development of better ways to assess, analyze, compare, design, and support systems change efforts.

On, Wisconsin!

In the winter of 2011, concerns were spreading at the University of Wisconsin (UW) about the possibility of upcoming cuts to the university in the state budget. The 2010 elections had resulted in a sweep of all branches of state government by conservative members of the Republican Party, many of whom had been vocal during their campaigns about the need to drastically reduce public spending. They described the need for budget cuts as a response to challenges posed by the Great Recession that was then wreaking havoc on the US and global economy. The newly elected governor, Scott Walker, had campaigned on a platform of cutting taxes and eliminating government waste. Like some European leaders urging austerity in the face of crisis, he argued that public sector cuts were necessary so that Wisconsin's economy would rebound and pledged that these policies would result in the creation of 250,000 new jobs in the state during his first 4-year term.

In the midst of the uncertainty about funding for higher education, the Teaching Assistants' Association (TAA) at the University of Wisconsin–Madison, a union representing graduate student employees of the university, launched a campaign to raise awareness and encourage continued public investment in education. The UW system had already absorbed substantial cuts in state funding during several of the preceding budget cycles. Handing out cookies and cards with a Valentine's Day theme: "I ♥ UW. Governor Walker, don't break my ♥," the TAA drew attention to concern that cuts would result not only in reduced pay and benefits for university employees (including for the teaching assistants in the TAA), but also in reduced opportunities and greater financial burdens on students through increased tuition and fees or reduced availability of courses and other forms of academic support. The Valentine's Day theme of this campaign is poignant in retrospect for its innocent appeal to the empathy and logic of decision-makers. The organizers of the campaign could not have known that they were about to be in the middle of a heated political battle in which such appeals would be flatly dismissed.

Act 10, the "Budget Repair Bill" was introduced on February 14, 2011. The bill included, but went far beyond, cuts in state funding for higher education. Through a long list of policy changes, it sought to fundamentally alter not only the ways that most public employees were compensated and evaluated, but also their rights to engage in workplace organizing and collective bargaining. In other words, it proposed to combine deep cuts in public spending (i.e., it contained a cut of more than $900 million to K–12 education) with legal changes that would effectively cripple the forces that might seek to resist such cuts in the future.

Since the bill sought not only budgetary changes, but also a fundamental modification to the balance of power in future budgeting decisions, the bill's authors were well aware that it was likely to create controversy. This was evidenced in a phone conversation that Governor Scott Walker believed he was having with conservative billionaire David Koch but was actually having with a reporter who recorded the conversation. On this call, Walker described the unveiling of this Budget Repair Bill as "dropping the bomb." He also made it clear that he saw the bill as an opportunity for significant and radical change, stating: "This is our moment, this is our time to change the course of history" (*Wisconsin State Journal*, 2011).

After a few days of fruitless attempts to negotiate portions of the bill, the state Senate's 14 minority Democratic Party members fled to an undisclosed location in neighboring Illinois to prevent the Senate from having the quorum necessary to pass the bill. Meanwhile, protests inside and around the state Capitol Building and Capitol Square in Madison were constant and growing. The TAA members, students, and residents had been joined by K–12 teachers from around the state. Busloads of concerned residents from the nearest larger city, Milwaukee, joined the fray. Within a week, the numbers of protesters swelled from thousands to tens of thousands each day. Many protesters occupied the Capitol Building around the clock. Despite the vastness of the Capitol Building, it could physically contain only a small fraction of the throngs of protesters (Figure 1.1). Those outside marched counterclockwise around the square, seemingly tirelessly, through falling snow and frigid February weather in Wisconsin, singing and chanting, "Kill the bill!" "This is what democracy looks like!," and call-and-response chants like: "What's disgusting? Union busting!"

The spectacle of this "Wisconsin Uprising" was riveting for national and international media. Radio and television networks established on-site stations for ongoing

Figure 1.1. Protesters fill the Wisconsin State capitol.

coverage, broadcasting the sights and sounds of the protests to audiences across the globe. The protesters represented a broad cross section of interests and concerns and brought a variety of modes of political expression and protest together. Some emulated labor organizing of the early twentieth century, while others borrowed slogans and songs from the protests of the 1960s that had defined the identities of a generation of Madisonians (Maraniss, 2003). Still others sought to creatively express the politics of the moment with new signs, songs, and activism on social media.

Scholars and observers of many stripes—from sociologists, anthropologists, and political scientists to musicologists and communications researchers—took interest (Collins, 2012; Yates, 2010). For instance, the ethnomusicologist Michael O'Brien (2013) analyzed soundscapes from the protests, arguing that "the protesters in Wisconsin created, mediated, and remediated soundscapes of popular protest that invoked the historical imagination while forging new contemporary political-regional identities through sonic performances in public spaces" (p. 2). Protests of similar scale were happening at the same time in Africa and the Middle East that would be known as the Arab Spring. Protesters in Egypt's Tahrir Square and Madison's Capitol Square exchanged messages of support through social media, emphasizing some commonalities in their respective struggles. For instance, one widely circulated image featured an Egyptian protester holding a sign in Tahrir Square reading "Egypt supports Wisconsin workers: One world, one pain" (see Chomsky, 2011; Kroll, 2011). Protesters in Madison similarly referenced the protests taking place around the world (Figure 1.2).

Figure 1.2. "A little bit of Egypt right here in Madison."

Figure 1.3. Firefighters marching in the protests around Capitol Square in Madison, Wisconsin, and receiving applause.

The Budget Repair Bill had exempted the uniformed services—the police and firefighters' unions—from the elimination of collective bargaining rights. Not incidentally, these unions had been supportive of Scott Walker's gubernatorial run, while teachers' unions and other public sector unions had been more supportive of his opponent. It was unclear at first how the police and firefighters' unions would react to the proposals in the Budget Repair Bill. Would they count themselves lucky to have been exempted and choose to sit the protests out quietly, or would they join in the fray on behalf of their fellow public sector workers?

I was part of the crowd on Capitol Square when a major firefighters' union made its appearance on a frosty evening in February (Figure 1.3). Marching in with banners and bagpipes blaring, the firefighters' arrival was cheered by the tens of thousands of protesters (Figure 1.4). One of their union leaders took to the podium on the southeast side of the Capitol Building to address the crowd from a microphone. Lights shining on the speaker's podium showed the steam coming off him as he spoke, at first softly. He explained that their union leadership had been busy consulting with their members and debating their stance on the bill. He said that their conversations kept coming back to the fact that this was clearly an attempt to divide and conquer organized labor in the public sector. When the chips were down, he proclaimed, now shouting loudly: They had decided that they would stand on the side of labor every time! This declaration of course drew exuberant and cacophonous applause and celebration from the crowd.

Figure 1.4. Bagpipers leading the way for the firefighters' union marchers.

Standing on the Capitol Square at that moment, and at many other times throughout the months that followed as these protests demonstrated uncommon staying power, it was tempting to believe the observers claiming that this was a watershed moment in which organized labor, long downtrodden in the United States, was asserting itself anew. I, for one, had never witnessed or been a part of demonstrations with such broad representation of various constituencies and such a fervent commitment to sustaining action. Nichols (2012), among others, has called these Wisconsin protests of 2011 "the most remarkable labor uprising in modern American history" (p. xi). Protests were held in other cities across the United States expressing solidarity with the Wisconsin workers, and people from more than 20 countries ordered pizzas—around 800 on one Wednesday in February (Greenhouse, 2011)—from a local pizzeria to be delivered to the crowds to help sustain the protests.

Conversations with colleagues and students at UW that spring would often turn to the topic of the protests and the likely outcomes of the underlying policy conflicts. Like many who were observing the protests from around the country and the world, most students that I encountered thought that the protests would, in fact, ultimately be effective in halting the Budget Repair Bill from passing. Surely, they reasoned, this massive uprising of residents would cause leaders in the state to re-think or moderate their austerity and antiunion agenda in the face of such profound discord and opposition. Others were not as convinced. Despite the impressiveness of the protests, could the effort really be effective in stopping the bill? Could the protests really build and maintain the kinds of organizations that could mobilize and hold decision-makers accountable for their actions over longer periods of time? Even those who were skeptical of the impact of the protests, however, would not likely have predicted the setbacks that followed.

Republican legislators ordered the arrest of the 14 Democratic senators who had fled the state, although the senators were not arrested since the Wisconsin police could not cross the state line to make the arrests. They leaned on the Capitol Police, unsuccessfully at first, to evict the protesters occupying the building. They searched for any hint of disorderly behavior to portray the peaceful protests as threatening or violent. Eventually, the senators returned to the state, and the Budget Repair Bill ultimately passed later that summer, with no changes from the original proposal. Opponents of the bill meanwhile channeled their efforts into an attempt to recall the governor and some of the state legislators who had supported it. Special re-call elections were triggered that fall and were held during the following summer (2012).

Ultimately, these recall efforts came up short. In fact, Governor Walker won the recall election by a larger margin than in his initial election in 2010, with more people voting in the recall election than in the previous gubernatorial election. Media portrayals of the protests varied in their characterizations. Although liberal radio and television stations had portrayed the protests as inspiring resistance to the onward march of the neoliberal assault on workers' rights, conservative radio and television had characterized them as politically motivated bullying by greedy and entitled union bosses unconcerned with the costs they imposed on taxpayers. In these outlets, Scott Walker was described as a courageous and principled rep-resentative of small businesses and private sector employees. In keeping with Tea Party ideology, he promised greater freedom from taxation so that the private sector could get the Wisconsin economy working again. This narrative triumphed and propelled Walker to national stardom among conservatives. Despite failing to reach the promised mark of 250,000 new jobs during his first term (J. B. Nelson, 2014), he was handily reelected to a second term in 2014 and began to be mentioned as a possible Republican presidential nominee for the 2016 election cycle.

Meanwhile, bill after bill was passed to roll back many policies and systems that had been in place in Wisconsin since the Progressive Era in the early twentieth cen-tury. For instance, despite giving indications during the battle with public sector unions that he would not pursue "right-to-work" legislation in the state that would damage private sector unions (likely an effort to build support among private sector workers for curtailing public sector bargaining rights), Wisconsin in fact did pass a right-to-work bill in 2015. Many of the same moves were made in Wisconsin that were made in other states with Republican-controlled governments, reflecting the priorities of the American Legislative Exchange Council (ALEC) and other national networks of conservative strategists and donors (see G. L. Anderson & Donchik, 2016). Drug testing for recipients of public assistance, curtailing of reproductive rights and women's preventive healthcare, and deregulating the payday loan industry in the state are examples.

The state forfeited funds that had been allocated by the US government to construct high-speed rail lines between urban areas in the Upper Midwest (Madison, Milwaukee, and Chicago), on the grounds that it was wasteful government spending. Likewise, Wisconsin declined to expand Medicaid or establish a state health insurance exchange in attempts to evade or hamper elements of the Affordable Care Act (i.e., Obamacare). Restrictions on carrying concealed handguns were rolled back. All references to a "living wage" were removed from state law. Many laws have been passed to prohibit localities from enacting progressive measures, such as minimum wage laws or tenant rights and protections from exploitative landlords.

Hundreds of millions of dollars were cut from the state's system of higher education, and there have been attempts to reorient the state's public universities toward performance-based assessment and funding (based primarily on employment outcomes for undergraduate alumni). These cuts and new budgeting approaches have been paired with a broader effort to bring public higher education institutions' governance and employment practices more in line with the private sector. The state park system's budget was cut. Environmental regulations have been weakened, and scientists' positions have been eliminated from the state's Department of Natural Resources. Those who remain in that department are forbidden from discussing climate change. Meanwhile, in what has been described as a "war on bikes," there have been proposals for new taxes on the sale of bicycles, while at the same time policies supporting the construction of bike lanes and paths are being eliminated (Ollstein, 2015).

These and other alterations of the state's policies and institutions have rolled through the legislative and executive branches, while those of us who participated in the protests or shared the sentiments of the protesters have seemed ever more helpless and dispirited. Perhaps even more damaging than each of these individual pieces of public policy, decision-makers in the state have taken numerous actions to ensure not only that unions have reduced power in the future, but also that workers, lower income residents, urban residents, and communities of color have reduced power. For example, a voter ID bill was passed, supposedly to counter the threat of voter fraud, though little evidence existed of a problem with voter fraud in the first place. Likewise, the state's legislative and congressional districts were redrawn in a highly partisan manner, bolstering the power of incumbency.

Not only did the Wisconsin Uprising—despite its historic magnitude and persistence—fail to stop the passage of the Budget Repair Bill, in fact it is often perceived as having had quite the opposite of its intended effect. Instead of losing support for their attacks on public sector employees, the backers of the bill emerged from the fight with greater popularity and credibility and with better organized support. They used these new assets to enact even greater change in the state, mostly in ways that were counter to the interests and preferences of the protesters. These policy enactments have diminished public goods and institutions and eliminated protections for vulnerable groups and individuals. They have also changed the ways that decisions are made in the state that will likely persist long into the future, creating a massive uphill battle for progressives, labor unions, public employees, and residents with lower incomes.

This is not to say that the protests caused these political outcomes that they were seeking to resist and oppose. It is striking, however, that one of the largest sustained mass protests in contemporary US history could be so ineffective in achieving its goals in terms of influence on decision-making. It is also telling that this was an unexpected outcome for many engaged citizens, activists, union organizers, political strategists, and observers, including those in the media and academia.

Blind Spots

In retrospect, there are many insights that might have enabled participants, strategists, and observers to better predict some of the outcomes of the Wisconsin Uprising. For instance, most urban residents at that time had very limited understanding of the mounting dissatisfaction in rural areas about perceived advantages enjoyed by residents of cities and suburbs, a phenomenon that Wisconsin political scientist Kathy Cramer (2012) has called "rural consciousness." These grievances and the sense of alienation among many rural voters are likely part of what undergirded the defiant stance struck by Republican elected officials in the face of the protests. This stance was startling to most observers who had expected more moderation and compromise, which would have been a continuation of long-standing norms in the state's government. Sociopolitical contexts, in other words, are constantly changing, and the outcomes of collective action are inherently difficult to predict in light of this. It is likely that in different circumstances, or even static circumstances that held certain aspects of the sociopolitical context constant, the Wisconsin Uprising could have produced divergent outcomes.

In addition to better understanding our changing context, however, we need better tools for understanding, analyzing, and comparing efforts to build power and exercise influence in civic affairs. How do we meaningfully compare and contrast something like sustained mass protests at a state capital with a variety of other forms of civic involvement and action—from participation in neighborhood associations, to forming coalitions, to joining advocacy groups, or engaging in boycotts/ buycotts, or signing online petitions? It will likely come as no surprise that social scientists lack (or disagree about) many of the most basic tools for distinguishing and comparing resident-led and community-driven change efforts such as these, much less to predict their effects and outcomes. One reason for this is that local and grassroots efforts have simply not had the same amount of close examination as other more macro-level social and political forces.

Many experts in universities, political campaigns, think tanks, and the media clamor to understand national and international politics and policymaking. The strategic decisions of politicians and elected officials and their effects on public opinion and voting behavior are the subject of much empirical analysis and extensive conceptual debate, especially at the national level. The effects of particular media or voter turnout strategies, for example, are scrutinized in detail, and results are fed back into professional campaign operations, where they are often used to inform strategy. In contrast, we have relatively few institutions and scholars dedicated to similar understanding of grassroots efforts of nonprofessionals and community organizations operating in the civic domain, particularly at the local level.

This is not to say that the professional observers and analysts of national politics and elections have mastered their craft. In fact, they are often wrong, sometimes alarmingly so.[2] The broader public also is often wrong, sometimes even about basic facts about sociopolitical systems. For instance, US whites who were opposed to President Obama tended to view their own economic distress in the wake of the Great Recession as being greater than that of Latinos and Blacks, and they placed blame on the government for tilting the playing field to their disadvantage. This is despite the fact that whites' financial outlook was actually better over this time period than other groups' (McKenzie, 2014).[3] In other words, if the wonks and pundits are often wrong about national politics in the United States, portions of the public even more regularly tend to make erroneous judgments about sociopolitical systems and processes.

These misunderstandings have ramifications for the ways that residents engage in efforts to make change in the systems and settings that they care about. People experiencing increasingly isolated and mediated lives often struggle to connect their concerns and enthusiasms to successful systems change efforts. Meanwhile, their support and action are continuously solicited by nonprofit organizations, businesses, and political candidates through direct mail, electronic media, and other forms of marketing. These attempts to channel concerns and enthusiasms for change most often position people as consumers, asking them in essence to purchase social or systems change that will ostensibly be executed by professionals. It is increasingly common for issue-focused or activist organizations to solicit support in the form of funds to enable professional advocates to advance a cause, rather than requesting people's direct action, much less their involvement, in decision-making.

When we are engaged as consumers, we often expect instant gratification, something that is increasingly common in the marketplace but very unusual in systems change processes. Even when we do become directly involved in participatory change efforts, unrealistic expectations for how easily change can be achieved can quickly give way to defeatism, nihilism, and a sense of personal inadequacy (Lerner, 1999; West, 2001). There is a risk that people who harbor misconceptions about how residents, organizations, and movements can make change in sociopolitical systems will move quickly from engagement and enthusiasm to burnout and alienation.

Mystification about how to change systems also pervades many professions whose missions depend on the ability to operate and intervene, at least in some cases, at a systems level. For example, public health researchers, policymakers, and practitioners are increasingly clear on the need to take action on the social determinants of health in order to combat persistent health inequities (Schulz & Northridge, 2004). Yet, researchers and practitioners alike struggle to produce actionable evidence and effective strategies for changing these macro-level systems (O'Campo, 2012). Likewise, although the discipline of social work has a long history of "macropractice" to engage in systems-level work in ways that benefit less powerful groups in society, this branch of the profession is miniscule and continues to face challenges of legitimacy and obstruction both within the discipline and in the practice settings where professional social work occurs, requiring vigilant advocacy from macropractice advocates (Rothman & Mizrahi, 2014). Other fields, such as education, community development, youth development, and community mental health, face similar struggles when it comes to changing the larger systems in which their work occurs, despite increasingly widespread recognition that this is what is required to make progress in their field's areas of concern.

Because our collective understanding of potential mechanisms for systems change is inadequate, many have a tendency to gravitate toward absolutes in thinking. For instance, according to some of the rosier popular accounts and appeals, we all can potentially be effective agents of sociopolitical change if we would only decide to take action. In one variant of this line of thinking, the geographic borders, hierarchies, and divisions that once separated and distinguished us are all vanishing as we enter a new hyperconnected era with unprecedented freedoms and possibilities for equality, creativity, and social entrepreneurship (e.g., Friedman, 2005). At the other end of this spectrum are observers who are convinced that political and economic systems are fundamentally rigged to suppress dissent, and that it is nearly impossible to effectively contest the interests of elites (e.g., Hedges, 2010). In this view, most forms of participation and engagement are ultimately futile.

The tension between these fundamentally critical and hopeful orientations must be navigated in many forms of social practice and research. On one hand, there are entrenched and evolving power structures that constrain opportunities for people to shape the systems that affect their lives. On the other hand, there are possibilities for individual and collective agency and concrete examples of successful systems change efforts. This dialectic has practical implications for how we address social issues and societal crises. Examining the nature and potential of community, or collective power, provides one requisite venue for this exploration.

Community Power and Empowerment

Effective engagement with the conditions and systems that affect people's daily lives is fundamental to functioning democracies. Yet in many cases, broad-based efforts to engage and create changes in policy or systems are ineffective. This was clearly evidenced by the Wisconsin Uprising, in which a sustained protest did not have the desired effects on policy, electoral representation, or public opinion. In retrospect, it is possible to identify some of the events that led to the failures of that specific effort. For instance, after weeks of sustained protests, the Wisconsin Democratic Party sought to redirect the energy of demonstrators into the recall elections. After the recall elections were initiated, protesters were encouraged to stop demonstrating at the Capitol Building and to instead dedicate their efforts to the electoral process (Rothschild, 2012). The party then proceeded to run a fairly typical professionalized political campaign.

Most of the resident-activists who had expressed so much passion about the issues at stake were effectively consigned to the usual roles: voter/supporter or perhaps donor or campaign volunteer (e.g., canvassing and phone banking). If instead of allowing the state's Democratic Party to capture and direct the process, the protesters had formed new organizations and decision-making structures, they could have built some more durable sources of power outside of (or even within) the preexisting political party infrastructure. Of course, it is not possible to say which outcomes would have been different in this kind of alternate historical scenario, but at the very least, there might be some additional powerful resident-led groups to fight for the concerns expressed by the protesters. As it stands now, there are few remaining vestiges of the Wisconsin Uprising. Groups do gather daily in the Capitol Building at noon for solidarity sing-alongs (see Kemble, 2013), and larger groups have gathered for marches on anniversaries of important events during the struggle. Although these demonstrations are a testament to the depth of commitment that fueled the protests (and the admirable persistence of the activists who continue them), these events understandably often have a mournful quality to them and appear to be nothing more than a nuisance to decision-makers in the state.

Local groups, however, sometimes do act as drivers of changes to address pressing social, economic, and environmental issues. Many such groups have sustained and built momentum for years or even decades, while other efforts are more short-lived. Furthermore, these groups tend to benefit their communities and societies in ways that go beyond the systemic and structural changes that they help to bring about. For example, they often create organizational settings that can support skill building, experiential learning, and positive psychosocial development among those who participate. Studies of these types of organizations can help us to think more critically and systematically about systems change efforts. For example, in the retrospective search for what might have produced different outcomes in Wisconsin, we could home in on what Maton and Salem (1995) and others have referred to as *opportunity role structure*, or the pervasiveness and accessibility of opportunities that are available for participants in community and organizational settings (Fedi, Mannarini, & Maton, 2009). Concepts like this can provide a common vocabulary and help us to establish indicators to compare and assess effects of different strategies across different times and places. Yet, research on concepts like opportunity role structures is not yet advanced enough to provide much evidence-informed guidance to community leaders and movement strategists. Meanwhile, the scale of social problems and the sophistication of institutions that can resist change have never been greater. Many people and organizations are engaged in some type of effort to build community power to make progress on pressing social issues, but how can we know when these efforts are likely to bring about desired outcomes?

To improve the likelihood that research can provide actionable insights into questions like these, we need greater understanding of community power and empowerment. *Community power* here refers to the social and structural relationships among local residents and organizations that shape outcomes when disputes or competition for resources might arise. Theoretical and empirical accounts of community power structure have spelled out some reasons why participatory action is sometimes ineffective and how powerful entities resist challenges. Further, scholarship on community power structures has sought to understand why resident-led challenges to elite domination arise in some instances and do not in others (e.g., Gaventa, 1980).

In essence, scholars of community power have asked the following questions: When can/do residents of local communities take action to meaningfully influence the conditions and systems that affect their lives? What are the factors and conditions that best predict successes or failures? What are the dimensions and configurations of community power that are most important in determining these outcomes? Despite the fact that many community leaders, organizers, and activists grapple with these same questions, much of this scholarship is not well known to those taking action in community settings. Furthermore, although it was once fairly prominent in several social science disciplines (primarily political science and sociology), scholarship on community power has diminished in recent decades.

In contrast, *empowerment* is a term that has soared in usage among practitioners, community leaders, politicians, and scholars alike. The term has become so widespread that it is now often used ambiguously to indicate nearly any type of positive development among members of a group, including increased feelings of connectedness, increased self-esteem, or increased access to information or services. These widespread but ill-defined uses of the term are often entirely disconnected from considerations of community power (Woodall, Warwick-Booth, & Cross, 2012). Yet, several decades of scholarship in community psychology, public health, community/international development, social work, and related disciplines have sought to define, measure, and understand aspects of empowerment processes (such as opportunity role structure, as described previously), with an eye toward a multilevel framework that can account for processes and outcomes linked to changes in community power structures (e.g., Gutiérrez, GlenMaye, & DeLois, 1995; Rappaport, 1987; Wallerstein, 1993; Zimmerman, 2000). *Community* here has most often referred to those shared contexts in which people experience a sense of belonging, emotional connection, shared values and norms, and mutual influence (D. Klein, 1968; Sarason, 1984). It is therefore typically geographically bounded (e.g., a neighborhood or community organization), although this is not necessarily the norm, as in cases of groups who build these types of ties across geographic boundaries like labor unions, racial or ethnic advocacy groups, or other interest groups (Israel, Checkoway, Schulz, & Zimmerman, 1994).[4]

These lines of scholarship have tended to define empowerment as the processes through which groups can gain greater control over their circumstances. Tools have been developed to assess and measure some elements of empowerment processes, primarily through survey methodologies. Some substantial gaps and oversights remain in this body of work, yet there are some concepts and measurement tools that have been tested and refined for use in a variety of contexts, and these are currently used to assess only a tiny fraction of the community work that claims empowerment as a goal or an outcome. This research–practice disconnect has helped to maintain the common perception among many practitioners, decision-makers, and scholars that empowerment and related community and organizational processes have not been well defined and are difficult or impossible to measure (Cattaneo & Chapman, 2010). This sometimes leads them to shy away from community-driven systems change efforts and instead to invest their energy and resources in efforts focused on changes that can be more easily measured, such as educational and health promotion programs to change attitudes, beliefs, and behaviors (Green, 2006).

In sum, many uses of the term *empowerment* have not been coherently linked to theory on empowerment, and even empowerment theory itself has not been sufficiently connected to considerations of community power. Likewise, scholarship on community power structure, while it has provided valuable insights into the maintenance of asymmetrical power relationships, has not articulated clear theories of empowerment (Stone, 2006). In addition to the cross-disciplinary disjointedness between scholars on these topics, there is a research–practice chasm that has limited the application of the research on community power and empowerment. There is therefore a great need to draw the parallel strands of research on community power and empowerment together, toward greater integration. The potential impact from integrating these lines of scholarship can be further enhanced if the findings and assessment frameworks can be clarified for multiple audiences, including those engaged in community practice, community-based research, and evaluation.

As a whole, this book is an attempt to advance the conceptual integration of community power and empowerment and to enhance the applicability of this integrated framework. As such, it is likely that scholars on these topics from various disciplines, and those whose work bridges research and practice, will be the primary audiences. As mentioned at the outset, however, my hope is that it will also be useful for some who are taking action and guiding participatory processes in communities and organizations. This book is therefore intended as a resource not only for researchers and evaluators, but also for those involved with nonprofits, foundations, voluntary associations, public agencies, social movements, community organizing initiatives, or coalitions who are interested in approaching questions of power, empowerment, and systems change more systematically.

Overview of the Book

Following this introductory chapter, the book consists of three sections. The first section unearths the conceptual histories of community power (Chapter 2) and empowerment (Chapter 3). Chapter 2 begins with power. Nearly universally identified as a fundamental force in community affairs and change processes, it is often acknowledged that it is difficult to define and investigate directly. Early social scientific attempts (beginning in the 1950s) to understand community power structure focused on which actors won and which lost in publicly visible debates and conflicts over policy. Later studies added conceptual depth to efforts to influence outcomes by drawing attention to gatekeeping, agenda setting, and other behind-the-scenes maneuvers that were not typically visible to the public or outside observers. Then, scholars who focused on the ways that power can be used to subtly shape and influence ideology, grievances, and quiescence added still further depth. Taken together, these three "faces" or "dimensions" of power in community decision-making comprise a framework for understanding community power. This chapter ends by considering how this three-dimensional framework can be updated and augmented to provide a contemporary conception of community power on which we can base considerations of empowerment.

In Chapter 3, I trace the rise of the term *empowerment* in the 1970s and 1980s and continue to the presently contested nature of this concept. A variety of historical trends helped empowerment to become a topic of great interest to activists, policymakers, and those in the helping professions alike. Examining early influences on empowerment theory and practice, I devote particular attention to the ecological framework for empowerment that was advanced in the 1980s and 1990s by community psychologists, social workers, and scholars of public health and community development. This framework posits inextricable and context-specific empowerment processes and outcomes at the psychological, organizational, and community levels of analysis. The conceptualization continues to be influential in interdisciplinary scholarship and practice, yet work is still needed to coherently link it to the concepts of community power discussed in Chapter 2, as well as to enhance its ability to illuminate dynamic organizational and community processes. Addressing these shortcomings of empowerment theory can help to recapture the value orientation and symbolism that initially animated discussion of the concept.

The second section of the book constructs an ecological model of empowerment with a focus on addressing the issues identified previously. Chapters 4 through 6 investigate human/psychological, organizational, and community empowerment processes, respectively. Where possible, I draw on previous research in assembling this model. Where the previous research is thin, scattered, or nonexistent, I propose new frameworks or modifications to existing ones, pulling in work from related fields of practice and branches of the social sciences.

Chapter 4 investigates psychological aspects of empowerment and their interplay with other human developmental and educational processes. Perceived control in the settings that a person inhabits is both an underpinning and an outcome of positive human development. This is no less true for the civic or sociopolitical domain than for the family, school, or workplace. It should come as no surprise, then, that perceived control in the sociopolitical domain—an important indicator of psychological empowerment—has been found to be related to other positive developmental outcomes. Yet, for psychological empowerment to be understood in a way that links it inextricably with organizational and community-level empowerment processes, it is not sufficient to focus only on perceived control. Critical awareness of the source, nature, and instruments of power, for example, must be taken into account. Although I pay particular attention to the role of empowerment in youth development in this chapter, psychological empowerment also continues to play vital roles in development and education during adulthood.

Chapter 5 takes up the topic of organizational empowerment. Voluntary associations and nonprofit organizations are the most common catalysts for empowerment processes and the exercise of community power. Yet, there are tremendous variations in scale, mission, composition, and structure among these organizations. How can stakeholders—from staff and volunteers to policymakers, funders, and evaluators—build more grounded understanding of their efforts to change systems? Organizational empowerment theory aspires to function as a framework that can shed light on these topics, yet it has inadequately considered how contemporary trends in political economy affect organizations and organizational networks. This chapter elaborates the characteristics of organizations and their networks of relations with other organizations that are conducive to building community power.

Most have treated empowerment at the community level in vague terms. Scholars in community development and health promotion have identified domains of community empowerment, but these were designed for—and are infrequently used beyond—programmatic contexts. Others have drawn in concepts from social movement studies and sociological work on neighborhood social processes to understand community empowerment, yet these frameworks have not been linked to community power structure or to psychological or organizational empowerment processes. Chapter 6 therefore constructs a new conceptual framework for community empowerment with dimensions that link to both community power and to organizational and psychological empowerment processes. This intent is to bring empowerment theory closer to being able to realize its fundamental goals of acting as an integrated orientation for action and an infrastructure for systematic research.

The concepts discussed in Chapters 4, 5, and 6 are primarily focused on empowerment processes rather than their outcomes. Chapter 7 distinguishes multiple hypothesized pathways through which empowerment processes produce impacts on health and well-being. The most direct outcome of empowerment processes is that social power is built and exercised. When this occurs, there are benefits for the participants in those processes, who often experience reduced stress and isolation. These *participant pathways* have been the most widely studied outcomes of empowerment processes. These pathways must, however, be clearly distinguished from the other ways that empowerment processes can enhance health and well-being in broader populations. For instance, empowerment processes often lead to changes in policies and systems, thereby addressing systemic inequities and contributing to community well-being. Through these *ecological pathways*, empowerment processes can influence outcomes for all residents of a community, not just those participating in the processes themselves. Finally, since empowerment processes can alter community power structures and make them more egalitarian, this may in itself lead to reduced vulnerability and insecurity and greater trust and cohesion. These *pluralist pathways* are not yet as well understood as the other two pathways but are a key piece of the puzzle for a clear understanding of how empowerment processes can promote health equity.

Taking account of this holistic framework for empowerment processes and outcomes, Chapter 8 provides recommendations in the form of a set of design principles that can apply to both empowerment research and the various forms of praxis that seek to catalyze, sustain, and multiply empowerment processes. Although there are common concepts that can guide and inform research and action, creative design is needed to tailor efforts for specific local contexts, issues of concern, and questions. The principles offered in Chapter 8 are therefore intended to provide a set of recommendations for translating the frameworks that are the primary focus of the book into context-specific plans for action and research. Chapter 9 offers some concluding thoughts, and the appendices contain scales that have been used to measure or assess aspects of empowerment processes. As I note in reference to many of these specific measures, work remains to refine many of these scales and to link them with methodologies other than survey research, but they are nonetheless extremely valuable tools when used strategically.

Notes

1. This quotation is often attributed to Margaret Mead, but this attribution is disputed. See https://en.wikiquote.org/wiki/Margaret_Mead.
2. This would apply to the nearly universal failure among observers and pundits to acknowledge the possibility that Donald Trump could be a competitive candidate in the 2016 Republican primary.
3. McKenzie (2014) based the comparison of racial/ethnic groups' financial outlook on several metrics, including poverty rates, changes in the unemployment rates by group, and percentage change in median wealth by group.
4. These concepts of community as they relate to power and empowerment are discussed in greater detail in Chapter 6.

Community Power

Introduction

It is common to hear that social research should pay more attention to power, for example, in the relationships of researchers and participants, or as determined by social location. Power, however, is a complex construct and can be considered with attention to multiple levels of analysis. It can refer to many different things, some easily observable and others very difficult to detect or describe. In this chapter, I trace the social scientific treatment of a particular form of power: community power. Several decades of work in multiple social science disciplines suggest a three-dimensional framework for community power. I present this framework and consider its applicability for understanding community power in an era characterized by globalized capitalism and deepening inequality. I consider the limitations that this emerging political–economic order is imposing on local action. Finally, I consider whether this type of framework for community power can function only as a tool for illuminating the use of power for oppression. Can it also be effective at guiding inquiry, strategy, and practice that are intent on building power to challenge elite interests? If so, what are the differences in how the framework should be applied? The goal of this chapter is therefore to work toward an understanding of community power that can inform and guide efforts to understand and promote empowerment.

Community Power Structure

Early discussions of power among social and political researchers focused on how power is wielded and where power resides in urban communities. Two competing theories emerged: those focused on pluralistic decision-making processes and those positing control by a smaller group of elites. In a 1953 study of Atlanta, Georgia, Hunter introduced the notion of a *community power structure* to social and political science. He interviewed business leaders, government officials, leaders of civic organizations, leaders in the Black community, and experts on the city's social services. Hunter's method was relational in the sense that he focused on leaders' understanding of who else in the community was capable of influencing outcomes. Specifically, he asked all interviewees to identify the most powerful and influential individuals in the city. In this way, he captured the reputational relationships among the city's leaders across various sectors. What he found is that most people understood the city to have only a small number of very influential power brokers, and there was broad agreement on who these people were. Chairs of major companies in Atlanta (like the Coca-Cola Company) were on this short list, as were local bankers and utility company chairs. Strikingly, many of these people lived in the same neighborhoods, belonged to the same social clubs, and sat on each other's boards of directors. For the most part, they all knew each other, and together they formed an informal network at the top of the community power structure.

Hunter found that these influential brokers within Atlanta's power structure in the mid-1950s had broad agreement on the most pressing issues facing the city. By far the two most frequently named priorities were a system of highways to move cars in and out of the city and a plan for downtown growth and redevelopment. Not all of the members of this elite group were actively involved in determining polices related to these priorities. The informal network as a whole, however, had at least one prominent member involved in each of the important policy debates taking place in the city. Furthermore, these issues seemed only to emerge as debates in public (i.e., in the newspapers or in proposals by civic organizations) *after* the network of power brokers had reached something approximating a broad consensus on the issues among themselves.

With collaborators, Hunter replicated the Atlanta study in a city in the northeastern United States, finding similar power structures in operation (Hunter, Schaffer, & Sheps, 1956). Hunter's findings led others to conduct similar studies of community power structure in other cities (e.g., Bonjean, 1963) and to consider community power structure in analyses of multiple cities (e.g., Hawley, 1963). They also sparked controversies and criticisms. Critics of Hunter's research believed that through methodological flaws or ideological blinders, he had either missed or misrepresented the city's power structure as monolithic (Polsby, 1960). In fact, the critics claimed, the power structures of American cities, Atlanta included, were more diffuse and democratic. These critics set out to conduct studies of US cities to test their claims (Dahl, 1961/2005).

Meanwhile, Mills's (1956/2000) book *The Power Elite* extended the notion of elite power structure to the national level in the United States and garnered even more attention in social science and the broader public. Taking stock of the post–World War II United States, Mills claimed that power was concentrated among national elites in three interconnected sets of institutions: the government, large corporations, and the military. According to Mills, this institutionally interconnected elite wielded more power together than the poor, working, and middle classes combined. The people who occupied high-level positions in one of these arenas tended to know the most powerful leaders in the other arenas. The borders between these types of institutions were porous for high-level officials, meaning that, for instance, a high-level military officer could become a leader in government and a government leader could become a leader of a major corporation. And, in many cases the interests of elites in all three institutional types were intertwined. Membership in the power elite was not constant. Instead, individuals rotated through roles, but the roles in the dominant institutions and the national power structure remained. Much like Hunter's account of community power structure, these members of the national power elite were not formally organized, and they did not agree on every issue. They nevertheless occupied the most powerful positions and collectively exercised broad control over the major policy debates of the day, especially as they related to their own power and interests.

Polsby (1960) and others took issue with the orientation of studies like Hunter's (1953) and Mills's (1956/2000), arguing that they represented "a general view of politics as an epiphenomenon of social stratification" (p. 475).[1] Polsby argued for an alternative "pluralist" orientation to the study of community power. He argued that Hunter and Mills had begun with the question of who constitutes the power structure in American communities (and therefore the presumption that there was such a hierarchical structure). In contrast, the pluralist orientation would insist that the starting point for inquiry on community decision-making should instead be whether community power is disproportionately held or exercised by anyone at all. The essence of this pluralist critique (methodological debates aside) was that those who had identified local and national power elites had fulfilled their ambition of identifying a minority holding a monopoly on community power precisely because they had set out to do so. Polsby asserted that studies conducted from a pluralist orientation would likely arrive at different outcomes in community research through what has been called the decisional approach: an "attempt to study specific outcomes, to determine who actually prevails in community decision-making" (p. 476). The critique resonated with many scholars of the day, likely at least in part because this pluralist orientation elevated classical liberal assumptions about democratic society.

In fact, using this decisional approach did yield different findings than studies using the reputational method that Hunter and others had used. Dahl's (1961/2005) book *Who Governs?* reported results from a study of decision-making in New Haven, Connecticut, becoming a touchstone in the debate between the pluralists and those arguing for the existence of more stratified community power structures (the pluralists took to describing these ideological opponents as "elitists"[2]). Dahl selected three issue areas in New Haven: public education, urban renewal, and nominations for elected political office. Having identified sets of economic and social "notables" in the city, he found these groups to be exerting much less influence on debates of public issues relative to, for instance, Hunter's 1956 account of Atlanta. In the issue area of education, for example, Dahl studied eight different policy decisions made during the 1950s in New Haven (e.g., increased purchasing of library books, systems for promoting teachers) and found that the mayor and the Board of Education were the most influential actors in decision-making on these community issues. Contrary to what Hunter's findings seemed to suggest, Dahl found that the Board of Education contained none of New Haven's social and economic notables.

In decision-making around urban renewal, a number of social and economic elites were involved, but Dahl (1961/2005) argued that their role was more of a passive advisory one than an active decision-making one. Instead of the elites calling the shots, the mayor and city staff were coming up with the specific policy proposals. They then did what they could to garner support from the economic and social notables, as from other parts of New Haven's citizenry. Like Hunter's study of Atlanta, the pluralist study of New Haven ignited debates on theory and methodology, including reexaminations of data on New Haven leading to different conclusions (e.g., Domhoff, 1978). The pluralist approach nevertheless became highly influential in American political and social science. Studies of other cities and other issues were conducted from the pluralist frame. With its emphasis on *who wins and who loses in publicly visible policy debates*, the pluralists had offered a clearly defined and empirically testable concept of community power structure.

Two Faces of Community Power

Against this backdrop of ongoing debate between pluralists and elitists, Bachrach and Baratz provided an overarching critique of the ways that community power was being conceptualized. Their 1962 article in the *American Political Science Review* was titled "Two Faces of Power." On some points, they sided with the pluralists. In particular, they joined the pluralists in rejecting elitists' suppositions that a structured power hierarchy would necessarily reproduce itself in all communities, and that these community power structures would be fairly stable over time (even if the individuals occupying the key roles in the structure were not themselves constant). Bachrach and Baratz also underscored the pluralist critique of the reputational method in elitist studies like Hunter's (e.g., Wolfinger, 1960) for the fact that the method took community members' perceptions that certain people were influential in community decision-making at face value. Along with the pluralists, they argued that a more critical examination of the supposed power and influence of the elites was warranted.

Two main criticisms of the pluralists' methods and underlying assumptions were leveled, however, by Bachrach and Baratz. First, the pluralist orientation of scholars like Dahl and Polsby, which focused on publicly visible issue area debates, did not take adequate account of "the fact that power may be, and often is, exercised by confining the scope of decision-making to relatively 'safe' issues" (Bachrach

& Baratz, 1962, p. 948). In other words, by examining only prominently debated public issues, they failed to take account of which issues were *not* up for public debate and why this might be the case. Second, the orientation and methods of the pluralists did not allow distinctions to be made between issues of great or little importance as they related to the interests of the notables or elite. Public education in New Haven, for example, was actually of little concern to economic and social notables except as it related to the issue of city finances. The notables tended to reside in the suburbs and send their children to private schools, so why should they be active participants in discussions around issues of public school library acquisitions and the like? Documenting the absence of the city's economic and social notables from the decision-making process in issue areas such as public education policy, as Dahl (1961/2005) had done, did not mean that they were not powerful and active in debates that were more directly related to their interests.

Furthermore, the apparent noncontroversy over other aspects of the status quo (i.e., in the distribution of resources or city services) was taken by the pluralists to indicate that these were "nonissues," or that broad consent to the status quo had been achieved. The decisional method of the pluralists was blind to the potential for the structure of power in communities to consciously or unconsciously prevent contestation of the status quo and preserve the semblance of consensus. With these points, Bachrach and Baratz identified a second "face" of community power, which is less easily observed and documented than the first face. The reputational methods of the elitists and the decisional methods of the pluralists, they argued, were only attending to the first face of power, which can be traced in careful studies of who has the most influence and most often achieves their desired outcomes in publicly visible policy debates. The second face of power is more concerned with events that *do not occur*, or "non–decision-making" (Bachrach & Baratz, 1962, p. 952), because of the exercise of power.

Intuitively recognizable mechanisms permit this second face of power to operate. Think of instances, for example, in which people or groups with legitimate grievances choose to avoid conflict for fear that they might jeopardize their already tenuous standing in institutional or community settings. Think of instances in which groups proactively moderate their proposals in anticipation of powerful backlash that would serve to undermine their public image. Bureaucratic wrangling can prevent certain topics from receiving public input or deliberation. Influential people act as gatekeepers to the settings where deliberation and decision-making do occur, effectively preventing views contrary to their own from appearing. Of course, these nonoccurrences that function covertly to preserve the status quo are more difficult to pinpoint and verify than the publicly visible occurrences that characterize the first face of power. Bachrach and Baratz (1962) suggest the study of the dominant values of institutions and the practices—such as the agenda setting and gatekeeping described above—by those interested in preserving the status quo that effectively limit the scope of public debate and decision-making to so-called "safe" issues. Consideration of these institutional values and practices permits identification of issues of true importance to the elites/notables. Determining elite influence over decision-making specifically within those issue areas is a better indicator of community power structure.

Some took up this call. Bachrach and Baratz (1970), for instance, elaborated on the concepts and explored methods for studying two faces of power, grounding the concepts in a study of poverty, race, and politics in Baltimore, Maryland, over several decades. Their findings challenged the pluralists' views on why some groups were less active than others in public decision-making. The pluralists had assumed that nonaction indicated acceptance of the status quo, inertia, or apathy. Polsby (1960), for instance, had reasoned that since it had been demonstrated that those who had middle- or upper-class incomes tended to participate in public decision-making more than the lower classes, that the lower classes must simply be finding their satisfaction in life through other types of activities. Participation, in other words, was assumed to simply be more of a cultural value of those with middle- and upper-class incomes. Of course, closer attention to the reasons for non-participation and non-decision-making helped avoid this potentially victim-blaming perspective of the pluralists. Salamon and Van Evera's (1973) study of Black voter turnout in Mississippi, for instance, found that, rather than apathy, discrimination and fear were inhibiting people from participation.

This second face of power expanded the possibilities for the study of community power structure. Understanding and documenting who prevailed in publicly visible policy debates (as pluralists did) was important, but not enough. For a deeper and more accurate understanding of how community power operates, it is also necessary to assess the relative importance of each issue to the interests of elites. Furthermore, it is crucial to pay attention to the ways that influence may be used to set the bounds of public decision-making, the ways that influence prevents some grievances and important challenges to the status quo from emerging in public debates and the ways that participation by nonelites is discouraged or suppressed. The results of taking these additional questions into account was of course to reveal a more complex community power structure that operated very differently from the classical liberal democratic assumptions of the pluralists.

The Three-Dimensional View

Still some argued that the second face of power did not go far enough to unmask how community power structures operate. In a 1974 book, *Power: A Radical View,* Lukes proposed a third face or dimension of power that built conceptually on the two faces of power concept. In addition to examining how contests to the status quo are prevented from emerging, Lukes called attention to the ways that power operates to shape people's very perceptions of public and community issues. Lukes's work drew attention to power as "the capacity to secure compliance to domination through the shaping of beliefs and desires, by imposing internal constraints under historically changing circumstances" (pp. 143–144).

This third dimension—the ways that power shapes ideology—is, according to Lukes (1974), the most foundational of the three dimensions of power. It is also the most difficult to detect because it is deeply rooted in people's worldviews and self-concepts through socialization processes that are often not apparent to the people themselves. In identifying this third dimension, Lukes was influenced in particular by Gramsci's notion of hegemony, in which the domination of one group over another is enforced not only through political and economic systems but also through cultural and ideological systems that serve to justify and naturalize the arrangement of power, in some cases achieving the active consent of those who are dominated (Gramsci, 2000). In a second edition to the book, Lukes (2005) also identified conceptual connections to works by Bourdieu and Foucault. The notion of *habitus*, for example, also concerns the unconscious internalization of social structures (Bourdieu, 2000). And, a central task of Foucault's genealogical work (e.g., Foucault, 1977, 1982) was illuminating the mechanisms of the third dimension of power in the evolution of social and institutional arrangements over time.

Early critics of Lukes's concept of power doubted whether this third dimension could ever be effectively studied empirically. This challenge was taken up by Gaventa in the book *Power and Powerlessness* (1980), which used all three dimensions of power to structure a detailed empirical analysis of decades of domination of an Appalachian valley and its people by a British mining company. Using the techniques of the pluralists, Gaventa first identified outcomes of publicly visible debates in issue areas including union elections and policies affecting the miners' working conditions and compensation and their job security over time. Miners and town residents were occasionally active, although not nearly to the extent that might have been expected given the degree to which their interests were at stake. And, in some cases, miners whose interests would be negatively affected by particular candidates and policies expressed support for those very candidates and policies.

If an observer of this Appalachian mining valley's history adhered to the pluralist approach, they might conclude that this nonaction and apparent consensus indicated apathy and ignorance on the part of the miners. Instead, Gaventa (1980) argued that these points of *apparent contradiction between interests and action* are precisely when inquiry into the second and third faces of power were most necessary. In fact, in this case, power was clearly operating to suppress grievances and produce the appearance of consent, as the two-dimensional view of power would indicate. Deeper investigation of this Appalachian mining case revealed many forms of either implied or explicit coercion taking place in the mining town and the miners' union. Corporate elites worked with the top leaders of miners' unions to organize apparent consensus and suppress possible complaints. The miners were of course dissatisfied as jobs were lost, pay and benefits were cut, and working conditions remained unsafe in the mines.

At one point, a challenge to the status quo did emerge with a candidacy for union leadership that gave voice to many of these grievances. In this context, Gaventa (1980) quoted miners who offered their support for the establishment candidate and the policies preferred by the establishment for fear that their pension benefits would be cut if they did not. The reform candidate was perceived as so much of a threat by the union establishment that they had him assassinated. Union leaders paid the assassins using union funds and convinced and reminded miners to stick to a false cover-up story in testimonies to law enforcement in the aftermath of the murder. Perversely, in this case, people were effectively coerced to perjure themselves to cover up the use of their union's funds to compensate the assassins of the candidate who had best represented their own interests.

Consistent with the gatekeeping function of the second face of power, conventions and committee meetings in which miners might have expressed grievances were held far away from the mining town. Financial assistance for travel to the meetings was provided to locals who would be most likely to acquiesce to the leadership. At these meetings, it was made clear by the organizers that critics of the status quo would be regarded as "enemies of organized labor" (Gaventa, 1980, p. 187). When such critical speakers took to the floor, their microphones were turned off, and they were beaten up and escorted out of the convention. Noncritical official reports expressing consensus were produced from these meetings, and, in the process, union leadership reinforced their dominance over the rank-and-file membership. Further, the established union leadership exercised extensive control over the electoral process, thwarting opposition from even gaining a hearing for their views through either in-person or print communications. Yet, Gaventa argued that even these overt instances of suppression of dissent through gatekeeping, agenda setting, and intimidation could not fully explain the degree of acquiescence to the status quo that could be observed in the valley. For example, even after evidence of corruption, embezzlement, and involvement in murder was clearly understood, 81% of votes from the town went to support the incumbent establishment union candidate.

The ways that power was being used to shape ideology (power's third dimension) could best be observed, Gaventa (1980) argued, through careful attention to two processes: (1) the ways that residents' sense of powerlessness worked to give a false sense of acceptance of the status quo and (2) more direct shaping of cognition by the holders of power. One example of the first process can be seen in the case of residents sticking to the false story to help cover up the murder of the reform candidate for union leadership. No overt threats had been made against the residents. Instead, there was an internalized feeling of vulnerability that led many to perceive likely risks for dissenting from the wishes of the establishment. Sufficient public examples of total domination—sometimes including outright violence—of the miners by the company and their collaborators in the union elite had led to a general sense of the futility and risk of taking action to resist domination. Miners who had not been directly threatened themselves either suppressed their own grievances or, in some cases, acted directly against their own interests because they perceived that doing so was a better option than being seen as an enemy or nuisance to the powerful elites.

The second process could be glimpsed in the ways that events and issues were framed and discussed. Myths about the reform candidate for union leadership (e.g., that his campaign was being financed by rich coal operators or that he planned to take workers' pensions away) were propagated and nurtured by the corporation. Advocates for miners' interests (e.g., Ralph Nader) were labeled as outsiders and threats to mining and organized labor. In short, the miners' beliefs about public issues were *more easily manipulated because of their dependency on the union and economic vulnerability*. Even in the rare instances when residents of the valley were able to organize autonomous sources of power, the threat to the company and local elites was effectively countered using a combination of mechanisms that can be analyzed using the three faces of power. Gaventa (1980) underscored the importance of the power relationship: "Power serves to create power. Powerlessness serves to reenforce powerlessness. Power relationships, once established, are self-sustaining" (p. 256).

The third dimension of power draws attention to our collective tendency to mistake causality in the flow of events by ascribing a greater role to rationality than it deserves. Through careful attention to common beliefs and the use of metaphors, language, and myths, we can discern that what appear to be rational choices by individuals and groups are sometimes masquerading ex post facto rationalizations that serve the interests of powerful entities. In other words, the third face of power is often the most difficult to detect because it requires observers to assiduously scrutinize the discursive moves and basic assumptions of participants in community power relations. Deeper still, it requires observers to rework some of the most commonly held conceptions of rationality, individualism, choice, and power.

Community Power Structure in an Era of Global Capitalism

The three-dimensional model (Table 2.1) can be a useful framework for studying the operation of community power at the local level, as Gaventa (1980) demonstrated. Yet, the power structures of local communities have changed in many ways since the middle of the twentieth century when this framework was developed. With the end of the Cold War, an era of global capitalism dawned, and the rise of free market economics has been seemingly inexorable. Companies whose brands were once synonymous with specific locations have established multinational systems of production and global systems of distribution. As a result of these and other changes

Table 2.1 **Example Questions for Insights Into the Three Dimensions of Community Power**

Dimensions of Community Power	Example Questions
1. Situational	• Who prevails in publicly visible conflicts over community issues? • Who is able to reward their allies and punish their adversaries?
2. Institutional	• How are issues being selected and prioritized for public debate? • Is expression of some grievances being prevented (e.g., by efforts by elites to confine discussions to "safe" issues or through instilled fear of backlash or reprisals)?
3. Systemic	• Which myths are useful for justifying the current distributions of resources and opportunities? • How are stories and language used to shift the bounds of what is considered rational, reasonable, or fair?

Note: Names for the dimensions of community power are from Alford and Friedland (1985).

in political economy, as well as technological developments, events are more interconnected across places than they once were, and private corporations are less likely to be tied to particular locations. Corporations are even less likely to be effectively regulated by the governments of those locations (Soja, 2000). Bargaining power has been reduced for residents and employees, but it has also been reduced for local and national governments, meaning that the public sites for democratic participation themselves have often either vanished or lost power (Stiglitz, 2006). The forms of mass media, surveillance, and mass society that some twentieth-century thinkers feared have now arrived, but they are often veiled and obscured by largely illusory forms of agency and democracy through consumer capitalism that holds out promises not only of satisfaction but also of identity and agency, including political agency.

Inequality has increased steadily for decades in many of the wealthier countries, such that presumptions about political and economic egalitarianism that were held in the mid–twentieth century are now viewed as historically specific forms of optimism about the nature of capitalism (Piketty, 2014). Inequalities in wealth have been steadily increasing within the United States (and, to a lesser degree, within other wealthy countries) since the 1980s. The magnitude of concentration of private wealth in relation to national incomes is not an anomalous occurrence but a result of durable changes in the global economy and the policies that govern it. Drivers of this wealth agglomeration include rapidly increasing top corporate salaries in comparison to worker pay. Meanwhile, returns on capital investment have outpaced growth in productivity and wages. And, changes in tax policies have favored corporations and the wealthy. These trends are leading to what Piketty called "the emergence of a new patrimonial capitalism" (p. 173), in which the incomes derived from previously accumulated wealth dwarf the potential earnings from even very highly compensated labor. Meanwhile, income and wealth generated by the poor and working classes has been stagnant or declining in real value.

In the United States, for example, levels of economic inequality have now been reached that have not been seen since before the Great Depression, but there is little reason to believe that inequality will not continue to rise as neoliberal policies are unceasingly advanced across a broader range of sectors, institutions, and levels of government (G. Nelson, 2013). Economics, class, and inequality therefore must occupy a more prominent place in conceptions of community power structure in this new era of global capitalism than they occupied in mid–twentieth century treatments. Some social theorists have developed frameworks for understanding the intersection of social/community power, state power, and economic power. Wright (1994), for example, provided a synthesis of how class shapes politics in a framework informed by Lukes's three-dimensional view of power.

Wright (1994) first argued for a view of class as relational (i.e., defined by relations between workers and the owners of capital who appropriate the value of labor) as opposed to a gradational phenomenon (e.g., lower, middle, or upper class). In the struggles that overtly arise in the power relationships that define class, capitalists are able to deploy disproportionate resources to achieve their goals at the expense of workers'. Because this asymmetry of power is not always exercised strategically or successfully within particular conflicts, it does not always result in greater exploitation of workers. This may be at least in part because capitalists are more dedicated to exercising power at the institutional rather than the situational level—power's second dimension rather than the first. In other words, those working to advance the interests of capital are often more invested in shaping the rules of the game (e.g., policies on taxation and electoral rules that function to exclude possibilities for contestation of their interests) than they are in the particular skirmishes that occur within that game. Further, exercise of power in the third dimension can be seen in the now-commonplace view that there are no plausible alternatives to global capitalism, and that it is a system whose functioning is natural (and therefore not amenable to modification or challenge). Wright concluded that class is likely to be a primary explanatory factor for the outcomes of political processes, whether or not overt conflict is evident, specifically when (a) what is being contested is more abstract/general and less fine-grained/particular and (b) class-based interests are more directly challenged.

This type of power analysis also has potential to yield insights into other systems of domination in contemporary society, such as race-based oppression. Attention to racism and racial disparities is conspicuously lacking in many of the studies of community power structures in the mid–twentieth-century United States. Despite the legal and symbolic gains for racial justice over the ensuing decades (e.g., the Voting Rights and Fair Housing acts of 1965 and 1968 and the election of Barack Obama as US president in 2008), stark disparities persist between racial/ethnic groups[3] in the United States in terms of rates of poverty, educational opportunities, health outcomes, and incarceration. Many of these disparities are rooted in the country's founding as a settler colonialist slave state (Baptist, 2014; Dunbar-Ortiz, 2015) and are being exacerbated by the neoliberal policies heightening inequality and diminishing public supports for less wealthy residents (Nkansah-Amankra, Agbanu, & Miller, 2013). Efforts to gain public support for these neoliberal policy reforms in the United States are often tacit appeals to racist sentiments. One conspicuous example was Ronald Reagan's invocation of the "welfare queen" to mislead the US public into believing that welfare fraud among people of color was rampant (see Levin, 2013).

Racism is particularly apparent in contemporary United States at the systemic and institutional levels or in power's second and third dimensions. An example of the operation of power at the systemic and institutional levels is the current system of mass incarceration in the United States. Since the 1970s, the population of incarcerated persons has grown by more than 500% (Cloud, Parsons, & Delany-Brumsey, 2014). The United States now accounts for more than 20% of the world's total of incarcerated people, despite accounting for only 5% of the world's population. Rates of incarceration are radically unequally distributed across racial and ethnic groups. For example, young African American men in the United States are currently more likely to be incarcerated than to graduate from college with a 4-year degree (Western, 2014). Much of this disparity is due to policies that have criminalized urban poverty, to disproportionate police contact in poor urban neighborhoods, and to differential treatment and outcomes in the prosecutorial and parole systems. Incarceration itself produces a number of negative social, economic, and psychological effects that ripple through families and generations (Schnittker, 2014; Wildeman, 2014), compounding existing racial disparities. As a whole, the system of mass incarceration can be viewed as a form of racialized domination and control or as a thinly disguised race-based caste system in an era in which more overt forms of racial domination (such as *de jure* segregation) are no longer possible in the United States (Alexander, 2010).

Some scholars have specifically explored the intersections of power and ideology that characterize the third face of power as it relates to mass incarceration. For example, scholars like Sloop (1996) and Steiner (2001) linked the discourses and stories that define public consciousness about crime, criminal justice policies, and prisons to underlying political forces. Steiner linked the "War on Drugs" to white supremacist fables about white innocence, African American crime, and the reasons for racial inequality. When aggressively punitive drug policies were passed in the 1980s and 1990s, large majorities of the public wrongly ascribed disproportionate levels of drug use to Blacks and even assigned blame to Blacks for economic disparities between races. Political discourse played on these myths to construct and reinforce notions of whites as innocent victims of drug problems that had their origin in "filthy city streets." Images of urban Blacks and Latinos as the "typical" users of drugs became frequent in media, helping to build support for militant policing and pitiless sentencing policies. Meanwhile, as Sloop showed, the public narrative about prisoners was transitioning from stereotypes of a hapless white male down on his luck to stereotypes of a Black male who has an essential violent criminal nature and should therefore be kept away from society. Steiner (2001) pointed out that "such political storytelling can be seen not only as a dominant methodology for promoting 'tougher' anti-drug policies but also as a tacit defense of existing dominant-subordinate relations (i.e. social and economic inequality)" (p. 201).

Myths and fables have also been very effectively deployed to suppress dissent and grievances during the decades-long march toward what Fraser (2015) called our "Second Gilded Age."[4] Much like Gaventa's Appalachian mining town—and unlike workers in the late nineteenth and early twentieth centuries—the US public has shown very little resistance to the reestablishment of an aristocratic plutocracy and have seemed in many respects to welcome it. In a wide-ranging cultural and historical analysis, Fraser identified three dominant fables that have served to make responses other than acquiescence difficult to sustain or, in some cases, even to contemplate.

First, there is the fable of the contemporary businessman as a populist hero: Disrupting old inefficient bureaucracies, taking risks, and dressing and behaving in unconventional ways for aristocrats (e.g., Steve Jobs, Warren Buffett), they became "our culture's plebian champions, our democratic plutocrats" (Fraser, 2015, p. 217). Second, there is the fable of mass consumption capitalism as the ideal vehicle for individual freedom. Appropriating the counterconformity instincts of the 1960s, consumer capitalism now offers infinite new avenues for individual "faux self-expression": "Consumer culture cultivates a politics of style and identity focused on the rights and inner psychic freedom of the individual . . . nothing could be more corrosive of the kinds of social sympathy and connectedness that constitute the emotional substructure of collective resistance and rebellion" (p. 305). Third, Fraser identified the fable of the free agent that has caused some to embrace the dismantling of the kinds of job security, workplace regulations, unions, and collective bargaining rights that the labor movement fought to establish during the New Deal. While some workers have resisted these changes, "many celebrated their new status, a fact that registers how deeply the notion of the free individual as a lone player in the marketplace had triumphed" (p. 330). According to Fraser, these three fables combine with fear of loss engendered by the declining fortunes of millions of Americans to induce both quiescence and the rise of the populist right.

The power of these fables obscures and naturalizes relationships of domination at a societal level, illustrating the central importance of the third dimension of power in establishing and maintaining the contemporary global order. Power has been exercised so effectively at the level of ideology that it renders many of the more publicly visible conflicts between competing interests (e.g., elections for the US presidency) much less important in terms of the effects of the outcome on the interests of the elite. Yet, some studies shine a light on the second face of power in action, demonstrating its continued importance. Hacker and Pierson (2010), for example, described the ways that wealthy and business interests in the United States from the 1980s onward have targeted contributions not only to Republican candidates and officeholders but also to members of the Democratic Party. This strategy allows them flexibility to control the agenda in turbulent policymaking processes:

> The main goal of channeling money to influential or swing Democrats was to minimize any prospect of distasteful policy drift. Carefully targeted contributions could effectively exploit the multiple channels American political institutions make available for diversion, dilution, or delay. Even grudging or quiet support from a handful of Democrats—particularly well-placed ones—could make a huge difference. Such allies could help keep issues off the agenda, substitute symbolic initiatives for real ones, add critical loopholes, or instigate unnecessary compromises with the GOP. (p. 178)

As these examples indicate, the contemporary exercise of power is frequently observed at the national or international levels, and decision-making is often influenced by societal myths that are perpetuated to reinforce systems of racial domination and the primacy of private-sector interests. To understand community power structure in the United States and many other parts of the world, it is necessary to orient the three-dimensional approach that Gaventa illustrated toward these specific manifestations of power. Critical race theory (Graham, Brown-Jeffy, Aronson, & Stephens, 2011) and an intersectional frame of analysis that examines multiple dimensions of identity-based oppression (Cho, Crenshaw, & McCall, 2013) are therefore especially vital when considering power's second and third dimensions operating at institutional/systems and ideological levels. Furthermore, understanding contemporary community power structure requires attention to the ways in which structural forces associated with globalization, global capitalism, and neoliberalism are affecting the ground on which local community power structures operate. In fact, some of these macro-level changes beg the question: What role is left for local community power and empowerment in an era of global capitalism that has aggregated many institutions—from businesses to news media—together into conglomerates? To what extent do these changes make attention to local community power futile from both scholarly and strategic standpoints?

Local Community Power

Autonomy and decision-making have been reduced for local communities as global capitalism has moved more of the levers of power to regional, national, and international levels. This fact presents challenges to those who seek meaningful changes. Many outcomes that are integral to people's daily lives, however, are still decided at the local level. For example, localities in the United States are the primary policymaking venues for education and law enforcement, and laws that govern employment and compensation standards such as the minimum wage are most often set at the local and state levels. Transportation and other forms of infrastructure (e.g., water and energy) are most often locally governed.[5] Moreover, due to the speed of communications, local conflicts now occur in more interconnected ways than they have in previous eras, creating possibilities for local collective action to galvanize national or even international change efforts. How do the dimensions of community power show up in more recent research on local change?

Situational

The influence of early community power theorists can be found in different strands of contemporary scholarship on local issues. The work of Hunter and Mills and the so-called elitists, for example, underpins conceptions of urban growth machines (Jonas & Wilson, 1999; Molotch, 1976) and urban regime analysis (Dowding, 2001; Stone, 2006). These concepts extend the notion of a community power structure to take account of the constant succession of governing coalitions that come together to exert influence in cities, typically in service of growth and publicly subsidized private development. And, of course, in an era replete with antielite sentiment (as exemplified by Occupy Wall Street and the Tea Party), Mills's basic position on the existence of a corporate and governmental power elite at the national level and the dangers that it posed is now widely shared, even if different ends of the political divide decry the domination of different forms of elitism.

The pluralists, meanwhile, have conceptual and methodological descendants in contemporary social science, which takes a naturalistic approach to the study of communities and political processes. Rational choice theory (see Kroneberg & Kalter, 2012) and punctuated equilibrium theory (Jones & Baumgartner, 2012), borrowing concepts from free-market economics and evolutionary biology, respectively, are examples. These approaches presuppose somewhat stable "rules of the game" and look for the influences that shape civic outcomes through systemic adaptations and the rational choices of interconnected actors. Scholars of social movements have adopted some of these perspectives in resource mobilization approaches that seek to explain movements and movement participation based on organizational incentives, cost-reducing mechanisms, and benefits to social movement participation (Klandermans, 1984; McCarthy & Zald, 1977; Oliver, 2015).

Institutional

The institutional second face of power can also be seen in some critical investigations of local decision-making processes. Studying local education systems, for instance, G. L. Anderson (1998) contrasted the rhetoric of democratic participation in these systems' community engagement strategies with the reality of how participation tends to take place in school reform efforts. In fact, he argued, educational institutions and more powerful groups of stakeholders tend to use the participation process to serve their own interests rather than the public's. Participation is often used by schools as a public relations strategy that persists only so long as the community members who are engaged do not wield actual control. Further, Anderson argued, participation can be a form of collusion as school administrators, teachers, and middle- and upper-class parents "capture" the participatory process and use it to advocate primarily for the interests of professionals and more advantaged students.

Local participation in community development processes can have similar dynamics. For example, contributors to a volume edited by Cooke and Kothari (2001) examined the ways that participatory practice by multinational development organizations—despite rhetoric about the transformative potential of so-called bottom-up processes—can actually serve to mask power differentials between the development organizations and local residents and to obscure differences in power among the local residents. Local participation is sought in venues that can subtly suppress candor and critique. Local input is often reinterpreted by outside facilitators in ways that ignore local power differentials. It can come to be understood in terms that are compatible with predetermined project deliverables. The staff who become the bearers and interpreters of local knowledge can use it to advance their own agendas within development initiatives and organizations. Local residents with advantaged positions will often learn to use the development processes to advance their agendas and standing in the community as well. In the worst cases, participatory development processes can afford development organizations additional justification for their predetermined agendas while feeding into local systems of patronage and reinforcing lopsided power relationships between locals. These insights into participation in community development and education policy demonstrate the critical importance of attention to the second face of power in local decision-making processes across a range of topics.

Systemic

There has been less attention to the systemic third dimension of power in studies of local community processes. Examples can be found, however, in critical urban geography such as Smith's (1992, 1996) work on gentrification on the Lower East Side of Manhattan (Speer, 2008). As developers sought to market the neighborhood to wealthier potential residents (rebranding it as the East Village), the existing residents, primarily with lower incomes, were inconveniently in the way. Smith documented how the area was routinely described as a "new frontier" (Smith, 1996, p. 7), with developments marketing "the taming of the wild west" (p. 13) to evoke both the opportunities and the potential dangers for those who would seize them. As evictions accelerated in the late 1980s, many existing residents became squatters in the area around Tompkins Square Park, and the park became a focal point for confrontations between antigentrification protesters and the city, especially the police. The park was eventually closed by the city and the squatters were evicted, clearing the way for the neighborhood to be resettled by "urban pioneers" (p. 11). The frontier myth was constructed by developers, but it became so pervasive that it was even used by those protesting the gentrification of the neighborhood. Smith demonstrated how it served to both obscure and rationalize the sometimes-violent displacement and opportunistic exploitation of the neighborhood.

Another example of insights into the second and third faces of power at the local level comes from Flyvbjerg's study of a comprehensive planning effort in the Danish town of Aalborg (1998, 2002). Through proposed improvements to public transportation, housing stock, and pedestrian and bike infrastructure, the plan initially aimed to reduce automobile traffic in the city by one third. The city government in Aalborg solicited public input on the plan. Observing these processes, Flyvbjerg concluded that there was both too little democracy and too much. There was too much democracy in the sense that certain groups (e.g., the Chamber of Industry and Commerce) were overrepresented to the point that they distorted the outcomes of the process. In contrast, there were insufficient efforts to engage local residents, an observation consistent with the second face of power.

Influenced by Foucault's conception of power as well as his genealogical method, Flyvbjerg probed deeper into this local planning debate and found that supporters and opponents of the plan were not only making different rational arguments but also they offering competing rationalities that could interpret specific facts differently. For instance, analyses of survey data were interpreted differently by supporters of the plan and the representatives of the business community, who opposed the reduction in automobile traffic. In the end, parts of the plan were implemented, but not the parts that would reduce the number of cars. In fact, automobile traffic increased as the plan was implemented. Flyvbjerg (2002) observed that the winners in the public deliberation were those who could—through multiple mechanisms and webs of power relations—put the most power behind their preferred rationality. He concluded that the relationship between rationality and power is mutually constitutive, yet unequal: "Power has a clear tendency to dominate rationality in the dynamic and overlapping relationship between the two. Paraphrasing Pascal, one could say that power has a rationality that rationality does not know. Rationality, on the other hand, does not have a power that power does not know" (pp. 360–361). This pithy statement on the relationship between rationality and power encapsulates the third dimension of community power.

As these examples illustrate, the three-dimensional view of power can be useful as a framework for organizing understanding of local decision-making processes and power relationships. In an era of global capitalism, however, it is imperative that understanding of power not be limited to the local level. In the mid-twentieth century, altering policies and practices at City Hall or at the headquarters of a local company might have constituted an ultimate victory in some cases. In the twenty-first century, the relationship of local businesses and governmental agencies to extralocal political and economic forces must be taken into account. Critical studies of multinational development like Cooke and Kothari's (2001) and critical urban geographers like Smith (1992, 1996) are good examples of studies of local power dynamics that are clearly situated within global political, economic, and historical context. An accurate understanding of contemporary community power dynamics will require more observers, practitioners, and strategists to make these connections in their work.

Liberation and Social Power

The theories and studies described so far in this chapter have been primarily concerned with illuminating the mechanics used to maintain asymmetric power relationships. Some critics of Lukes and other community power theorists have pointed out that their emphasis is nearly entirely on domination ("power over") and not on power relationships with the potential to be positive or transformative ("power to").[6] Yet, power is used not only for domination and oppression but also for transformation of oppressive structures or liberation (Prilleltensky, 2008). A core principle of grassroots community organizing speaks to this fact—organizers argue that power itself is inherently neutral—it can be exercised for many different purposes, ranging from domination to liberation (Mondros & Wilson, 1994). The nearly exclusive focus on explanation of power relationships of domination may help to explain why many strands of community power theory have remained primarily academic discussions (Swartz, 2007); the three-dimensional view of community power structure, for example, is not frequently used by practitioners, grassroots groups, advocates, and strategists.[7]

Yet, community power theory offers insights that can apply readily to liberation-oriented efforts to build and exercise community power. Just as it can be useful for tracing the exercise of power by elites seeking to maintain their advantages, it can be useful for planning action and contestation of elite interests. Like power itself, which can be used for oppressive or liberatory ends, nothing prevents this framework from being used in the study of liberation processes as well as the maintenance of asymmetric power relations. The framework provides a lens that can be applied in pursuit of various ends. The exercise of community power for liberation and achievement of social justice, however, is not always simply the mirror image of the exercise of power for the purposes of domination and oppression. Examining both types of processes, some differences become apparent.

Specifically, the three-dimensional framework does not account for some of the fundamental processes that build residents' power to mount challenges. These can be thought of as the *sources* of community power for resisting and overcoming domination and asymmetry (Speer, 2008). The sources of elite power often hinge on greater access to resources, while those who contest elite interests must rely on social power. In Gaventa's (1980) study, for example, it is clear that the same tools are not available to the Appalachian miners that those in control of the company have at their disposal. The company deploys its disproportionate resources to exert influence and advance its interests. The company is able to wield resources, for instance, to influence or even suppress news coverage of particular community issues. The miners' interests were repeatedly repressed by the company's deployment of these resources.

Fortunately, this same outcome does not occur in every other case of conflict arising within asymmetric power relations. In fact, in many cases, those with fewer resources prevail, often due to their ability to organize larger numbers of people. As Saul Alinsky (1971) famously claimed, there are two forms of power: organized money and organized people (p. 127). Most groups seeking to exercise power for liberation and social justice face opponents with access to more money and institutional resources than they have themselves and must therefore seek to build power primarily through organizing people. Community organizing and movements for civil rights and Black liberation in the United States, for example, provide many vivid examples of the power of organized people.

Organizing people, however, requires countering some dominant societal myths. Individualism, in particular, is an obstacle to organizing people. Especially in the West, where individualism is among the strongest cultural values, we tend to gravitate to interpretations of events that center on the agency of individual actors. The civil rights movement in the United States, for instance, is often described as if its successes were catalyzed primarily by the charismatic leadership of Martin Luther King, Jr. In reality, the movement's successes depended on decades of organizing, training, and direct action taken by thousands of people whose names rarely appear in history books (Preskill & Brookfield, 2009). In the words of Ella Baker, "The movement made Martin, and not Martin the movement" (see Fairclough, 2001, p. 409). This misperception that social and political change happens when individuals take action has grave consequences for those seeking to build power in the form of organized people. Many people tacitly expect transformative leaders to be able to make social and political change,[8] and their own approaches to engagement in public issues are fundamentally individualistic and consumerist. Unless they are in control of large amounts of money that can be strategically deployed, however, isolated individual actors in the public arena are unlikely to have much effect. Countering these dominant societal myths, which requires operating in power's third dimension, is critical for developing social power.

In fact, this basic insight about the source of social power goes back much further than Alinsky and models for grassroots community organizing. Among democratic nations, Tocqueville wrote, "All the citizens are independent and feeble; they can hardly do anything by themselves. . . . If men living in democratic countries had no right and no inclination to associate for political purposes, their independence would be in great jeopardy" (1840/1945, p. 115). Although the fact that people must organize to be effective is a cornerstone of democratic theory, it is often either ignored or obscured. Hacker and Pierson (2010), for example, made the case that contemporary political science has failed to adequately attend to the central role that organized groups play in struggles over specific policies. "In our fragmented political system, victories without enduring organization are almost always fleeting. Struggles over policy—over what the government actually *does* for and to its citizens—are usually long, hard slogs" (p. 172).

When considering community power from the perspective of liberation and transformation, we must therefore attend not only to the mechanisms by which power is exercised, but also to the preconditions for social power in the form of organized people. Distinguishing between social power, state power, and economic power, Wright (2013) defined social power as "power rooted in voluntary cooperation through collective action" (p. 19), which has varying relationships with economic and state power in different sociopolitical arrangements. Just as we would seek to understand economic and political power as a precondition for understanding the establishment or maintenance of oppressive power relationships, we must attend to the organizational and relational sources of social power to understand how power operates in processes of liberation.

Cooperation is a cornerstone of social power. This reality, however, can serve to obscure the fact that conflicts are typically necessary to bring about social and political transformation. Drawing on Freire (1973), Niebuhr (1932), and Alinsky (1971), Speer (2008) identified this paradox: Although cooperation is an essential element of community change efforts, "the issue of cooperation is complicated by the fact that any efforts that successfully challenge oppression and injustice in the status quo will meet strong resistance" (p. 205). Efforts to change systems by building social power must therefore be able to balance the needs for cooperation and conflict (Christens & Inzeo, 2015). This paradoxical insight into the *nature* of social power is critical for an understanding of community power as it operates in pursuit of liberation and transformation.

Conclusions

Drawing on theory and research from social and political sciences, this chapter has traced the contours of a theoretical framework for understanding contemporary communities' power structures. Lukes's three-dimensional view of community power urges us not to stop at identifying the winners or losers of publicly visible conflicts over issues (situational, first dimension) or even to stop at understanding the agenda-setting and gatekeeping processes that seek to influence which conflicts emerge in public debate and which do not (institutional, second dimension), but to interrogate the assumptions that undergird public understanding of issues and the ways that power is operating to shape and promote particular rationalities and interpretations of information and events (systemic, third dimension). In fact, how power is operating in this third dimension is particularly meaningful since it shapes and constrains opportunities for the exercise of power in the second dimension, which in turn shapes possibilities for overt contestation and, ultimately, the outcomes of these conflicts. Studies by Gaventa, Flyvbjerg, and others demonstrated the utility of this three-dimensional view for critical insights into asymmetrical power relations.

If anything, attention to all three of these dimensions of power has become more essential in an era of global capitalism. The seemingly inexorable rise of a new power elite with global reach is constraining the possibilities for local action. Corporations are using ever more intrusive forms of communications media to shape conceptions of public issues and ever more money to influence political outcomes. People's identities are being purposefully shaped into individualistic consumers rather than participatory members of local communities. Meanwhile, oppression and injustice are promulgated through systems such as banking, public education, housing, policing, criminal justice, and incarceration. Yet, it is possible to identify and contest the ways in which our political, social, economic, and institutional systems have been built to protect the interests of some groups, while excluding, exploiting, and even killing others. And, it is increasingly possible to identify connections between marginalization and economic exclusion of different populations around the world and to understand similarities in the logic used to rationalize these injustices (Sassen, 2015).

Understanding that power is inherently neutral and can be used for both domination and liberation opens possibilities for a multidimensional view to be less determinist and more dynamic. Yet, the sources and nature of social power differ from those of state and economic power. Democratic theory and grassroots community-organizing models provide additional insights into the source of social power: collective action. Building social power requires countering individualist myths to build social power through organizations. Community organizing and democratic theory also stress the likelihood of conflict when institutional and systemic changes are pursued, providing insight into the nature of social power. By drawing on the perspectives described in this chapter—the three-dimensional view of power, an understanding of structural forces such as racism and neoliberal globalization, and insights into the source and nature of social power from community organizing and democratic theory—we arrive at a framework for community power that can account for the multiple dimensions of domination and oppression while also allowing possibilities for agency, development, and transformation. Although it can certainly be further detailed, enhanced, and refined, this chapter has sought to identify some of the major components of a framework for community power that can inform and guide empowerment theory and practice.

Notes

1. This critique of power structure and power elite theories is similar to liberal critiques of Marxism, yet elite theorists and community power structure theorists have tended to be less focused on class-based stratification and more focused on the political power within and between organizations and institutions. There will be more on this further in the chapter.
2. The "elitist" label conferred by the pluralists on their ideological opponents is somewhat misleading. So-called elitists have tended to be critical of the concentration of power in elite groups.
3. Racial identities are socially constructed, not biologically based, yet they are often deeply meaningful social categories in race-conscious societies (Jones, 2000).
4. The first Gilded Age ran from the late nineteenth century through the Great Depression.
5. However, corporate interests are impinging on local control of these resources in some cases.
6. In the second edition of *Power: A Radical View*, Lukes (2005) acknowledged that his thinking on this point had changed in the intervening 30 years since he first published the book; he now believed that the study of power should not be limited to asymmetric relations or domination, but should also include power as capacity and ability.
7. The three-dimensional view of power has been applied in work on international development by nongovernmental organizations. Gaventa (2006) has specifically adapted the model for work with practitioners in this domain, and there has been some limited adaptation of this model for use in other forms of civic action.
8. The euphoria among many liberals and progressives during the 2008 election of Barack Obama, for instance, quickly turned to disappointment when the limitations of his individual power, even from the office of US president, became apparent.

|| 3 ||

The Rise of Empowerment

The term *empowerment* was once much less pervasive than it is today. It seems to have first come into common use in association with social movements of the 1960s, such as feminist movement organizations and the Black Power movement (McAdam, 1999; Rogell & Olsson, 2011). By the late 1970s and early 1980s, it was just beginning to be used in discussions on social theory and social policy, as well as in the helping professions (e.g., psychology and social work) (Simon, 1994). Rappaport (1987), a psychologist, provided an influential definition of empowerment as "a process by which people, organizations, and communities gain control over their affairs" (p. 122). Yet, the term simultaneously began to appear in popular culture and advertising. The term has become ever more common and popular in the early twenty-first century and is now deeply ingrained in the vocabulary of local politics, educational and health promotion programs, community organizations, and even self-help books. In many instances, empowerment is invoked as a catch-all term for feeling good, strong, and capable of managing one's individual concerns in life, love, and work.[1] This terminological expansion and dilution has led to a reciprocal trend—a growing disaffection with the term among scholars, practitioners, and civic actors, who would prefer the term to mean something more specifically social and political, as it did decades ago. Many of them tire of explaining the distinctions between the ways that they intend the meaning of the term and the ways that it pops up in everyday life.[2] In fact, some have recently argued that it is time to discard the term altogether.

Has empowerment had its moment? Should the term simply be ceded to the advertisers and self-help gurus? What is it about the origins of the term and the concepts that it can communicate that might make it worth fighting for (and over)? In this chapter, I attempt to rediscover the conceptual roots of the term and identify some of its initial appeal. To do so, I identify some of the underpinnings of empowerment ideology from long before the term itself became common. I then trace the evolution of the concept through to empowerment's current crisis of meaning and dig into what I believe are some of the most pressing current issues with the concept. These are (a) a lack of definitional clarity, (b) the growing tendency for empowerment to be understood as an individualistic phenomenon, (c) the weakened links between contemporary conceptions of empowerment and a coherent theory of power, (d) a lack of clarity on roles in empowerment processes, and (e) tensions between collaboration and conflict. Only by addressing these interrelated issues can the theory of empowerment grow beyond current shortcomings to realize more of its long-recognized potential to act as a guiding framework for community practice and research.

Roots of Empowerment Ideology

Even when it is watered down, empowerment has connoted decentralization, reductions of stratification and hierarchies, and belief in the capabilities of everyday people. These basic ideas of course pre-date the arrival of the term *empowerment* in the late twentieth century. Simon (1994), for instance, traced the roots of the approach in social work to some of the profession's earliest practices in the 1890s. Further, she argued that some of the inclination toward empowerment among the field's founders was due to influences by much earlier political and intellectual movements. In this account, the cultural and ideological origins of the concept and approach can be found, for example, in the 1600s in the Protestant Revolution and in responses to early industrial capitalism. In the early 1800s, some elements of an empowerment approach are evident, for instance, in Jeffersonian democracy, with its emphasis on self-rule and active citizenship. Simon traced similar cultural threads through nineteenth and twentieth-century intellectual movements, including utopianism, transcendentalism, pragmatism, populism, unionism, progressivism, feminism, anarchism, and the social and political thought of African American scholars and leaders such as W. E. B. Du Bois and other founders of the NAACP (National Association for the Advancement of Colored People).

The settlement house movement, beginning in the late 1800s, is often viewed as a foundation of an empowerment orientation to social work. Settlement houses were established in poor neighborhoods in industrializing cities to provide social and educational opportunities to recently arrived immigrants, particularly women and children. Although much of the work of settlement houses was charity oriented,[3] practitioners also worked alongside residents to pursue systemic changes in their communities—an approach that is a harbinger of empowerment. Jane Addams, the most visible leader in the movement and the founder of Chicago's Hull House, had some instincts that were empowerment oriented, most evident in her idea that Hull House could function to help not only meet the material, social, and educational needs of poor families, but also operate as an anchor institution for collaborative inquiry into the causes of poverty and sustained efforts to address them. These instincts were nurtured and advanced over time by her collaborations with leaders for civil rights, workers' rights, and women's rights, including Florence Kelley, Julia

Lathrop, and Mary Kenney O'Sullivan (Knight, 2010). For example, collaborating with Florence Kelley persuaded Addams to adopt a more progressive stance, to aim more of her efforts at the causes of poverty and associated social problems rather than treating their symptoms, and to side more often with exploited groups in social and political conflicts (Preskill & Brookfield, 2009).

One element of the empowerment approach that is evident in the settlement house movement is the attempt to address both the rights and needs of vulnerable populations. In addition to providing opportunities for residents, the "settlers" were committed to collaborating with residents to become

> transformers of housing, schooling, workplaces, the Constitution, government, sanitation, health care, consumers' rights, and public spaces. The settlers of the three decades before World War I worked to make the social and physical environment of cities more habitable for poor and vulnerable people and to extend the realm of American social justice to include them. (Simon, 1994, p. 67)

The work of these Progressive Era settlement house leaders was the foundation of a nascent empowerment-oriented branch of the field of social work, which has held fluctuating levels of influence over the field as a whole throughout its history.

While Jane Addams pursued these goals through social work, John Dewey (one of her collaborators and supporters) was formulating and testing philosophies of psychology and education that would exert profound influences on the notions of empowerment that would develop later in the twentieth century. His philosophy built on the work of earlier pragmatists William James, Charles Peirce, Oliver Wendell Holmes, and others (Menand, 2001). This line of thought is characterized by rejection of the view that we can achieve certainty about foundational principles of reality. Instead, pragmatism argues that the human cognitive apparatus is inherently geared toward successful adaptation to circumstances. How we understand the world to function is therefore shaped by how we learn to survive (and possibly thrive) in it. Truth should not be adjudicated through abstract logic but should instead be determined by how well an idea or principle works to further particular goals in specific sets of circumstances. This viewpoint makes it imperative that people are clear about their values so that we can measure the utility of certain ideas through a scientific approach to action in service of those values.

Dewey understood political involvement and action as intrinsic to the duties and role of citizens in a democracy. Democracy, he argued, was not just a mode of governance, but an ethical imperative because of the ways that it shaped people through the educative process of collective decision-making (Dewey, 1916). Publics were formed when groups of people were affected by social problems. These publics not only were vehicles for the resolution of particular social problems but also provided experiences that enhanced people's ability to think and participate effectively as members of democratic society (Dewey, 1927). Democracy and education therefore were not just interdependent processes for Dewey; in a functioning democracy, they would be the same thing. This pragmatic view of the public, of democracy, and of education advanced by Dewey and other scholars like George Herbert Mead formed the intellectual bedrock of much of what would later be formulated as empowerment theory.

Progressive era pragmatism made another vital contribution to what would become empowerment theory with the notion of transaction (Dewey & Bentley, 1949). From Dewey's perspective, it was fruitless to talk about individuals and communities as if they were distinct entities. He pointed out that every time you talked about individuals, you ended up talking about communities as well. And, every time you talked about communities, you ended up talking also about individuals. These were the kind of "dualisms"—individual and community, subject and object—that Dewey saw as unproductive conceptual representations of the world. People and groups could more productively be conceptualized as thoroughly connected to each other through what he termed *transactions*. This transactional–ecological worldview (see Altman & Rogoff, 1987) influenced the psychologists and social workers who later formulated an ecological model of empowerment.

The ideological groundwork for empowerment not only was laid by philosophers, social reformers, and educators but also drew many influences from social movements. International labor movements, people's movements, and women's movements developed many of the building blocks, but perhaps no single movement has been so influential on empowerment theory as the US civil rights movement to end legalized segregation, voter suppression, and discrimination in housing, education, and employment (Carson, 1995; McAdam, 1999). Through decades of relationship building, education, and training, leaders built the organizational infrastructure for broad-based and sustained mobilization utilizing various tactics for direct action, including boycotts, sit-ins, civil disobedience, and nonviolent resistance.[4] This was coupled with civic education and voter registration, for example, through Citizenship Schools started in local communities and supported by regional training organizations. Although it tends to be portrayed as a singular or unified movement, in fact it was a sustained effort that was enabled by the creation of hundreds of independent local and regional organizations and institutions, many of which used different methods and tactics.

Civil rights leaders who worked to build organizational and community capacity provide some of the best examples for contemporary empowerment theory. Leaders like Septima Clark helped to support the development of Citizenship Schools in South Carolina. Ella Baker, a seasoned organizer, taught and practiced a distinctive model of collective leadership for democratic self-determination in the movement (Ransby, 2003). As Preskill and Brookfield (2009) pointed out, "The nature of collective leadership militates against any one person clearly standing front and center as some sort of leadership figurehead. For Baker, leadership was never about charisma and always about helping people realize the power of collective solidarity" (Preskill & Brookfield, 2009, p. 95). This type of behind-the-scenes leadership deserves a greater share of the responsibility for the movement's successes than it is given in most popular accounts. It is also more akin to an empowerment orientation than the charismatic or "messianic" leadership model that dominates many retellings of movement successes. Baker's practice of collective leadership provides a highly relevant model for building grassroots power and empowerment in contemporary communities (West, 2014).

Influenced by social theory as well as by labor movement successes, Saul Alinsky (1971) also developed new models for broad-based social action in poor urban neighborhoods in the 1930s through the early 1970s. This method sought to knit together diverse organizational constituencies in neighborhoods (churches, social clubs, labor unions, etc.) through identification of shared self-interest and intentional development of relationships across lines of faith, ideology, and ethnicity. Residents worked together to examine the causes of community problems and to build and sustain campaigns for change on strategically selected issues. Public actions were held in which residents called on decision-makers to commit to specific actions. The groups maintained pressure as necessary to see policy and systems changes implemented while consolidating their gains and undertaking action on other quality-of-life issues. Throughout the process, new residents became engaged in cycles of relationship development, action research within their own communities, strategic mobilization and collective action, and collective reflection and analysis on the results of actions. Groups influenced by Alinsky's model for community organizing now exist in almost every city in the United States and in many other countries,[5] and the approach was influential on the early development of empowerment theory.

Like Ella Baker's collective leadership, the model of grassroots community organizing that Alinsky practiced and described in *Rules for Radicals* (1971) prioritizes leadership by the people who are most directly affected by public issues. Even more than Alinsky himself (who seems to have had a love for the limelight), many of the professional organizers that he taught and inspired tend to operate as catalysts and behind-the-scenes supporters of grassroots community organizing campaigns rather than as spokespeople or advocates. "Never do for people what they can do for themselves" is a principle that helps remind practitioners of neo–Alinsky-style organizing to err on the side of staying out of the way as volunteer leaders deliberate, strategize, and mobilize. Through these grassroots democratic processes, residents gain a deeply experiential form of practical civic education.

Community organizing—when practiced as described—is also akin to another significant influence on empowerment theory: popular education. Paulo Freire (1973) advanced popular education as a mechanism for building the awareness and capacities for action that could lead to liberation from oppression. Like Dewey, Freire viewed education as inherently linked to politics, although he was less idealistic than Dewey was about the possibilities for inquiry and action in the public realm to resolve issues through democratic collaboration. This is likely in part because of his formative experiences in northeastern Brazil during the Great Depression. Like many of their neighbors, his family was plunged into poverty, and Freire observed that class-based relations of domination caused those who were marginalized to suffer silently and passively through extreme poverty, even to the point of starvation. He would later study the ways in which oppression is experienced, and the roles that education can play in perpetuating this "culture of silence" or in disrupting it (Ledwith, 2011, p. 55). Freire saw traditional educational practice as a form of domestication and sought instead to develop methods for education focused on critical consciousness (*conscientização* or "conscientization") and action to achieve liberation from poverty and political oppression.

The philosophy and methodology of popular education is described in Freire's book *Pedagogy of the Oppressed* (1973). Influenced by Gramsci's concept of hegemony as well as other educators like Dewey, Freire described a form of critical educational praxis that not only embraced the democratic and collaborative model of progressive education but also explicitly oriented the educational process toward critical consciousness. Popular education is concerned not only with knowledge, literacy, and skills, but also specifically with the ability to "read the world" or to understand arrangements of power in society and take collective action to transform the status quo. According to Ledwith (2011), "Freire's great strength is the way he locates critical pedagogy within an analysis of power and the way that it becomes woven into the structures of society. In this way, Freirean pedagogy is not segregated from life in the false structures of a classroom, but is all around us in the places that people live their lives; an engagement with people in context" (p. 58). Freire's ideas and his model of popular education are some of the most direct influences on the notion of empowerment. These roots and influences make it clear that the concept of empowerment and the philosophy that it connotes did not spontaneously emerge when the term was coined or was taken up in various contexts. The degree to which these historical and philosophical roots of the term are conveyed by the term's current usage, however, has been continuously contested.

Empowerment Arrives

The first time that empowerment appeared in academic literature was in Barbara Bryant Solomon's 1976 book *Black Empowerment: Social Work in Oppressed Communities*. Solomon described empowerment as a process that should be a goal of collaborative problem-solving between professional social workers and their Black clients. Empowerment in social work practice could not only solve concrete problems for Black clients but also simultaneously work to undo the sense of powerlessness that was a result of a legacy of oppression.

One year later, Berger and Neuhaus's (1977/1996) influential monograph *To Empower People: From State to Civil Society* was published. Seizing on a moment in which the US public sentiment was shifting markedly toward disaffection with government and public-sector programs, Berger and Neuhaus argued for an alternative to large bureaucracies with one-size-fits-all programs. Mediating structures (local nonprofits, religious institutions, neighborhood associations, etc.) could play more central roles in solving social problems and providing social services. Mediating structures were not fully private or fully public, and they could bridge the gap between private lives and remote and impersonal societal institutions. "Public policy should recognize, respect, and, where possible, empower these institutions" (p. 164).

This call was taken up primarily by right-wing and centrist reformers, who steadily reduced the role of government over the decades to come, in some instances replacing government programs with more decentralized grants and contracts to local nonprofit organizations.[6] This neoliberal turn was not purely a co-optation of the idea of empowerment. In fact, these threads had been present in the ideals of Jeffersonian democracy and other ideological underpinnings of the concept. Ella Baker, Saul Alinsky, Jane Addams, and other influences of an empowerment approach certainly worked in and through mediating institutions. Part of the complexity of the concept of empowerment therefore involves a nuanced contextual analysis of the roles and responsibilities of government and citizens and the roles of private nonprofit organizations and other civil society institutions. Indeed, even though empowerment became a rallying cry for those seeking more egalitarian social systems, part of its conceptual appeal is that it emphasizes the potential of smaller decentralized organizations and groups to take meaningful and productive actions in the sociopolitical arena. A paradox of the empowerment approach, then, is that it can sometimes serve as a cover for the neoliberal goal of demolishing the social welfare state in the name of freedom or can at least be fairly compatible with this aim.

The concept of empowerment became particularly influential in the field of community psychology. This field has done much to advance a coherent theory of empowerment that is oriented toward egalitarianism and community well-being. In some ways, the field's founding in the 1960s was an embrace of an empowerment ethos even though the term itself did not show up in the field's literature until Hoffman's 1978 study of the United Farm Workers was published in the *Journal of Community Psychology*. Community psychology began as a movement among psychologists to address social/community problems and promote well-being in nonclinical contexts. As in the macropractice branch of social work, empowerment was quickly acknowledged as an aspect of the practice and research of community psychologists.

In a presidential address to the American Psychological Association's division for community psychology (now the Society for Community Research and Action),

Newbrough (1980) articulated a vision for "the participating society" concluding that "the public interest is the empowerment of people" (p. 15). Giving the following year's presidential address, Rappaport (1981) suggested that empowerment should be at the conceptual core of the field as it sought to balance the needs that people have for services and supports with their inherent rights, capacities, and freedoms. In his address, he faulted the Progressive Era philosophy that spawned many of the helping professions for overemphasizing needs over rights. Speaking shortly after its dawn, he correctly anticipated a new neoliberal era that would mobilize against the achievements of the Progressive Era. He was duly critical of the neoliberal fixations with freedom and the rights of individuals to the neglect of needs. For the field to navigate the paradoxical nature of social and community problems without overemphasizing rights or needs, Rappaport suggested, *"we need to find a renewed symbolic and ideational goal and a renewed sense of urgency"* (emphasis in original, p. 15). Empowerment, he contended, could provide both the necessary plan for action as well as that symbolic ideology.

Prevention has also been a conceptual cornerstone of community psychology, and Rappaport (1981) strongly contrasted empowerment ideology with the prevention orientation to community problems. The prevention approach "implies experts fixing the independent variables to make the dependent variables come out right" (p. 16), while an empowerment approach could recognize capabilities that existed in individuals and communities, viewing social and community problems in terms of barriers that prevented these capabilities from being exercised.[7] Rappaport suggested that there were likely psychological benefits to individuals gaining greater control over their lives, but that this was not itself the primary goal of empowerment. "I am, frankly, willing to argue that the programs and policies which make it more possible for people to obtain and control the resources that affect their lives are per se what empowerment is all about" (1981, p. 18). For Rappaport, like Berger and Neuhaus, this logic pointed toward a focus on "mediating institutions" that bridged the gap between remote and bureaucratic societal institutions and individual (often alienated) people. For community psychology to maintain its sense of urgency and not become lopsided in its approach to people's rights and needs, it would need to pay particular attention to community organizations, voluntary associations, and other social settings in which relationships were built, capacities were developed, and control of resources was enhanced.

Although Rappaport identified empowerment as an ideology that ran counter to the logic undergirding the helping professions and their traditions of service provision, he was clear that it was not as an avenue for abdication of social responsibilities or the governmental and societal infrastructure to help solve social problems and provide services. Instead, empowerment for Rappaport implied a repositioning of the helping professional from the role of expert service provider to the role of collaborator in search of solutions to community problems. And, he stressed, solutions to these problems might take shape differently in different community contexts, just as the process of empowerment itself might look different in different communities. This "symbolic ideology" of empowerment permitted professionals to operate more flexibly in dealing with diverse local problems rather than searching for one-size-fits-all solutions.

In subsequent articles, Rappaport (e.g., 1987) elaborated an ecological theory of empowerment. He stressed that empowerment was neither solely an individual psychological construct nor solely a macrosocial phenomenon concerned only with policy and social changes. Empowerment, he argued, should be understood as a multilevel construct in which change at one level (e.g., psychological, macrosocial) might have radiating influences at other levels of analysis. He sought to build empowerment from a vague notion into a theoretical framework by posing critical questions for future investigations in the field, such as: "What are the limits of empowerment in one sphere of life as opposed to another?" and "What is the nature of settings in which empowerment is developed or inhibited?" (p. 129). Referencing Trickett's (1984) work on ecology, Rappaport outlined an agenda for building and testing this ecological theory of empowerment that would investigate processes at different levels of analysis, search for radiating influences across levels, and take account of the historical and cultural contexts in which empowerment processes were unfolding. Research conducted in this framework, he argued, should—to the extent possible—examine, document, and compare these empowerment processes over time, treating participants in the settings as collaborators in searches for locally developed solutions to community problems.

Empowerment theory as articulated by community psychologists has inspired and informed research and practice not only in community and applied social psychology, but also in public health, social work and social policy, community development, and other professions seeking to address social problems. Many of these iterations and implementations of empowerment theory have also drawn on earlier influences. For instance, Wallerstein and Bernstein (1988) and Wallerstein (1992, 1993) used Rappaport's work, but also drew particularly on Freire's model of popular education in proposing empowerment as a framework for health education and health promotion. Swift and Levin (1987) crafted an empowerment orientation for work in prevention and mental health promotion that used these same approaches as well as feminist theory and critiques of Western epistemology and assumptions about power (e.g., Marayuma, 1983).

In the late 1980s and early 1990s, empowerment frameworks were developed for practice and research with particular groups or populations and in many different settings. For example, Gutiérrez (1990) outlined the implications of an empowerment orientation specifically for social work with women of color. Checkoway and Norsman (1986) adapted it as an orientation for collaborative community development work with differently abled people. Empowerment became an influential framework for community-based HIV prevention work (e.g., Gutiérrez, Oh, &

Gillmore, 2000; Levine et al., 1993). Some authors sought to adapt the concept for more general use in organizational psychology and business management (e.g., Conger & Kanungo, 1988), while others used it as a frame for understanding community capacity building (e.g., Bond & Keys, 1993), international development, and poverty alleviation (see Ellis & Biggs, 2001).

The field of public health became broadly interested in how empowerment could guide a variety of types of efforts toward health promotion, as well as research and evaluation. The influential *Ottawa Charter for Health Promotion*, adopted by the World Health Organization (WHO, 1986), declared community empowerment to be a core tenet of health promotion. Many large-scale public health initiatives, such as WHO's European Healthy Cities Network, have accordingly emphasized empowerment in their guiding frameworks for local action (Heritage & Dooris, 2009; Tsouros, 2009). In the early 1990s, public health scholars also took up Rappaport's call for greater specificity and testing of an ecological model of empowerment. For instance, contributions by Israel et al. (1994) and by Rissel (1994) drew clearer conceptual distinctions between empowerment at psychological, organizational, and community levels of analysis and sought to achieve greater clarity on empowerment processes and outcomes. Public health practitioners and evaluators also adopted empowerment approaches for their work during this time (Eng & Parker, 1994; Labonte, 1994).

The field of community development, meanwhile, was also drawing on and contributing to empowerment theory in unique ways. Calvès (2009), for instance, identified the origins of the term in international development not only in some of the North American scholars and practitioners described previously, but also, more potently, in feminist movements in the Global South in the 1980s (Sen & Grown, 1987). The term was taken up by movements for alternative approaches to development in many parts of the world. In this context, empowerment became a key term for advocates for less "top-down" or externally driven approaches to development and for anticolonial approaches. Empowerment became a conceptual mainstay of alternative development practices that sought to establish more democratic decision-making processes, placed a greater value on local knowledge, and challenged justifications for inequality.

Although empowerment was initially perceived as too radical for the major development and finance institutions (United Nations, USAID [US Agency for International Development], World Bank, etc.), as Calvès (2009) documented, the term began appearing more in mainstream development discourse in the mid-1990s. By the turn of the millennium, empowerment was even often prominently used in the titles and covers of the plans of the largest international development institutions. Many critical scholars and activists welcomed this broader recognition of the empowerment approach to community development, while some also feared that it was simply being assimilated into existing development approaches, representing a co-optation of the term.

A noteworthy example of community development embracing empowerment, at least at the level of rhetoric, was a US federal program to promote economic and community development through designated "empowerment zones" in urban neighborhoods with high rates of poverty.[8] The designation paired an older model of "enterprise zones" (tax breaks and other incentives for economic development) with a mandate for a more comprehensive and participatory approach. In applying for the designation as an empowerment zone, cities were required to propose plans for collaborations across sectors and broad engagement of residents. In actual implementation, very few of these goals were realized. This was in part because the participatory and collaborative aspects of the zones were funded at much lower levels than were the incentives for private economic development and in part due to local governments' attempts to control the administration of these resources (J. McCarthy, 2003). Most studies of the empowerment zones' approach to community development have concluded that they produced very little employment or socioeconomic gains compared to similar urban neighborhoods without empowerment zones over the same time period (Oakley & Tsao, 2006).

Em–ment: Empowerment's Crises of Meaning

As these examples discussed demonstrate, by the mid-1990s empowerment had become ubiquitous in discussions on health and social service professions, social policymaking, community and urban development, organizational studies, and politics. In some cases, concerted efforts were being made to clearly define empowerment and to study and compare its development across diverse contexts, as Rappaport and others had advocated. Alongside this applied empirical work, scholars were critiquing and debating assumptions of various formulations and applications of empowerment theory. In a variety of other contexts, however, the term was being invoked in ill-defined ways, taking little or no notice of theory and research on empowerment. The term had vigorously materialized in the popular lexicon, yet it seemed to mean different things when different people used it. It is also clear that among the more ambiguous uses of the term lurked political and commercial motivations and attempts at co-optation, manipulation, and distortion of the concept's original strong grounding in struggles for equal rights and social justice.

Critiques of various notions of empowerment started to crystallize during this surge of interest in the concept and are continuing today. There have been persistent questions about the definition and appropriations of the term. Some debates have centered on the extent to which empowerment processes were (or should be) defined by collaboration and consensus as opposed to struggle and conflict (e.g., Riger, 1993). Some critique the growing tendency for the term to be understood primarily in an individualistic way (e.g., D. D. Perkins, 1995). Still others center on difficulties in negotiating the roles of professional practitioners or facilitators of empowerment processes (e.g., Gruber & Trickett, 1987; Toomey, 2011). Finally, in light of the assimilation or co-optation of the term, some argue either for discarding it in favor of less commonly used terms or for concerted attempts to recapture the more radical and transformative origins of the term (e.g., Cattaneo, Calton, & Brodsky, 2014; Woodall, Warwick-Booth, & Cross, 2012).

These debates persist in multiple scholarly and practice-focused venues and outlets, sometimes in relative isolation from parallel debates in other fields and sometimes in response to each other. Here, I delve into several issues within these debates that I believe are currently the most pressing. The first is the lack of clarity in the definition of empowerment. Second is the growing tendency for empowerment to be understood as an individualistic phenomenon. Third are the weakened links between power and conceptions of empowerment. Fourth is the lack of clarity on roles, particularly for practitioners, in empowerment processes. Fifth and finally are the tensions between collaboration and conflict. All five of these issues are related to each other, and together they pose interrelated challenges for empowerment theory and practice.

Definition

Many observers have concluded that empowerment is a poorly defined concept, and there are at least two ways to interpret this claim. On the one hand, scholars have sought to define empowerment and to specify how it can be identified and measured at the psychological, organizational, and community levels (Zimmerman, 2000). Although there have been threads of consistency throughout this literature, it can still be critiqued on the grounds of definitional specificity. A recent definition was provided by Maton (2008), who defined empowerment as "a group-based, participatory, developmental process through which marginalized or oppressed individuals and groups gain greater control over their lives and environment, acquire valued resources and basic rights, and achieve important life goals and reduced societal marginalization" (p. 5). Maton's definition was intended as a synthesis of earlier works, and it is similar to others' such as Rappaport's (1987) definition of it as "a process by which people, organizations, and communities gain control over their affairs" (p. 122) and Wallerstein's (1992) definition of it as "a social-action process that promotes the participation of people, organizations, and communities towards the goals of increased individual and community control, political efficacy, improved quality of life, and social justice" (p. 198). Despite some consistencies in these definitions of empowerment as an overarching term, as we will we see in the next few chapters, conceptual debates continue on psychological empowerment, organizational empowerment, and community empowerment (e.g., N. A. Peterson, 2014). Particularly as it relates to organizational and community contexts, there is much work that remains to be done on empowerment theory to refine and consistently apply conceptual frameworks and measures.

On the other hand, the critiques of empowerment as a poorly defined construct have tended to focus less on the concept as it has been used in the research referenced previously, which together only constitute a sliver of the total use of the word *empowerment*, and have tended to target somewhat more common uses of the term. To be sure, empowerment has a variety of meanings as it is promulgated in advertisements, political campaigns, religious teaching, business management, self-help books, and a variety of other contexts (see Note 1 for this chapter). It would seem that what has been particularly vexing for scholars seeking definitional clarity, however, is less this broader array of uses than it is the murky borderland between these vernacular uses and the research on the topic and its applications in practice. For instance, Cattaneo and Chapman (2010) reported that a search of the PsycInfo database (of published psychological research articles) for the term yielded 6,266 results—appreciably more than a similar search for the term *self-confidence*. Woodall et al. (2012), in a review of the uses of the term in health promotion programs, concluded that "the term has been used with reckless abandon, with many health promotion projects and interventions (seemingly regardless of their function) aiming to 'empower' the populations they are working with" (p. 743). Thus, the infiltration of the poorly defined term from colloquial use into the language of health promotion, community development, psychology, and other helping professions remains a prevalent issue and fuels periodic questioning by scholars and practitioners (e.g., Brodsky & Cattaneo, 2013), some of whom wonder whether the term has become so ambiguous that it should be abandoned altogether.

Individualism

The conceptual creep of empowerment has sometimes simply been toward ambiguity; in other cases, however, there has been notable slippage toward a more individualized concept. Although the foundations of empowerment theory are clear that feelings of empowerment are inextricably linked with setting and community-level processes, as well as changes in behavior and cognition, the term is much more often used in ways that do not make these connections clear (D. D. Perkins, 1995). Note that in all of the definitions provided previously (by Rappaport, Wallerstein, and Maton), empowerment is defined as a process involving *people and groups*, such as organizations and communities. In many vernacular uses of the term, however, there is no consideration of a group or of participation in collective action, and empowerment is reduced to a feeling or perception of individual mastery and self-determination.

In many cases, this notion of *individual empowerment* has influenced conceptions of empowerment in theory, research, and practice. For instance, although Zimmerman (1990a) made it clear that psychological empowerment should be distinguished from individual empowerment by the former's inextricability from group process and context, strands of the literature on empowerment continue to focus either primarily or exclusively on individuals. For example, Cattaneo and Chapman (2010) defined empowerment as

> an iterative process in which a person who lacks power sets a personally meaningful goal toward increasing power, takes action toward that goal, and observes and reflects on the impact of this action, drawing on his or her evolving self-efficacy, knowledge, and competence related to the goal. Social context influences all six process components and the links among them. (p. 647)

Although it acknowledges the influence of social context, this definition centers on the experiences and actions of a particular person to the neglect of any group, much less of collective action. In this regard, it stands in contrast to definitions by Rappaport, Wallerstein, and Maton. Individualized notions of empowerment also risk overemphasizing agency, mastery, and control at the expense of community and connectedness (Riger, 1993).

Weak Links Between Power and Empowerment

The individualization of empowerment has, in many cases, been associated with (and served to advance) particular ideological and political ends. In particular, individual empowerment is less strongly linked to power than a truly ecological concept of power would be. Put simply, feelings of power and individual action are not social power. Riger (1993) argued that emphasizing individual perceptions of power might lead to a version of empowerment characterized by illusory notions that individuals have power to make change. As Woodall et al. (2012) pointed out: "Individual empowerment does not consider or challenge the social determinants of people's health and in our view does not constitute full empowerment in the sense of transforming the relations of power" (p. 743). Further, by making empowerment primarily about individual-level phenomena, the concept also becomes more compatible with neoliberal ideology, which emphasizes individual rights and responsibilities while eroding collective rights and responsibilities.

The association between individualized notions of empowerment and neoliberal policy agendas is especially evident in the field of community development, where the term, once considered too radical due to its transformative aspirations and origins in feminist movements in the Global South, has been taken up assiduously by mainstream development institutions. Calvès (2009) pointed out that organizations such as the World Bank have sought to recast empowerment in terms of financial markets. For example, a 2001 World Bank report states that the goal of empowerment is to "build the assets of poor people to enable them to engage effectively in markets" (p. 39). These sorts of appropriations of the term led Sardenberg (2008) to draw a contrast between "liberal empowerment," which is primarily about increased economic and legal power for individuals and groups, and "liberating empowerment" (p. 20), in which transformation of power relations and the development of collective capacity are central considerations. According to Cornwall and Anyidoho (2010), the original vision for liberating empowerment has been misappropriated and diluted with concepts of liberal empowerment: "For many feminists, 'women's empowerment' represents a sorry—but not unfamiliar tale of how a once-radical concept was stolen by the priests of neo-liberalism only to be foisted onto women in the Global South as their putative salvation" (p. 145).

Roles in Empowerment Processes

The roles that different people play in empowerment processes have been a source of continual debate. What role do practitioners—social and youth workers, public health practitioners, nonprofit staff, researchers, teachers, and so on—play in empowerment processes? Can one person ever "empower" another? Or, should empowerment be thought of purely as an autonomous group process that can be expected to take place in some types of settings? Gruber and Trickett's (1987) study of decision-making in a policy council for an alternative public high school took up this question directly. The school's culture placed a strong emphasis on egalitarianism, and parents, students, and teachers were equally represented on the policy council. Yet, the study details the ways in which the fundamental inequalities in power in this context (teachers held more) made the policy council itself less powerful over time. Teachers, for instance, possessing greater access to information than parents or students, chose not to bring key decisions to the policy council. Gruber and Trickett's article is "Can We Empower People?"; their answer to this question based on their case study of the policy council is an emphatic "no." To the extent that empowerment took place in this case, it was largely an illusory feeling that parents and students had based on the school's rhetoric of egalitarianism and shared decision-making.

This tension remains in many discussions of empowerment. Many use the term in ways that imply that it can be done by one person or group to another, as in adults claiming to empower young people or social workers claiming that they empower community residents, and so on (e.g., Lindqvist, Mikaelsson, Westerberg, Gard, & Kostenius, 2014). In most cases, these claims are at odds with the symbolic ideology of empowerment as described by Rappaport and other empowerment theorists. At its core, empowerment should be understood as an iterative process that people and groups go through that both depends on and builds their own capacities. This is not something that can be done to someone by someone else. On the other hand, some empowerment processes can be helped along in meaningful ways by practitioners or other members of groups who hold more power or privilege. Typically, this facilitation is more about supporting, maintaining, or co-creating structures, settings, and venues in which empowerment processes can unfold, although it may also involve some teaching, mentoring, and advocacy in certain contexts. This balancing act can be fraught with all the tensions of collaborations between more marginalized and more privileged groups. This complex reality is misrepresented in the unfortunately commonplace claims that one person or group is "empowering" another.

Collaboration or Conflict?

Finally, there have been debates about the roles of collaboration and conflict in empowerment processes. On one hand, some have advanced conflict-free concepts of empowerment in which struggle and conflict are seen as detractors from empowerment, and social change is held to be a result only of collaborations (e.g., Fawcett et al., 1995). These views on empowerment processes stand in clear contrast to the community power theory described in the Chapter 2 that sees conflict as likely when seeking to transform the status quo (see also Christens & Inzeo, 2015; Speer, 2008). Yet, even among those discussing empowerment who do understand that the model needs to account for conflict as well as collaboration, it is not always clear which actors are entering into conflict and which are collaborating and under which circumstances. For example, Riger (1993) critiqued empowerment theory from a feminist perspective for what she regarded as an excessive focus on struggle and conflict, arguing that empowerment should be more about community building and less about "fighting with others for power and control" (p. 290). In many empowerment processes, however, community building and collaboration can take place within a group while conflict is pursued with other groups or decision-makers as a strategy for change. Consistent with the insights into the nature of social power discussed in the Chapter 2, theories of empowerment must address both collaboration and conflict within and between empowerment processes.

The Enduring Conceptual Appeal of Empowerment

Each of these interrelated debates—over the definition of the term, individualism, weakened links to power, and roles and conflict—have contributed to the sense shared by many observers that the term is now "a tired buzzword" (Toomey, 2011, p. 183). It is not uncommon to hear claims that the concept is primarily about individuals and their feelings. Sometimes, this is meant as a critique, and other times it is simply an assumption based on how people have heard the term used. Many critical scholars feel that the term has been co-opted and lost or has abandoned some of its original connections to social justice and transformation. Some sense that it has become associated with naive presumptions about power and social change processes. In spite of these concerns with the misappropriations of the term, however, the appeal of the concept has largely endured. Why is this the case? What is it about the concept and framework of empowerment that makes it so seemingly indispensable for researchers and practitioners in social work, health promotion, community organizing, and community development?

Rappaport (1981) argued for empowerment as a guiding orientation for social theory and practice, yet it was clear that he did not intend for it to be a perennial construct of central importance. He saw empowerment theory as a response to particular historical trends in the United States. In particular, he identified the concept's potential to guide a balanced approach to rights and needs through divergent rather than convergent problem-solving. He cautioned that "should empowerment become a dominant way of thinking I have no doubt that it too will force one-sided solutions" (p. 21), as opposed to the balanced approach he advocated. In the years since, it could be argued that empowerment has become a dominant way of thinking based on the prevalence of the term. As we have seen, however, much of this usage of the term is superficial, individualist, and, in some cases, distorted. This raises the question of whether the concept of empowerment as described by community psychologists has ever truly been dominant, even in social theory and practice. Nevertheless, the term and its uses must be continually scrutinized for effectiveness in reaching espoused goals: real progress toward greater egalitarianism in the power relations that determine allocations of resources, as well as increased capacity of the groups and individual people who are leading efforts in pursuit of these changes.

Most of those who offer ardent critiques of the abuses of the term do want to reclaim it for transformative community-driven work. Calvès (2009), for example, urged feminist community development researchers and activists to

> protest and resist the ways that empowerment has been neutralized and thrown off track. . . . [This resistance] must be local as well as global, and it must be a part of a larger protest against the neoliberal, patriarchal and neocolonial development model that perpetuates and reinforces inequitable power relations. (p. xiii)

Scholars across a number of fields have called for similar forms of resistance to misappropriation and co-optation and reclamations of the core concept of empowerment (e.g., Cattaneo, Calton, & Brodsky, 2014; Ledwith, 2011), and many have also called for rigorous work to define and measure various aspects of empowerment processes (e.g., N. A. Peterson, 2014). There are some, however, who have advocated the development of new alternative guiding frameworks. Woodall et al. (2012) sought to "move beyond the rhetoric associated with empowerment" (p. 745), for example. There are likely many others who are tentative or reluctant about engagement with the concept because of the political murkiness and perceived individualism associated with it.

Along with others who urge resistance to cooptation of the term, I believe that there is much to recommend conceptual reclamation as well as continued theoretical development of empowerment. Simply put, the symbolic ideology of empowerment is worth some conceptual wrangling. The concept is particularly valuable for what Simon (1994) called a "dual focus" (p. 15) on people and their social and physical environments. The ecological model of empowerment holds out the promise of a holistic understanding of the interplay between psychological, organizational, and community action. Empowerment has pragmatic underpinnings, and many who have used the concept have been declarative about its orienting social justice values. There is benefit in using a term with roots in social movements as well as education, philosophy, social reform, and community organizing. There is also a body of research that continues to advance and refine measures for various facets of empowerment. All of these are reasons not to easily cede the conceptual ground.

Yet, to reclaim empowerment's symbolic ideology and to position it as an orienting framework for action toward social justice, it will not be enough to loudly proclaim that use of the term should more closely adhere to theory and research on the topic. First of all, I suspect that regardless of how well empowerment is understood and used in social science and the professions, there will always be more colloquial uses of the term that are murky, diluted, or even in some cases directly contrary to some basic tenets of empowerment theory. Those who take up the term for use in scholarship and practice will therefore need to maintain patience for explaining that they mean something more or something different when using the term.

Second, it will not be enough to point to the current research literature on the topic as an alternative or an antidote to the poorly defined, diluted, or co-opted notions of empowerment. The scholarship on the topic has itself been uneven. Much of it has been fundamentally individualistic. Some of it more closely resembles colloquial uses of the term than the empowerment theory that Rappaport described. Moreover, although some recent work has taken strides to connect empowerment theory more coherently with power (e.g., Cattaneo et al., 2014), much of the research on the topic has not been coherently linked to power, and very little of it has considered community power. The concepts investigated in Chapter 2 have influenced some strands of empowerment theory (e.g., Speer, 2008), but it would be too much to claim that empowerment theory has an adequate understanding of power. The task of reclaiming the term and reinvigorating empowerment theory, then, will require not only revisiting some of the early work on the topic and rekindling the concept's links to its ideological precursors but also at least as much new work to construct and test the framework in ways that enable the concept to more effectively guide action. Before taking this on, however, it is worthwhile to contemplate the overarching idea that has structured much of empowerment theory and sought to connect micro-, meso-, and macrolevel processes: the ecological metaphor.

Ecology of Empowerment

When Rappaport (1987) proposed an ecological understanding of empowerment, he specifically cited the influence of J. G. Kelly and Hess's (1986) work on the ecology of prevention and Trickett's (1984) work on the ecological metaphor as it relates to community research. In fact, the concept of ecology has long been employed in sociology and psychology to describe complex human systems.[9] Community psychologists (Kelly, Trickett, and others) took principles derived from the ecological study of biological systems—cycling of resources, adaptation, interdependence, and succession—and applied them to the study of people in communities. These theorists were influenced in turn by Barker's (1968) application of ecological psychology to the study of behavior settings in a small town, as well as by Bronfenbrenner's (1979) application of an ecological perspective to human development. In the simplest terms, what these perspectives have in common is a keen sense of the interrelatedness of people, settings, and communities.

An ecological understanding has become the standard organizing framework in empowerment theory. Zimmerman's (2000) synthesis provided definitions and descriptions of psychological empowerment, organizational empowerment, and community empowerment. This designation of empowerment at different "levels" of analysis responds to Rappaport's call for an ecological understanding of empowerment that is specific enough to be measured and rigorously assessed in different contexts. At the same time, it introduces new challenges. For instance, although Zimmerman and others have stressed that empowerment processes at different levels of analysis are interrelated and inextricable, it is extremely difficult to empirically capture this dynamic holism. A result is that most studies of empowerment take a narrower view, most often emphasizing the psychological level over other levels of analysis.

Another challenge with studying different "levels" of empowerment is that it is often accompanied by a kind of definitional rigidity. Specifically, there is a tendency for individuals, organizations, and communities to be conceptualized simplistically as though they are discrete entities. In fact, psychological dynamics are not only individual but also relational and group based. Similarly, organizations contain many different settings that each change over time, and some of these settings are at the intersection of different organizations (e.g., coalitions). Communities are notoriously difficult to define consistently as bounded entities. Unlike Dewey's concept of transaction, then, which questions the usefulness of divisions such as individual and community, the designation of discrete levels of analysis can, somewhat paradoxically, obscure the holism that many empowerment theorists have sought.

Despite these challenges, the psychological, organizational, and community-level distinction has served to advance specificity in studies of empowerment. This multilevel understanding is now deeply engrained in empowerment theory. In the next section of this book, I elaborate on empowerment at each of these levels, drawing on existing research when possible and advancing new thinking and frameworks where necessary. One theme that runs through each of the chapters that follow is the potential for relational and network perspectives to advance empowerment theory beyond a rigid conceptual framework that treats each level of human ecology separately. Another theme, of course, is the connections between community power and empowerment as it manifests in psychological, organizational, and community dynamics.

Conclusion

This chapter has investigated the history of the concept of empowerment as it has been invoked in theory and practice in multiple fields. Empowerment theory has appeal because it seeks to account for both the capacities and the needs of less powerful or advantaged people and groups. In other words, it can accommodate both structure and agency. It is also attractive because it aspires toward a holistic or transactional view of psychological and group processes. The multifaceted appeal of the concept, however, has led to its overuse in the language of multiple fields of practice, as well as in the broader society, particularly in the United States and Europe. This overuse has exacerbated and accentuated tensions that are inherent in the concept.

Putting the shortcomings of present-day empowerment theory as well as the abuses of the term aside for a moment, risks remain that are inherent to an empowerment approach. First, it is informative to distinguish the potential risks that are a result of misunderstanding or misuse from those that are not because the latter are more likely to endure even if empowerment theory and practice realize its full intended potential. Comparing the values, assumptions, and practices of an empowerment approach with those of traditional Western psychological approaches, postmodern approaches, and emancipatory communitarian approaches, Prilleltensky (1997) concluded that each approach has potential risks as well as benefits. Acknowledging the potential of an empowerment approach to restore personal and collective power and control, he nevertheless pointed out the risk that in the pursuit of these goals, empowerment will place excessive emphasis on self-determination and control, to the neglect of compassion and social responsibility. "In seeking power for oneself or one's group, there is a risk of becoming less sensitive to other equally or more disempowered groups. . . . When more control for oneself or one's group means less control for others, or when enhanced autonomy means less tolerance for diversity, we have to question the moral grounds of empowerment" (p. 527). This insight represents a fundamental challenge for empowerment theory, and some recent work is bringing this issue to the fore (Kaiser & Rusch, 2015).

Empowerment is a symbolic ideology that seeks to address inequities. Yet, when empowerment processes are successful, they change power relationships and the allocation of resources such that new imbalances may arise. In the pursuit of social justice, therefore, it will not be sufficient simply to demand more and more empowerment. It is not the only goal of community building and action. In the current sociopolitical situation, however, it is imperative to pursue empowerment in response to systematic injustices, stark and worsening inequality, and the associated concentration of power.

Notes

1. A quick scan of books with empowerment in their titles reveals the ways that empowerment is often invoked. One popular genre promotes belief in the power of positive thinking (often intermingled with religious belief) to produce quick gratification. For instance, Gershon and Straub's *Empowerment: The Art of Creating Your Life as You Want It* (1989) explains that we can craft our reality with thought. In Price's *Empowerment: You Can Do, Be, and Have All Things* (1992) prayer and principles will lead to power, love, and money. Another genre explains business management practices that can improve employee motivation and profitability, such as Bernoff and Schadler's *Empowered: Unleash Your Employees, Energize Your Customers, and Transform Your Business* (2010), which emphasizes the potential to harness the social media activity of employees to market a company's products.
2. The label on my current shampoo bottle makes a claim about empowerment.
3. And, as many have pointed out, settlement houses functioned, in some ways, as ethnocentric assimilationist institutions (Lasch-Quinn, 1993; Lissak, 1989).
4. Although the movement is sometimes characterized as entirely nonviolent, movement leaders actually held a range of viewpoints on the roles that violence could play in putting an end to oppression, even well before the rise of prominent militant and separatist elements in the late 1960s and 1970s. There were many violent encounters with white supremacists. Movement leaders sometimes used violence, either as self-defense or occasionally as a form of direct political action (see Cobb, 2015).
5. Although many forms of organizing are influenced by Alinsky in some respects, the influence is most pronounced in several organizing networks that today operate primarily through faith-based institutions of multiple faiths. These include local initiatives that are part of the Industrial Areas Foundation, which Alinsky started, as well as the PICO National Network, the Gamaliel Foundation, and others. A field scan by Wood, Partridge, and Fulton in 2013 identified approximately 300 active local congregation-based organizing initiatives in the United States.
6. Berger and Neuhaus's book influenced right-wing thought leaders at the Heritage Foundation as well as initiatives to support charitable organizations while cutting the social welfare state, such as US President George H. W. Bush's emphasis on charities and voluntary associations as "a thousand points of light" or the Big Society efforts in the United Kingdom.
7. In his presidential address, Rappaport (1981) presented empowerment and prevention in conceptual opposition. In later work on the topic (1987), he modified his argument on the basis of debate that his address had prompted and his own further reflection. Instead, he suggested that empowerment refers to the phenomena of interest for theory in community psychology—it "is what we try to define, understand, explain, predict,

and create or facilitate by our interventions or policies" (p. 127)—whereas prevention provides exemplars of implementation of concrete problem solutions. Some preventive interventions could therefore be implemented in ways that would be consistent with empowerment's symbolic ideology and implications for action, while other preventive interventions might not be.

8. Administered by the US Departments of Housing and Urban Development in urban areas and the Department of Agriculture in rural areas, the Empowerment Zone and Enterprise Community Initiative was passed by Congress in 1993. To qualify for designation as an empowerment zone in the initial selection process, an area of less than 20 square miles needed to have a population between 50,000 and 200,000 and poverty rates higher than 20% in each census tract, 25% in 90% of the census tracts, or 35% in at least 50% of the census tracts.

9. Early examples of application of the ecological metaphor to social systems include Park's (1936) and Wirth's (1945) articles on "human ecology" and Long's (1958) article on the local community as an ecology of games, all in the *American Journal of Sociology*. Today, the social–ecological model is a conceptual foundation of public health and related disciplines.

|| 4 ||

Human Development

Chapter Overview

The previous two chapters examined the conceptual foundations of the main topics for this book: community power (Chapter 2) and empowerment (Chapter 3). Specifically, Chapter 2 examined both the dimensions and some of the contemporary dynamics of change in local community power structures, and Chapter 3 delved into the concept of empowerment, defined (following Rappaport, 1987) as a mechanism by which people, groups, and communities gain control over their affairs. Empowerment processes are vital at a societal level for democratic functioning, but they are also imperative at the level of groups for organizational effectiveness. In addition, empowerment can play important roles in human development. *Psychological empowerment* can be defined as "the psychological aspects of processes through which people, organizations and communities are developing critical awareness of their environments, building social networks and social movements, and gaining greater control over their lives" (Christens, Peterson & Speer, 2014, p. 1766).

This chapter examines theory and research on the psychological aspects of empowerment and their interplay with other human developmental and educational processes. Although particular attention is devoted to the role of empowerment in youth development, psychological empowerment continues to play a meaningful role in development and education during adulthood. The first half of the chapter lays out psychological empowerment theory, then examines the multiple components of psychological empowerment, the ways they have been measured by researchers, and ongoing debates about the ways that they connect to an overarching concept of psychological empowerment. Then, the second half of the chapter examines the existing evidence on the ways that psychological empowerment is developed among young people and adults, culminating in a developmental framework for psychological empowerment processes and outcomes.

Psychological Empowerment

A basic key to understanding psychological empowerment is to distinguish it from individual empowerment. As mentioned in Chapter 3, Zimmerman (1990a) pointed out that an individual-oriented conception treats empowerment as a personality variable and tends to neglect context. In contrast, psychological empowerment is oriented to context and is conceptually inseparable from empowerment as a multilevel construct. That is, psychological empowerment is not an individual attribute that is context-invariant, but is instead a psychological process that manifests as part of community and organizational empowerment processes. Someone could therefore, for example, display characteristics of psychological empowerment in the context of his or her workplace, but not in the context of a faith-based setting. Many discussions of empowerment remain unclear on this distinction and therefore treat empowerment as an individual-level construct with little or no connection to organizational or community-level phenomena (Christens, 2013).

It is likely that this individual-oriented conceptualization of empowerment is prevalent in part because it is resonant with the individualist ethos common in Western societies, and psychology in particular (Prilleltensky, 1994; Riger, 1993). From a research perspective, the individual-oriented conception of empowerment may also owe some of its prevalence to the challenges of integrating levels of analysis by studying psychological phenomena in ways that are attentive to person–environment fit (Rappaport, 1981). Indeed, it is much simpler to design research that assesses people as if they were discrete and self-contained entities than it is to capture complex phenomena operating at multiple contextual levels. Yet, a holistic theoretical and assessment framework is precisely what is necessary to gain an accurate understanding of psychological empowerment.

As with many psychological constructs, theorists suggest that psychological empowerment, while it cannot be directly observed or assessed, can be understood as an underlying (or latent) construct with multiple components. Zimmerman (1995) proposed an influential model for understanding and assessing psychological empowerment according to its manifestation in three components: an emotional component, a cognitive component, and a behavioral component. This model for a latent construct with affective/emotional, behavioral, and cognitive components is common for studying psychological constructs (e.g., Breckler, 1984), yet very few studies have confirmed this three-component/factor model of psychological empowerment.[1] Noting the emphasis on interpersonal relationships in research on psychological empowerment processes, I have proposed consideration and investigation of a possible relational component of psychological empowerment (Christens, 2012b). Some recent studies have built on this conceptualization of a relational component (e.g., Cheryomukhin & Peterson, 2014; Langhout, Collins,

& Ellison, 2014), with findings suggesting that a relational component may be operating in some psychological empowerment processes.

Many questions remain, however, about the component structure and nature of the underlying construct of psychological empowerment and its relationship to measurable components (N. A. Peterson, 2014). Furthermore, it is clear that empowerment—particularly at the level of psychology—is not necessarily a concept that is conducive to development of universal global measures. Rather, it is at least to some extent a context-specific process that may require tailored tools to understand in different settings, cultures, or populations (Zimmerman, 2000). Before investigating these overarching theoretical questions in greater depth, let us first examine the definitions and research on measurement of each of the components that have been studied to date.

Emotional Component

The emotional component[2] of psychological empowerment refers to the feelings and self-perceptions that one is capable, through participation in organizational and community settings, of influencing decision-making and collective social change processes. Wallerstein (2002) captured some of the essence of this component of psychological empowerment in selected quotations from focus groups of young people involved in advocacy for changes in state policy: "Most youth were just there to watch, but we were there to speak, to be heard!" and "What I want to do . . . is to make a difference and effect change in [driving while intoxicated] policy in New Mexico to make this state a safer and better place for youth" (p. 76). This emotional component has been studied for several decades, primarily using a concept and measure of sociopolitical control, a concept that has built on psychological research suggesting that perceived control and efficacy differ across various life domains (e.g., work, family, sociopolitical domains). Sociopolitical control therefore relates to one's perceived political efficacy and sense of civic duty. In a sense, it can be thought of as a dimension of self-efficacy (Bandura, 1982), as well as motivation to control one's environment (De Charms, 1968) as these concepts relate to the sociopolitical arena.

Zimmerman and Zahniser (1991) first operationalized sociopolitical control, defining it as a latent construct with two dimensions: (a) leadership competence and (b) policy control. The leadership competence dimension is defined as the skills and confidence needed to exercise leadership in community and organizational contexts. The policy control dimension captures the perceptions that one is competent and able to influence decisions in community and organizational contexts. Together, these two dimensions reflect the overarching definition of sociopolitical control—the perception that one is capable of operating effectively and effecting social, systems, and policy change.

The two-dimensional model for sociopolitical control has been tested as a measure in samples from different countries and populations. Zimmerman and Zahniser's (1991) initial study reported on analyses from three different samples that varied by age and geography. The 17-item scale that they used to measure the construct was revised in more recent literature (N. A. Peterson et al., 2006) and demonstrates improved fit in most samples while similarly indicating a two-factor structure (Appendix 4.1: Sociopolitical Control Scale, SPCS-R). The sociopolitical control scale has been either directly translated or adapted for use in a number of countries, including China (Wang, Chen, & Chen, 2011); Spain (Ramos-Vidal & Maya-Jariego, 2014); Israel (Itzhaky & York, 2000); Estonia (Kasmel & Tanggaard, 2011); and Azerbaijan (Cheryomukhin & Peterson, 2014). The measure has also been adapted recently for use specifically with young people in the United States (N. A. Peterson, Peterson, Agre, Christens, & Morton, 2011); Italy (Vieno, Lenzi, Canale, & Santinello, 2014); and Malaysia (Christens, Krauss, & Zeldin, 2016) (Appendix 4.2: Sociopolitical Control Scale for Youth, SPCS-Y).[3]

Importantly, this concept of sociopolitical control should not be thought of as an individual personality characteristic, such as optimism. Rather, it is a capacity that develops as people become more engaged in civic life. Sociopolitical control can therefore be considered as a domain-specific form of perceived efficacy, but because civic action requires collective action, it is perceived efficacy that is predicated on—and inextricable from—participation in group-based action.

Behavioral Component

The behavioral component of psychological empowerment has been conceptualized as the actions one takes to exert influence or gain control in the sociopolitical domain. Theory on the behavioral component of psychological empowerment has built on earlier research on citizen participation. The concept of citizen participation was once more narrowly focused on participation behaviors that were directly linked to collective decision-making processes (e.g., voting, writing a letter to an elected official). Taking an empowerment perspective, Zimmerman and Rappaport (1988) expanded the scope of citizen participation by including participation in community and organizational activities. Their measurement of the concept also included efforts to organize people or influence public debate through, for instance, writing a letter to the editor of a newspaper. In the research literature today, the behavioral component is most often referred to as *community participation* (e.g., Christens, Peterson, et al., 2011; Heritage & Dooris, 2009) and is assessed by indicators of multiple forms of community and organizational involvement.

Most empirical assessments of the behavioral component of psychological empowerment have treated and measured it as a one-factor/dimensional construct (e.g., Speer & Peterson, 2000) (Appendix 4.3: Behavioral Empowerment Scale). These measures have generally performed fairly well from a psychometric standpoint and have consistently demonstrated relationships with theoretically linked concepts, such as sociopolitical control. There is reason to believe, however, that civic and community participation encompasses various types of behaviors that might more accurately be treated as distinct dimensions. For example, Speer, Jackson, and Peterson (2001) made distinctions between three types of community participation: (a) organizational membership, indicated by the number of types of community groups (e.g., school/parent groups, civic/community organizations, etc.) of which one is a member; (b) organizational participation, indicated by the number of times a person participated in organizational activities during the recent past; and (c) individual civic participation, which encompasses forms of civic action that are accomplished without the mediating role of a community organization, such as attendance at informational meetings or writing a letter to the editor. Furthermore, because many civic behaviors are directly observable, there is the possibility of directly observing and recording certain types of community and organizational participation rather than relying on retrospective self-reporting through survey data collection.

Some research (conducted in developmental psychology and to some extent in political science, communications, and education) on younger people has explored distinctions and relationships between different forms of community participation and civic engagement. Examples of these different types include volunteer, political, community, and religious activities (Metzger & Smetana, 2009); engagement through social media (Lee, Shah, & McLeod, 2013; Oser, Hooghe, & Marien, 2013); discussion of social and political issues with parents (e.g., Wray-Lake, & Flanagan, 2012) and family members (Mahatmya & Lohman, 2012), with peers (Ekström, & Östman, 2013), and with nonfamilial adults (e.g., Camino & Zeldin, 2002); discussions of controversial issues in classrooms (e.g., Hess, 2002) and schools (e.g., Torney-Purta, 2002); community service (e.g., C. A. Flanagan, Kim, Collura, & Kopish, 2015); program and religious activity participation (e.g., Zaff et al., 2011); political consumerism (e.g., Stolle, Hooghe, & Micheletti, 2005); and participation in social action (e.g., Diemer & Li, 2011). As part of an effort to measure critical consciousness, Diemer, Rapa, Park, and Perry (2017) have developed a measure for critical action (Appendix 4.4) that provides a unified measure of participation similar to the community participation scales most frequently used for adults.

It is therefore likely that many of the measures of community participation that have been used in studies of psychological empowerment to date are too simple and are aggregating what ought to be considered multiple different forms or dimensions of behavior that are part of empowerment processes. Research and evaluation seeking to assess the behavioral component of psychological empowerment could therefore benefit from adopting some of the distinctions between types of civic behavior that have been made in the broader interdisciplinary literature cited previously. Furthermore, continued efforts to measure these behaviors in more direct ways, rather than solely through retrospective self-reports, are likely to yield accuracy and additional insights (see Christens, Speer, & Peterson, 2016). Developments in mobile technology and social media make breakthroughs likely on this front, especially since many civic and political organizations are seeking to more accurately record and understand patterns in specific types of behavior among their participants and stakeholders. These types of organizationally-generated data can also yield contextual information about participatory behaviors, helping to avoid overly individualized assessments.

Cognitive Component

The cognitive component of psychological empowerment involves critical understanding of systems, environments, and the forces that shape them, as well as strategic understanding of what is required to make change.[4] An example from a qualitative study that captures some of the essence of the cognitive component is from an adult involved in community organizing who explained that, in their efforts, it is becoming more important to think about "changing the balance of power, and in terms of changing systems, and in growing local economies and local community . . . creating places for people to be able to come together" (Christens & Collura, 2012, p. 602). Zimmerman's (1995) framework described the cognitive component as encompassing the norms and values associated with commitment to collective interests, the skills to lead and make decisions, and knowledge of the options for social and political action. Other scholars (Speer, 2000; Speer & Peterson, 2000) have built on this framework by proposing a three-dimensional construct involving knowledge of the source, nature, and instruments of social power (Appendix 4.5: Cognitive Empowerment Scale). The notions of social power that influenced this work include those by Lukes (1974) and Gaventa (1980) that are discussed in Chapter 2, as well as those that are taught in models for grassroots community organizing (e.g., Gutiérrez, & Lewis, 1994; Speer & Hughey, 1995).

First, knowledge of the source of social power involves the understanding that individuals are unlikely to be able to create changes in social and political systems through independent action. Instead, changes in these systems are more likely to be achieved through collective coordinated efforts. This relates to a basic tenet of community organizing, which is that power comes in two forms: organized money and organized people (Alinsky, 1971). Therefore, in order for residents and grassroots groups to make changes through the exercise of social power, they must be organized. This understanding regarding the source of social power comprises the first dimension in the three-dimensional conceptualization of the cognitive component of psychological empowerment.

Second, knowledge of the nature of social power involves the understanding that efforts to change the status quo are likely to result in conflict. This tenet, which is common to both models for community organizing (e.g., Gutiérrez & Lewis, 2012) and studies of social change and social conflict (e.g., Gaventa, 1980; Ledwith, 2011), rests on the supposition that powerful individuals and groups benefit disproportionately from the status quo and are likely to take issue with proposals to change it. When groups organize for meaningful changes to the status quo, therefore, they must be prepared for the likelihood of conflict, often in rough proportion to the degree of systemic transformation that they are pursuing. In contrast, a naïve approach would be one based on the premise that significant change can be accomplished simply through the presentation of compelling logic or through a relatively harmonious compromise process. Hence, the understanding that conflict is likely to occur during systems change processes comprises the second dimension of the cognitive component of psychological empowerment.

Third, as described in detail in Chapter 2, Lukes (1974) theorized three dimensions or "faces" of social power, the first face being the most visible and the third face being the most hidden. The conceptual and measurement model by Speer and Peterson (2000) for the cognitive component of psychological empowerment uses these three faces to assess knowledge of the instruments of power. To recap in brief, the first face concerns the role of power in determining who wins and who loses in publicly visible disputes over policy or systemic changes. The second face involves the roles that power plays in gatekeeping and agenda-setting processes that shape not only the outcomes of publicly visible disputes, but also which disputes arise or do not. The third face involves the roles that power plays in shaping the ideology of the public and the participants in social and political systems. An understanding of all three "faces" of social power comprises the third dimension of the cognitive component of psychological empowerment: knowledge of the instruments of social power.

Critical consciousness (Freire, 1973), as discussed in Chapter 3, is a concept that is closely related to psychological empowerment and has been influential, particularly in studies of young people. When compared with psychological empowerment, it is clear that critical consciousness places greater relative emphasis on learning and the cognitive aspects of capability to produce social change. Watts, Diemer, and Voight (2011) proposed a multicomponent framework for critical consciousness, encompassing critical social analysis or reflection, political efficacy, and critical action and participation. Although these dimensions map fairly well onto cognitive, emotional, and behavioral components, respectively, key substantive differences between psychological empowerment and critical consciousness exist (see Christens, Winn, & Duke, 2016). Critical reflection is especially substantively distinct and may provide additional insights relevant to the cognitive component of psychological empowerment (Appendix 4.6 provides an example of a scale to assess critical reflection with subscales for perceived inequality and egalitarianism). Further exploration of the relationships between cognitive aspects of psychological empowerment and critical consciousness may yield valuable insights into empowerment processes.

Relational Component

Some studies have identified processes that might be considered a relational component of psychological empowerment. For example, Russell, Muraco, Subramaniam, and Laub (2009), in their study of youth empowerment in high school gay–straight alliances, identified one dimension through which empowerment was experienced as a relational or interpersonal empowerment. This dimension included the commitment to passing on the values associated with the group's activity to future members. It also involved a desire to enhance the skills and motivations of other members of the group. An example of a quotation by a participant in that study that captures some of the essence of the relational component of psychological empowerment is "you can't be empowered or stay empowered for very long if you're not . . . connected with other people" (p. 899). Similarly, Langhout, Collins, and Ellison (2014) captured some of the essence of relational empowerment in their analysis of qualitative data collected from interviews with children involved in a youth participatory action project: "As Vanessa explained, 'We decided on what we were going to do next together and we decided that doing things together always made it easier. . . . We decided that, we needed to make a change and we decided on what we were gonna make the change on together" (p. 374).

Drawing on similar findings from these and other studies, I suggested consideration of a relational component of psychological empowerment in future research (Christens, 2012b). I noted the fact that at other levels of analysis (community, organizational), empowerment theory had been more clear about the roles that relationships play in empowerment processes (e.g., mutual support in organizations) and the ways that relational characteristics can be understood as empowered outcomes (e.g., interorganizational relationships and coalitions). Investigating a relational component, I reasoned, could be a way not only to more fully capture psychological empowerment processes, but also to strengthen links between psychological empowerment and empowerment at other levels of analysis. Examining interpersonal processes in psychological empowerment may also help to address Riger's (1993) critique of empowerment as an overly individually oriented concept. Furthermore, consideration of a relational component of psychological empowerment connects empowerment theory with discussions about the role of relationships in psychology, more generally, and critiques of psychological theory as overly individualistic (e.g., Gergen, 2009; Prilleltensky, 1994).

In "Toward Relational Empowerment" (Christens, 2012b), I sought to distinguish a relational component of psychological empowerment from other conceptually relevant concepts, such as social capital, sense of community, and social support. Then I identified some elements that might comprise a relational component of psychological empowerment, including collaborative competence, bridging social divisions, facilitating others' empowerment, mobilizing networks, and passing on a legacy. *Collaborative competence* refers to the ability of individuals to forge group membership and solidarity. Bridging social divisions refers to the set of competencies necessary for building trust and reciprocity across lines of difference. Facilitating others' empowerment involves the ability and propensity to strategically catalyze empowerment processes for others in a group. Mobilizing networks involves the ability to strengthen others' commitments to involvement and to galvanize them toward more engagement and participation. Finally, passing on a legacy refers to the ability and propensity to identify newcomers and instill in them a sense of the organizational history, identity, and strategies.

Although no well-established measures exist yet for assessing the relational aspects of psychological empowerment, conceptual work on the topic is informing ongoing empirical work. For example, a study by Langhout et al. (2014) examined elements of relational empowerment among elementary school students involved in a youth participatory action research program, finding that students' experiences could be analyzed using the dimensions of relational empowerment described previously. Likewise, Cheryomukhin and Peterson (2014) used a relational empowerment framework to assess components of psychological empowerment among participants in Azerbaijan. Furthermore, some researchers (e.g., Z. P. Neal, 2014) are using social network analysis to assess relational aspects of empowerment, an effort that has implications not only for psychological empowerment, but also for linking psychological empowerment with empowerment at other levels of analysis (J. W. Neal & Christens, 2014).

Putting the Pieces Together

As mentioned, there is by no means agreement that psychological empowerment can best be understood according to the four components that we have just explored. In fact, although many studies have examined various components, few studies to this point have found support for a multifactor structure for psychological empowerment as an overarching construct. Most studies of psychological empowerment have instead examined one or more of the components in relation to other components and to other conceptually related variables.

Many of these studies have, for example, treated community participation as a distinct variable that is related to psychological empowerment but does not comprise a component of it, rather than as an indicator of the behavioral component of psychological empowerment. In fact, this has become so common in the research literature that it may reflect an emerging consensus (N. A. Peterson, 2014). Moreover, in many studies, indicators of the cognitive component of psychological empowerment have shown complicated and sometimes-inverse relationships with indicators of the emotional component (Christens, Speer, & Peterson, 2011; N. A.

Peterson, Hamme, & Speer, 2002). This has raised questions about whether both can rightfully be considered as components of the same underlying construct of psychological empowerment. Undoubtedly, this lack of clarity is a contributor to the frequent misuses of the term *empowerment* in many academic disciplines and fields of professional practice (Cattaneo et al., 2014; Woodall, Warwick-Booth, & Cross, 2012).

N. A. Peterson (2014) has stressed the importance of clarifying the nature of the higher order multidimensional construct of empowerment and that of its components, including psychological empowerment. The conceptual distinctiveness of the different components of psychological empowerment—as well as the many studies that have found them not to be correlated with each other or to share similar relationships with other variables—led Peterson to question whether psychological empowerment should be considered as an *aggregate* latent construct, rather than a *superordinate* latent construct as it has often been portrayed in the conceptual and measurement literature. An aggregate latent construct is one that is formed by, rather than reflected in its components. In other words, if psychological empowerment is considered as an aggregate latent construct, we could assume that multiple components (perhaps including more than those that have currently been identified), when considered together, make up the different parts of psychological empowerment. In contrast, a superordinate or reflective latent construct should be fully indicated by its components, and leaving a component out would be particularly detrimental to understanding the construct.

Following this logic, we might consider sociopolitical control, for example, to be a reflective construct that is indicated by the two dimensions of leadership competence and policy control, which have consistently been found to be highly associated with each other. Yet, we might also hypothesize that sociopolitical control—as an indicator of the emotional component of psychological empowerment—might not be a reflective indicator of psychological empowerment, but instead one of potentially multiple noninterchangeable facets, which together form an aggregate construct of psychological empowerment. These distinctions are needed for ongoing theoretical and measurement work on psychological empowerment, as well as for an accurate understanding of empowerment at other levels of analysis. Examining the research that has been conducted to date, it appears likely that psychological empowerment should be considered using a *formative,* rather than reflective, measurement model. This also permits examination of the various components of psychological empowerment as antecedents and consequences of other components without calling into question the validity of the underlying latent construct of psychological empowerment. As discussed in the next part of this chapter, this notion that certain components of psychological empowerment are predictors or consequences of other components is entirely consistent with the current evidence on the development of psychological empowerment.

This chapter has so far examined the concept of psychological empowerment according to its different components. Because empowerment involves changes in behaviors, relationships, emotion, and cognition, efforts have been made by researchers to understand empowerment processes in each of these facets of psychology. Empowerment, however, is a context-dependent process, so there are likely differences in how it manifests across different groups, processes, and cultures. It is also a process that is specific to the sociopolitical domain, although it is likely intertwined with changes in other domains as well. For example, studies of young people's sociopolitical development often find that it is related to educational and career aspirations (Christens & Dolan, 2011; Kirshner, 2009). The next part of this chapter considers psychological empowerment as a developmental process that is interrelated with other aspects of human development.

Development of Psychological Empowerment
Developmental Frameworks and Concepts

Many signs point to psychological empowerment being a key aspect of human development. As discussed previously, empowerment theory has been influenced by Bronfenbrenner's (1977) notions of ecology in human development. Accordingly, developmental approaches to empowerment have emphasized interactions between humans and the organizational and community contexts in which empowerment occurs. An influential study that advanced a clear developmental perspective on psychological empowerment was Kieffer's (1984) qualitative study of citizen empowerment processes among established adult participants in grassroots community-organizing groups. This study, which drew on the narratives of established grassroots leaders, identified distinct *eras* in their sociopolitical development.

The first era is one of *entry* into sociopolitical involvement. This era is characterized by initial provocation to become involved in one's community, often through an issue that directly negatively affects (or threatens to affect) a person or their family. Of note, none of the leaders in this study became involved through intellectual analyses, education, or other consciousness-raising interventions. They all became involved in civic action because of some social force that was intruding into their daily lives and provoking them toward outrage and confrontation. The second era in the development of civic leaders involves *advancement* through supportive peer and mentored relationships. The role of a community organizer or other mentor for community involvement is particularly vital during this era to support experimentation in the sociopolitical arena and demystify social and political relations. The role of peers in the organization is also important to provide arenas for mutual support and problem-solving. A cycle of reinforcement occurs during this stage of advancement in which gains in critical analysis and understanding lead to deepening and broadening of civic involvement, which in turn leads to deeper understanding and the honing of skills. Kieffer saw aspects of this era as analogous to the developmental tasks of childhood.

The era of advancement is followed by the third era of *incorporation* and the maturation of leadership skills. Perennial involvement is needed during this era to confront the persistent nature of systemic barriers. Participant leaders must sort through social strains associated with continuous involvement. Resolve to remain involved and continual reflection on one's own roles and identities in organizational efforts are developed in this era. These tasks are akin, Kieffer argued (1984), to some of the developmental achievements of adolescence. The final era, analogous to adulthood, is one of *commitment*, in which participatory competence is fully realized, but citizen leaders continue their commitment to engagement in struggles for social and political change. This is not an endpoint but an attainment of capacities that are continually applied proactively through struggles in the sociopolitical arena.

Across these developmental eras, Kieffer (1984) emphasized the importance of contradictions and *dissonance*, for example, in the initial provocations to become involved and continual conflicts that stimulate dialogue that can refine understanding and skills. Likewise, he identified the central importance of *praxis* (or continuous experience that is characterized by cycles of action and reflection) that can advance the empowerment process through cycles of behavioral change and cognitive and emotional development. Although this model of stages or *eras* has heuristic value for conceptualizing and retrospectively describing empowerment processes, it is nevertheless an oversimplification of behavioral and psychological processes that do not often unfold in ways that are evenly sequential. In practice, civic leaders cannot often be easily identified according to particular eras or stages, but move through complex processes that might better be understood as cyclical or helical rather than linear (e.g., Cattaneo & Chapman, 2010). Nevertheless, this developmental model provides some of the basic contours that often differentiate the early stages of psychological empowerment processes from later stages and offers insights into temporal patterns and relations between different components.

Although Kieffer's study is a rare example of a developmental model for psychological empowerment among adults, many studies of empowerment among younger people have taken a developmental perspective. Many of these studies have considered psychological empowerment as an aspect of *positive youth development*, a perspective that is focused on children's, teenagers', and young adults' strengths and potential, in contrast to perspectives on youth and adolescence that place a greater emphasis on risks, problems, or disabilities (Damon, 2004). Although deficit-focused perspectives are still widespread and influential, they were much more pervasive during the twentieth century before the influence of positive youth development. The positive youth development perspective aims to understand and engage young people's capacities to explore the world around them, build skills and abilities, and take productive actions which may also overcome deficits and risk factors. Viewed within this framework, aspects of psychological empowerment have been studied as youth civic engagement, including the many forms that this takes (see the summary in the previous section on the behavioral component of psychological empowerment), as well as civic commitments (Martínez, Peñaloza, & Valenzuela, 2012); civic efficacy (e.g., M. J. Boyd, Zaff, Phelps, Weiner, & Lerner, 2011); civic identity development (e.g., Kirshner, 2009); civic education (Youniss, 2011); and sociopolitical development (Watts, Williams, & Jagers, 2003).

Taken together, these various strands of research literature can be termed *youth civic development*. C. A. Flanagan and Christens (2011) traced the evolution of this concept and emerging field of study, which has involved contributions by scholars and practitioners from disciplines including psychology, education, and political science, and synthesized the major findings to date. These included (a) the fact that young people who have opportunities to participate in civic activities alongside peers and adults are more likely to go on to be active civic participants as adults; (b) that a sense of social incorporation and identification with community institutions is related to young people assuming responsibility and civic participation in adulthood; (c) that opportunities for civic engagement are not distributed equally across racial, ethnic, or social class groups, and the compounding lack of civic opportunity compounds over time to depress civic incorporation and civic actions among marginalized groups; (d) that there are some traits, including confidence, optimism, and extraversion, that predispose youth toward civic engagement; and (e) that civic engagement is positively associated with other positive psychological outcomes, including psychological well-being and mental health. Many of these themes are supported by evidence from multiple countries, as are the importance of community organizations as mediating institutions for civic opportunities and civic development (C. A. Flanagan, Martínez, Cumsille, & Ngomane, 2011).

Several of these points warrant more detailed explanation for present purposes. One is the issue raised in the third point, sometimes referred to as the *civic opportunity gap* (Kahne & Middaugh, 2008) or the *civic empowerment gap* (Levinson, 2012). This phenomenon is particularly imperative to consider given empowerment theory's focus on liberation and the agency of marginalized populations. Social hierarchies exert a strong influence on the number and quality of civic opportunities that young people have. Young people in households with lower levels of income and formal education, for example, are less likely to be involved in organizational activities or the civic arena, in large part because they have fewer of the opportunities to engage that are associated with, for instance, attending a college or university (C. Flanagan & Levine, 2010). Immigrant youth in contemporary United States are either as active or nearly as active in the civic domain as their peers who were born in the United States when the effects of social class are taken into account. Undocumented immigrant youth, however, have particular restraints on their civic activities. Nevertheless, many immigrant youth demonstrate high levels of participation and engagement, particularly in organizing and advocacy efforts related to human rights, including their own rights to access education and employment

(Seif, 2011). The opportunity gap, however, is compounded by the decline of institutional settings for engagement such as labor unions that have served as primary mediating structures for civic participation of many workers.

Another point from the literature on youth civic development that has been frequently noted in studies of youth empowerment concerns the role of adults. For example, Cargo, Grams, Ottoson, Ward, and Green (2003), in a study of youth and adults involved in a community health promotion project, emphasized that youth empowerment is a transactional process that can be facilitated by working partnerships between youth and adults. These are sometimes termed *youth–adult partnership*, which Zeldin, Christens, and Powers (2013) defined as "the practice of (a) multiple youth and multiple adults deliberating and acting together, (b) in a collective [democratic] fashion, (c) over a sustained period of time, (d) through shared work, (e) intended to promote social justice, strengthen an organization and/or affirmatively address a community issue" (p. 388). Recent studies have empirically examined these elements of youth–adult partnership and linked these to indicators of psychological empowerment among youth (Krauss et al., 2014; Zeldin, Krauss, Collura, Lucchesi, & Sulaiman, 2014). Youth–adult partnership is also a contributor to adult development (Zeldin, 2004) and can build adults' sense of efficacy within organizations.

Research on Development of Psychological Empowerment

Taking a look at the research that has been conducted on psychological empowerment as a set of developmental processes, what has been learned so far about which components of psychological empowerment tend to precede and influence development of the others? Relatively few studies have examined the relationships between the components over time in the same groups of people, yet the longitudinal studies that do exist can be viewed alongside evidence from cross-sectional studies to begin to sketch out a developmental framework for psychological empowerment, which can then be further refined in ongoing research.

In one longitudinal study (Christens, Peterson, et al., 2011), we examined community participation (the behavioral component) and sociopolitical control (the emotional component of psychological empowerment) at two time points in a sample of adult participants in community-organizing initiatives. We found that community participation was a better predictor of gains in sociopolitical control over time than the reverse. In other words, although there is undoubtedly some degree of reciprocal causation between the emotional and behavioral components, the *socialization* that occurred through community participation appeared to exert a stronger influence on perceptions of control in the sociopolitical domain than the selection effects of those who perceived themselves to be capable of achieving social and political change choosing to become more involved in their communities. This finding in support of strong socialization resonates with observations from qualitative studies, such as Kieffer's (1984), which made clear that many people will become empowered through community participation, and that this is more common than people who already feel empowered becoming involved as a result of their preexisting levels of psychological empowerment. This suggests, of course, that a promising way to promote psychological empowerment processes is to increase opportunities for people to participate, as opposed to, for instance, seeking to enhance people's feelings of empowerment in hopes that these feelings will lead to greater levels of participation.

As mentioned previously in this chapter, the cognitive component of psychological empowerment has complicated relationships with the behavioral and emotional components. Studies have consistently found that the cognitive component and the emotional component are not positively associated, and in some cases are negatively associated, with each other. Moreover, the cognitive component and the emotional component tend to be higher or lower in different groups according to demographic characteristics such as social class and race. For instance, N. A. Peterson et al. (2002) found that, among a sample of adults in the northeastern United States, people identifying as African Americans had higher levels of all three dimensions of the cognitive component of psychological empowerment than did those identifying as Caucasians, with significant differences on the measures for the source and the instruments of social power. Moreover, in contrast with the many studies that have found strong relationships between the behavioral component and the emotional component, the cognitive component is not often found to be strongly correlated with community participation.

Other studies have found similarly complex results when examining the cognitive component of psychological empowerment and differences in social class, as indicated by household income and level of formal education. For instance, in a cross-sectional study of adults involved in five community-organizing initiatives (Christens, Peterson, et al., 2011), we found that those reporting lower socioeconomic status (SES) indicated higher overall levels of the cognitive component of psychological empowerment, and that for the group reporting lower SES, there was a positive association between community participation and elevated levels of the cognitive component. In contrast, for the group reporting higher SES, which indicated lower overall levels of the cognitive component, there was no positive association between community participation and elevated levels of the cognitive component of psychological empowerment. What this means, practically speaking, is that some psychological empowerment processes and outcomes often differ by groups according to positions in social and economic hierarchies—a finding consistent with the foundations of empowerment theory, which has maintained that such differences are likely given the context-specific nature of empowerment (e.g., Rappaport, 1987).

In simpler terms, the existing evidence suggests that those with more relative privilege or advantages are likely to feel a greater sense of sociopolitical control (the emotional component of psychological empowerment) compared to those who are members of disadvantaged groups or those with less relative privilege. In contrast, those who identify as members of less advantaged groups are more likely to have keener understandings of the source, nature, and instruments of social power (the cognitive component of psychological empowerment) than those who identify as members of groups with more advantages. This makes intuitive sense when you consider two points: First, those in more advantaged groups may feel a greater sense of control in the sociopolitical arena because these systems serve in many ways to maintain and legitimize their advantages and to serve their interests. Of course, these perceptions of control are likely illusory if they are not combined with consistent participation in community and organizational settings and informed by critical awareness of social and political power dynamics. The second point is that many individuals who are disadvantaged by sociopolitical systems have more pressing reasons to develop a keen understanding and awareness of how those systems operate, while many of those who are advantaged by them may prefer to avoid such awareness.

In fact, when more privileged individuals do develop greater awareness of how power operates in society, it can erode their sense of the legitimacy of some of their relative advantages over others and thereby lead to alienation. And in fact, we have seen indications of this in analyses of data. For instance, in one study, we found that relatively advantaged people (those reporting higher SES) who were more critically aware of the source, nature, and instruments of social power appeared to have relatively elevated levels of alienation or hopelessness (Christens, Speer, et al., 2011). In another study, we found that the combination of high levels of sociopolitical control and cognitive empowerment was relatively rare (Christens, Collura, & Tahir, 2013).[5] These points indicate the need for tailored supports for empowerment processes. Techniques that have successfully catalyzed or supported empowerment processes in one type of setting may not necessarily translate well to another and particular attention should be paid to the demographic composition and backgrounds of participants in a setting when selecting strategies or approaches.

Distinction should also be made between the different roles that community participation (the behavioral component of psychological empowerment) can play in the development of the cognitive and emotional components among members of different groups (e.g., according to income, immigration status, or racial/ethnic identity) for practical purposes. As mentioned, in terms of causal influence, the behavioral component is more likely to lead to gains in the emotional component than vice versa (Christens, Peterson, et al., 2011). Importantly, this appears to hold true for members of less advantaged groups as well as more advantaged groups (Christens, Speer, et al., 2011). In other words, although those with less relative privilege or advantage have tended to report lower overall levels of perceived efficacy in the sociopolitical domain, getting involved in community and organizational settings seems to exert a strong positive influence on sociopolitical control through a socialization mechanism. In fact, studies have found that this relationship between the behavioral component and the emotional component is strongest for those reporting fewer advantages (Christens & Lin, 2014), underscoring the value of getting people involved in civic activity as a starting point for psychological empowerment.

The civic opportunity gap is therefore of paramount importance and likely helps to explain some of the widespread differences in perceptions of sociopolitical control between more and less marginalized groups. In other words, poorer people, less educated people, or those who are members of more oppressed groups are less likely, on average, to feel a sense of control in the social and political arena. These same people, however, are the very ones most likely to exhibit strong gains in their sense of control when they become more involved in community organizations. Progress toward greater levels of psychological empowerment, and the interrelated systems change goals of empowerment processes, are therefore likely particularly hampered by the fact that less advantaged people tend to be presented with fewer opportunities to become involved in civic and organizational contexts (C. Flanagan & Levine, 2010). Indeed, in some cases, opportunities for civic participation are deliberately restricted or destroyed by those with greater relative power, for instance through laws that restrict democratic participation (Bentele & O'Brien, 2013).

The role of community participation in the development of the cognitive component of psychological empowerment is additionally complex, particularly when considered alongside people's racial and/or class backgrounds. As mentioned, studies have often found a lack of a relationship between community participation and the cognitive component of psychological empowerment (e.g., N. A. Peterson et al., 2002). Yet, this is at least in part because of the fact that among individuals identifying as members of more advantaged groups, findings have indicated a slight negative association between community participation and the cognitive component of psychological empowerment, while for those who are members of less advantaged groups, there appears to be a positive relationship (Christens, Speer, et al., 2011). It is therefore likely that community participation encourages gains in both the cognitive and emotional components of psychological empowerment for many members of less advantaged groups and populations. These findings can be layered onto empowerment theory to posit a developmental process model for psychological empowerment.

A Developmental Process Model for Psychological Empowerment

Community participation is most often the starting point for empowering processes to take place and for gains to occur in the other components of psychological empowerment. Community participation takes a variety of forms, as discussed previously, and may unfold in eras or stages like those identified by Kieffer (1984).

The relational aspects of psychological empowerment can be considered as process, or intermediate, outcomes[6] of the socialization that can occur in these contexts (Christens, 2012b; Kieffer, 1984; Zeldin, 2004). Through socialization in supportive organizational and community contexts, gains can also be realized in the emotional component of psychological empowerment, sociopolitical control. This socialization mechanism may be detectable using measures that are often studied alongside psychological empowerment, including social cohesion, sense of community, and social support (Christens & Lin, 2014; Christens & Peterson, 2012; N. A. Peterson, Lowe, Aquilino, & Schneider, 2005). In Figure 4.1, socialization is indicated as a praxis mechanism, referring to the continuous cycle of action and reflection that characterizes empowerment processes (Cattaneo & Chapman, 2010; Kieffer, 1984).

A parallel praxis mechanism is experiential learning. This mechanism is akin to conscientization (Freire, 1973), which indicates experiential education for critical consciousness. As we have seen in the research reviewed in this section, these mechanisms for development of psychological empowerment are likely to be moderated by relative privilege or marginalization and by the cultural and sociopolitical contexts in which empowerment processes are taking place. These factors likely influence differences across these two parallel processes and in the outcomes associated with psychological empowerment processes. Finally, the development of psychological empowerment is not likely to unfold in a linear fashion but is likely to involve cycles of action and reflection, as indicated in the reflection praxis mechanism.

Like Kieffer's stage-based model that identified four distinct eras in the development of psychological empowerment, the developmental process model presented

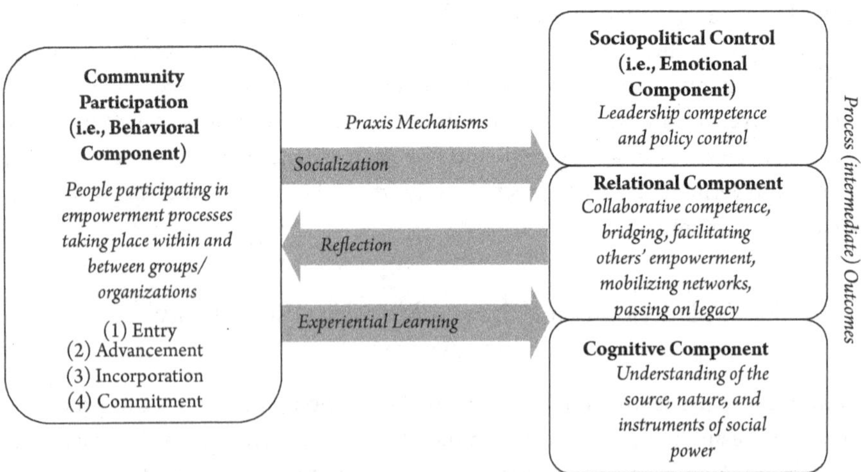

Figure 4.1. A developmental process model for psychological empowerment.

here has heuristic value as well as limitations in its ability to capture and reflect the complex reality of empowerment processes, which often unfold unevenly for particular individuals as well as across different groups and contexts. It is nevertheless useful to attempt overarching syntheses of the conceptual and empirical work that has been conducted on psychological empowerment over several successive decades to assess what these scholarly efforts have shown us as a whole and to trace the contours of this body of knowledge.

Understanding of psychological empowerment and its development remains limited. Refinement of the available tools to measure the components of psychological empowerment, as well as discussion of the nature of the component structure of the construct should continue (see N. A. Peterson, 2014). Meanwhile, studies examining empowerment processes in a variety of community and organizational contexts, as well as among diverse populations, are valuable for building on and challenging existing models. Unfortunately, few data sets currently provide the ability to trace the development of psychological empowerment over time. Furthermore, representative studies would be useful to provide insights into psychological empowerment in larger populations and to test hypothesized links between the development of psychological empowerment and a variety of other indicators of population characteristics and well-being. Although much of this work is conceptually and technically complex, advances in understanding of psychological empowerment hold enormous potential for advancing the effectiveness of systems change efforts.

Psychological Disempowerment

Finally, a comprehensive understanding of psychological empowerment should also account for the processes that lead to its absence. What are the most likely markers of psychological disempowerment? The sociopolitical control scale that assesses the emotional component of psychological empowerment was developed with reference to learned hopelessness (Seligman, 1975). Sociopolitical control, in contrast, was formulated as a kind of domain-specific learned hopefulness (Zimmerman, 1990b), so we would expect for its opposite to be hopelessness as it relates to the civic or sociopolitical domain. Some studies of psychological empowerment have also included measures of alienation (often using Dean's 1961 measure) and found it to function as a divergent indicator for sociopolitical control (e.g., N. A. Peterson et al., 2006), but this measure is not specifically oriented to the sociopolitical arena. It is therefore likely that future efforts could develop an improved contraindicator for the emotional component of psychological empowerment.

For the behavioral component, apathy and disengagement are the opposite of community participation and civic action. Drawing on the understanding of community power outlined in Chapter 2, however, we should be attentive to the possibility that the second face of power is operating to prevent or suppress participation. In other words, fear of reprisals and discrimination should be examined as well as individual lack of motivation to participate (Salamon & Van Evera, 1973). Legacies of subjugation and historical trauma may also inhibit engagement (Gone, 2013). Furthermore, participation in civic and community affairs through venues or organizations that serve to maintain oppressive aspects of the status quo or that engage communities in tokenistic and manipulative ways should be seen as possible indicators of psychological disempowerment processes.

Cognitive aspects of disempowerment include a lack of understanding of the source, nature, and instruments of social power as identified by Speer and Peterson (2000). We might also identify a lack of critical reflection as understood in the framework for critical consciousness (Watts et al., 2011; Watts & Flanagan, 2007). A promising contraindicator that has not yet been examined alongside psychological empowerment is *system justification*, or the legitimation of existing social relationships, even if at the expense of the person doing the legitimizing (Jost, Banaji, & Nosek, 2004). System justification is therefore one potential indicator for the pernicious psychological effects of power's third dimension. Furthermore, as demonstrated in Gaventa's (1980) analysis of the third dimension of power, community power structures may operate to constrain people's ability to imagine plausible alternatives to the status quo. This also points to a gap in psychological empowerment theory: To what extent are empowerment processes opening up people's ability to imagine alternatives to the status quo? Concepts such as radical imagination (e.g., Haiven & Khasnabish, 2014; Kelley, 2003) could be instructive for future studies seeking to address this gap.

For the relational component, we would of course expect to see sociopolitical isolation or the absence of the kinds of relationships that build community power (Christens, 2010) as indicators of psychological disempowerment. Yet, just as simply having interpersonal relationships is not necessarily indicative of relational empowerment, certain types relationships may be detrimental to psychological empowerment. For example, Jost, Ledgerwood, and Hardin (2008) argued that system justification has a relational basis with those with motives to justify the status quo working, sometimes subtly, to reward system-justifying responses in their friends and family members and to punish system-challenging responses. There may be certain qualities of relationships and network configurations, therefore, that impede psychological empowerment processes. Future research could examine these sorts of disempowering processes and perhaps provide insights that could help inform efforts to avoid them.

Conclusions

Psychological empowerment can be understood as a set of change processes that occur as people grow and develop through their participation in systems and policy change efforts in community and organizational contexts. For instance, cognitive change is occurring as experiential learning takes place. Emotional changes and self-perceptions occur as certain types of relationships grow and deepen. These processes are related to each other. For instance, both cognitive and emotional empowerment processes depend on active community participation and relational processes. Likewise, behavioral and relational processes often serve to stimulate emotional and cognitive changes. Yet, they do not always unfold evenly together, and the ways that they unfold are related to identity, SES, and experience of oppression, as well as context.

It is therefore necessary for future research and practice to become ever more sophisticated and comprehensive in designing and implementing approaches to enhancing psychological empowerment. There is no avoiding the fact that we have a long way to go before such comprehensiveness and sophistication can be claimed. As Cattaneo and Chapman (2010) pointed out, much of the research up to this point has only been able to capture pieces of empowerment processes, rather than studying the processes as a whole. And, as discussed in Chapter 3, many practitioners and researchers continue to use the term *empowerment* in ways that connote the individual orientation that Zimmerman (1990a) argued against. Nevertheless, conceptual and empirical work on psychological empowerment has resulted in considerable gains in actionable knowledge. Furthermore, there is now a foundation of concepts, measures, and basic findings that can be built on in future work. With this foundation established, the task of the next two chapters is to consider empowerment processes in organizational and community settings, while remaining cognizant of the inextricability of those processes and psychological empowerment.

Appendix 4.1   Measure of the Emotional Component of Psychological Empowerment Among Adults: Sociopolitical Control Scale—Revised (SPCS-R)

Stem: *Please rate your agreement or disagreement with the following statements:*

Item	Item Wording
SPCS-R1	I am often a leader in groups.
SPCS-R2	I would prefer to be a leader rather than a follower.
SPCS-R3	I would rather have a leadership role when I'm involved in a group project.
SPCS-R4	I can usually organize people to get things done.
SPCS-R5	Other people usually follow my ideas.
SPCS-R6	I find it very easy to talk in front of a group.
SPCS-R7	I like to work on solving a problem myself rather than wait and see if someone else will deal with it.
SPCS-R8	I like trying new things that are challenging to me.
SPCS-R9	I enjoy political participation because I want to have as much say in running government as possible.
SPCS-R10	A person like me can really understand what's going on with government and politics.
SPCS-R11	I feel like I have a pretty good understanding of the important political issues which confront our society.
SPCS-R12	People like me are generally well qualified to participate in political activity and decision making in our country.
SPCS-R13	It makes a difference who I vote for because whoever gets elected will represent my interests.
SPCS-R14	There are plenty of ways for people like me to have a say in what our government does.
SPCS-R15	It is important to me that I actively participate in local issues.
SPCS-R16	Most public officials would listen to me.
SPCS-R17	A good many local elections are important to vote in.

Note: Items SPCS-R1 through SPCS-R8 are indicators for the leadership competence dimension, while Items SPCS-R9 through SPCS-R17 are indicators for the policy control dimension of sociopolitical control.

Source: N. A. Peterson et al. (2006).

Appendix 4.2 Measure of the Emotional Component of Psychological Empowerment Among Young People: Sociopolitical Control Scale for Youth (SPCS-Y)

Stem: *Please rate your agreement or disagreement with the following statements*:

Item	Item Wording
SPCS-Y1	I am often a leader in groups.
SPCS-Y2	I would prefer to be a leader rather than a follower.
SPCS-Y3	I would rather have a leadership role when I'm involved in a group project.
SPCS-Y4	I can usually organize people to get things done.
SPCS-Y5	Other people usually follow my ideas.
SPCS-Y6	I find it very easy to talk in front of a group.
SPCS-Y7	I like to work on solving a problem myself rather than wait and see if someone else will deal with it.
SPCS-Y8	I like trying new things that are challenging to me.
SPCS-Y9	I enjoy participation because I want to have as much say in my community or school as possible.
SPCS-Y10	Youth like me can really understand what's going on with my community or school.
SPCS-Y11	I feel like I have a pretty good understanding of the important issues which confront my community or school.
SPCS-Y12	Youth like me have the ability to participate effectively in community or school activities and decision making.
SPCS-Y13	My opinion is important because it could someday make a difference in my community or school.
SPCS-Y14	There are plenty of ways for youth like me to have a say in what our community or school does.
SPCS-Y15	It is important to me that I actively participate in local teen issues.
SPCS-Y16	Most community or school leaders would listen to me.
SPCS-Y17	Many local activities are important to participate in.

Note: Items SPCS-Y1 through SPCS-Y8 are indicators for the leadership competence dimension, while Items SPCS-Y9 through SPCS-Y17 are indicators for the policy control dimension of sociopolitical control.

Source: N. A. Peterson, Peterson, Agre, Christens, and Morton (2011).

Appendix 4.3   Measure of the Behavioral Component of Psychological Empowerment Among Adults: Behavioral Empowerment Scale (BES)

Stem: *How frequently have you done the following in the last 3 months?*

Item	Item Wording
BES-1	Signed a petition.
BES-2	Wrote a letter or made a telephone call to influence a policy or issue.
BES-3	Attended an event that provided information about community services.
BES-4	Arranged an agenda for a public meeting
BES-5	Had an in-depth face-to-face conversation about an issue affecting your community.
BES-6	Attended a public meeting to press for a policy change.
BES-7	Attended a meeting to gather information about a neighborhood issue.

Source: Speer and Peterson (2000).

Appendix 4.4   Measure of the Behavioral Component of Psychological Empowerment Among Young People: Critical Action Dimension of Critical Consciousness Scale (CCS)

Stem: *How frequently have you done each of the following?*

Item	Item Wording
CCS-14	Participated in a civil rights group or organization.
CCS-15	Participated in a political party, club or organization.
CCS-16	Wrote a letter to a school, community newspaper, or publication about a social or political issue.
CCS-17	Contacted a public official by phone, mail, or email to tell him or her how you felt about a social or political issue.
CCS-18	Joined in a protest march, political demonstration, or political meeting.
CCS-19	Worked on a political campaign.
CCS-20	Participated in a discussion about a social or political issue.
CCS-21	Signed an email or written petition about a social or political issue.
CCS-22	Participated in a human rights, gay rights, or women's rights organization or group.

Source: Diemer, Rapa, Park, and Perry (2017).

Appendix 4.5   Measure of the Cognitive Component of Psychological Empowerment Among Adults: Cognitive Empowerment Scale

Stem: *Please rate your agreement or disagreement with the following statements*:

Item	Item Wording
CES-1	When there is a problem in this community, I am better able to deal with it on my own than as a member of a group.*
CES-2	Only by working together can people make changes in a community.
CES-3	I can impact community issues only by working in an organized way with other people.
CES-4	To improve my community, it is more effective to work with a group than as an individual.
CES-5	The effectiveness of activists and corporate leaders is really due to the quality of their organizations, not from their personal characteristics.
CES-6	The only way I can act to improve the community is by connecting to others.
CES-7	Changing a community almost always results in conflict.
CES-8	Because the interests of the powerful are so different from the interests of common people, sooner or later conflict is to be expected.
CES-9	When community groups work to improve schools, housing, public safety and the like, then they must be ready for conflict with local institutions.
CES-10	Community groups should not strive for conflict, but they must be ready for conflict with local institutions when making change to improve community conditions.
CES-11	When community groups work to improve things like public health or crime, they sooner or later come into conflict with business leaders or public officials.
CES-12	Things happen in my community because those with power reward their friends.
CES-13	The powerful punish their enemies.
CES-14	The powerful control what information gets to the public.
CES-15	Those with community influence keep many issues out of the news.
CES-16	Those with power shape the way people think about community problems.
CES-17	Influential groups shape the way a community interprets local events.

Note: Items CES-1 through CES-6 are indicators for the dimension: source of social power; Items CES-7 through CES-11 are indicators for the dimension: nature of social power; Items CES-12 through CES-17 are indicators for the dimension: instruments of social power.

* Indicates reverse-coded item.

Source: Speer and Peterson (2000).

Appendix 4.6   Measure of the Cognitive Component of Psychological Empowerment Among Young People: Critical Reflection Dimensions of the Critical Consciousness Scale (CCS)

Stem: *Please rate your agreement or disagreement with the following statements*:

Item	Item Wording
CCS-1	Certain racial and ethnic groups have fewer chances to get a good high school education.
CCS-2	Poor children have fewer chances to get a good high school education.
CCS-3	Certain racial or ethnic groups have fewer chances to get good jobs.
CCS-4	Women have fewer chances to get good jobs.
CCS-5	Poor people have fewer chances to get good jobs.
CCS-6	Certain racial or ethnic groups have fewer chances to get ahead.
CCS-7	Women have fewer chances to get ahead.
CCS-8	Poor people have fewer chances to get ahead.
CCS-9	It is a good thing that certain groups are at the top and other groups are at the bottom.*
CCS-10	It would be good if groups could be equal.
CCS-11	Group equality should be our ideal.
CCS-12	All groups should be given an equal chance in life.
CCS-13	We would have fewer problems if we treated people more equally.

Note: Items CCS-1 through CCS-8 are indicators for the critical reflection: perceived inequality dimension, while Items CCS-9 through CCS-13 are indicators for the critical reflection: egalitarianism dimension of critical consciousness.

* Indicates reverse-coded item.

Source: Diemer, Rapa, Park, and Perry (2014).

Notes

1. One recent study has found evidence supporting this three-component structure among a sample of youth of middle school age in the United States (Eisman et al., 2016).
2. This emotional component has been referred to as the intrapersonal component or affective component in some of the research literature on psychological empowerment.
3. The Sociopolitical Control Scale for Youth (SPCS-Y) has also recently been adapted to a phrase completion format, rather than a Likert-type response scale, with promising results (see N. A. Peterson, Gilmore Powell, Hamme Peterson, & Reid, 2017).
4. This cognitive component has been referred to as the interactional component in some of the research literature on psychological empowerment.
5. In this study (Christens et al., 2013), we found that only 7.5% of adults in the sample could be grouped into a cluster indicating high levels on both the cognitive and emotional components of psychological empowerment.
6. See Chapter 7 for more on empowerment processes and outcomes.

5

Organizational Development

Introduction

Community power and empowerment almost always have an organizational context. More specifically, community power is most often built and exercised through nonprofit organizations and voluntary associations and through networks of such organizations. Thus, it is crucial to examine the ways that empowerment manifests and power is mediated through organizational contexts. Nonprofit organizations include social and recreational organizations, labor unions, advocacy organizations, faith-based institutions, community development corporations, social change and social movement organizations, and organizations dedicated to the arts. Many hospitals, universities, and providers of social and human services are also nonprofits. The nonprofit sector also includes private foundations, from small family foundations and local community charities to the largest global and national foundations (e.g., the Bill & Melinda Gates Foundation or the Ford Foundation). Collectively, the nonprofit sector has grown rapidly in recent decades, particularly in industrialized and postindustrial countries (Frumkin, 2005; Salamon, 1994).

In the United States, for instance, there were an estimated 1.44 million nonprofit organizations operating in the year 2012. These organizations are supported by more than $300 billion in annual private charitable contributions, which along with other sources of revenue total more than $2 trillion dollars annually (McKeever & Pettijohn, 2014). The US nonprofit sector has grown more rapidly in recent decades than either the private/business or the public/governmental sector. More than a quarter of US adults volunteer with nonprofit organizations each year.

Although detailed comparative data are difficult to obtain, it is clear that the nonprofit sectors of many countries around the world have experienced similar growth. The Johns Hopkins Comparative Nonprofit Sector Project has assembled data from 40 countries around the world and established definitions that allow cross-national and historical comparisons (Salamon, 2010). The annual operating expenditures by nonprofits in those 40 countries add up to more than the gross domestic product of all but the 6 wealthiest countries. Many European countries have a larger share of paid workers in nonprofit organizations than does the United States, yet it is clear from comparative data that wealthier countries do tend to have a larger percentage of their workforce employed in nonprofits than poorer countries.

What explains the development of this "global associational revolution," as it has been called (Salamon, 1994, p. 109)? And, since nonprofit organizations and voluntary associations contain key settings for empowerment, what are the implications of this revolution for community power and empowerment? Consistent with an understanding of community power, theory on *organizational empowerment* seeks to identify, distinguish, and understand organizations, organizational settings, and interorganizational networks that are capable of mounting and sustaining challenges to unjust conditions. Yet, closer examination reveals that it is not sufficient to take terms like *nonprofit, voluntary, public interest, philanthropic, nonpartisan,* or *grassroots* at face value. Instead, there is a narrower subset of nonprofit and voluntary associational organizations that provide real opportunities for empowerment to occur and for community power to be built. Before examining the specific ways that empowerment occurs and power is built in organizational contexts, then, it is helpful first to take a bird's-eye view of the societal and global ecology of organizations that shapes opportunities for community participation and civic engagement and enables and constrains the ability of organizations to exert influence in their communities through empowering processes.

In the next section, I make a case that understanding the rapid increases in inequality is indispensable for a clear view of the organizational contexts in which power is built and empowerment occurs. Specifically, it is fruitful to consider several trends in the types of organizations that make up civil society and their roles in political economy. These include seemingly contradictory trends, such as the aforementioned rapid growth of the nonprofit and voluntary sector, in contrast to well-documented, long-term declines in some of the most common forms of associational activity (Putnam, 2001). Insights can be gained into paradoxes like these through analyzing relationships between increasing inequality and shifts in civil society, including declines in labor organizing, increased business organizing, and increases in both philanthropy and wealth-driven political action.

Civil Society and Inequality

Civil society refers broadly to the organizations, institutions, and associations that are neither the state nor the market, but shape both of these other sectors through reinforcements and challenges (C. A. Flanagan, Martínez, & Cumsille, 2011). Civil society includes nonprofit and nongovernmental organizations (NGOs), but also encompasses voluntary associations that may not be formalized as corporate entities. The functions of civil society exist in fundamental tension with the democratic ideal of equality among citizens, for although civil society organizations are both a source and a consequence of civic engagement, they are also a source of factionalization, polarization, and attempts by small groups to achieve policy victories, a number of which may advance narrower private interests, sometimes at the expense of the common good. Indeed, there is a long history of skepticism, worry, opposition, and legal limitations on private philanthropy in the United States, particularly concerning associations and institutions with large private endowments (Hall, 2013). One fear has been that these entities, which in many countries effectively receive public subsidies in the form of advantaged tax treatment in perpetuity, might be used by the wealthy to shape institutions, policies, and public opinion to suit their purposes.

Civil society as a whole, however, has long been regarded as a fundamental component of a capitalist democratic society. Most contemporary observers tend to view it primarily as a necessary and beneficial feature of society, so much so that broad declines in participation in associational activities are widely held to be causes for concern on behalf of democracy (e.g., Putnam, 2001). Despite these concerns about declines in civic activities, such as individual memberships in organizations and meeting attendance, there is some evidence that civic engagement is not declining over time but is simply evolving into newer forms of engagement, such as participation in collective events that blend expressive functions with social action and protests (Sampson, McAdam, MacIndoe, & Weffer-Elizondo, 2005). Regardless, two headline trends about changes in US civil society—(a) that there is an ongoing major expansion of the nonprofit and voluntary sector and (b) that there have been long-term declines in at least some of the most common forms of associational activity—constitute a conundrum. What explains this apparent discrepancy?

One part of the answer is that the nonprofit sector plays increasingly vital and complex roles in public governance from urban affairs to international affairs (Anheier, 2009). In fact, nonprofits in the United States now act as the providers of the majority of government-funded services (Lecy & Van Slyke, 2013), typically through grants and contracts. This is due, in part, to government agencies' moves to save money by outsourcing the provision of health and human services to nonprofit organizations, which must then compete for limited-term grants and contracts. Around the world, the rise of so-called new public management in the 1980s has led to such a degree of governmental devolution through outsourcing of health and human services that some now refer to the central aim of public administration as managing the "hollow state" (Milward & Provan, 2000, p. 359). This is true even in countries with well-developed social welfare states. For example, in spite of the common image of northern European countries' social welfare systems as governmental, many services in these countries are managed and provided by NGOs (Salamon, 2010). Some of the growth of the nonprofit sector globally can therefore be understood as an extension of the competition-based free market mentality into the provision of social goods and services (Eikenberry & Kluver, 2004), including healthcare, education, and in some cases, even police and fire services (M. W. Anderson, 2014).

The evolution of contemporary civil societies cannot be adequately understood, however, without a more fine-grained analysis of the relationships between civil society and steadily increasing inequality. What is the relationship between the escalating inequality among households discussed in Chapter 2 and the growth and evolution of nonprofit sectors across nations? Examining several trends in the composition and functioning of the US nonprofit sector (in labor organizing, business organizing, and philanthropy and political action) provides insights.

Trends in Labor Organizing

In spite of the expansion of the nonprofit sector in recent decades, some of its traditional pillars have steadily eroded. Labor unions in the United States, for instance, have declined precipitously in number and in overall membership. In contrast, labor unions increased in prevalence, membership, and importance after the National Labor Relations Act was signed into law in 1935 during President Franklin D. Roosevelt's New Deal. By 1973, in the US private sector, 34% of men working were members of unions, along with 16% of women, whereas today the rates for both genders are in the single digits (Western & Rosenfeld, 2011).

For most of the mid-twentieth century, unions played pivotal roles in electoral politics. Today, their influence on policy debates and elections has greatly diminished. The decline in US labor unionization was not a naturally occurring economic phenomenon. Corporate interests began to have success at eroding the power of labor unions through, for example, right-to-work legislation passed in numerous states beginning in the 1960s, which was enabled at the federal level by the Taft–Hartley Act of 1947. Clawson and Clawson (1999) detailed the ways that employers, beginning in the 1970s, more aggressively targeted unions.[1] In the workplace, for example, there was a steep increase in the number of union elections that were contested through the National Labor Relations Board. Employees were treated vindictively for union involvement, including through loss of their jobs. Employers invested disproportionately in worksites that were not unionized and failed to invest in expansion at unionized sites. At a policy level, it became clear to employers and union leaders alike that governmental authorities were unlikely to update labor laws to protect workers' right to organize and collectively bargain, as in the 1978 failure of a labor relations bill to pass the US Congress despite Democratic majorities in both chambers and a Democratic president.

Across nations, the existence of collective labor rights has been empirically linked to declines in income equality (Kerrissey, 2015). Moreover, in the United States, labor unions have been able to achieve policy shifts and changes in norms that have increased wages for unionized workers and non-unionized workers alike (Western & Rosenfeld, 2011). Thus, the declines in labor union activity in the

United States can be understood as a potent precipitator of recent surges in inequality. Hacker and Pierson (2010) argued that this decline in labor union power left openings for free-market and antitax groups to exert influence on tax policies and the ways that these policies were enforced. The result is that policies have increasingly favored corporations and the wealthy at the expense of lower wage and middle-class workers.

Trends in Business Organizing

At the same time that labor unions were being extinguished and subdued, Hacker and Pierson (2010) detailed a marked uptick in US business organization beginning in the 1970s. This intensification was partly a response to what many employers perceived as a series of blows to private enterprise in the late 1960s and early 1970s: Environmental preservation policies, occupational safety regulations, and consumer protections all were widely perceived as damaging incursions into business models. Strikingly, the number of businesses with registered lobbyists in Washington increased from 175 to 2,455 between the years 1971 and 1982. Over this same time period, the membership of the national Chamber of Commerce more than doubled and its budget tripled. New business organizations were also formed, such as the Business Roundtable, founded in 1972. A variety of organization types were formed at different scales. As Hacker and Pierson described:

> Building networks of employees, shareholders, local companies, and firms with shared interests, they [businesses] could soon flood Washington with letters and calls. Within a few years, these classically top-down organizations were to thrive at generating bottom-up style campaigns. . . . these emerging "outside" strategies were married to the "inside" ones. (pp. 176–177)

This increased business organization contributed to the declines in labor organizing through policies and restrictions that made operating and negotiating more difficult for unions. The tipping of the scales in civil society from labor organizing to business organizing has set the stage for many specific alterations within the US policy environment in the decades since.[2] Top tax rates for corporations declined from 52.8% in 1969 to 34% by 1988, where they remained until recent cuts brought them down to 21%. The top individual marginal income tax rates followed, declining from 70% in 1981 (it had been as high as 92% in the 1950s) to less than half of that rate by the early 1990s. In the years since, the top rate has fluctuated between 31% and 39.6%. Reductions in capital gains taxes and estate taxes have compounded these gains for the wealthy.

"But Nobody Pays That" is the title of the Pulitzer Prize-winning series of *New York Times* articles (Kocieniewski, 2012). This series exposes the ways that corporations and households with higher incomes shelter their assets and earnings from even these reduced levels of taxation and the obscure legal loopholes that enable them to accomplish this. These combined changes in tax policies and practices alone are believed to account for up to a third of the growth in US wealth inequality since the mid–twentieth century (Hacker & Pierson, 2010; Piketty & Saez, 2007).

Trends in Philanthropy and Political Action

As large fortunes have snowballed and found ways to avoid taxation, the wealthy have increasingly made contributions to nonprofit organizations and private foundations. These contributions are often tax deductible, especially for wealthier donors.[3] The organizations receiving them can also operate exempt from corporate taxes. The large-scale philanthropy of billionaires and celebrities now routinely makes headlines. In spite of many beneficial uses to which some of these charitable resources have been put, these donated funds represent some funds that would otherwise be public funds if tax policies had not shifted so dramatically to the benefit of the wealthy. It is clear that the wealthy prefer the continued control that they exercise over their charitable contributions to the alternative of contributing to the public through taxation, which of course has more democratic systems of control.

In fact, the standards by which charitable contributions are judged to be operating in the public interest and thus eligible for tax advantages (a public subsidy) are incredibly broad. Piketty (2014), for example, called into question the purposes of many of these funds as being in the public interest, pointing out the following:

> Families often use foundations for both private and charitable purposes and are generally careful to maintain control of their assets even when housed in a primarily charitable foundation. . . . In some cases, a family trust whose purpose is primarily to serve as an inheritance vehicle exists alongside a more charitable purpose. . . . There is a certain porosity between public and private uses of these legal entities. (p. 452)

In some cases, then, apparent increases in flows of capital to civil society actually represent elaborate tax shelters for private individuals, families, and corporations.

Beyond these purely private and more covert uses of foundations, wealthy donors openly shape the charitable activities of foundations and organizations to advance their worldviews and priorities for society. For example, the Bloomberg Foundation uses its billions of dollars to carry out philanthropic activities broadly consistent with the worldview of founder Michael Bloomberg; likewise, the Walton Family Foundation, the Bill & Melinda Gates Foundation, and many other large foundations operate with the intent of advancing their founders' priorities. Because these forms of donor-directed philanthropy are embraced by elites across the political spectrum in the United States, they are not as controversial as they were in earlier eras when they were disproportionately utilized by one side of the political spectrum or the other (Hall, 2013).

Taken as a whole, however, large foundations do privilege the perspectives and priorities of the elite, potentially at the expense of the priorities of the public.[4] Ostrander (2007), for example, chronicled the growth in donor control that has occurred in the nonprofit services sector and the accompanying declines in possible inputs by other stakeholders, especially the clients or recipients of the goods or services that the organizations provide. This rise in donor control has been accompanied by a shift detailed by Skocpol (2004) "from membership to management." Volunteer-run organizations, which were once prevalent, have given way to professionally managed associations and interest groups, reducing the availability of meaningful roles for nonprofessional volunteers and members.

Meanwhile, particularly in the United States, large donor-driven nonprofit organizations' importance in policy debates and elections has skyrocketed as restrictions on money in politics have eroded or been removed entirely. The controversial Supreme Court ruling in *Citizens United v. Federal Election Commission* (2010) holds that financial backing of entities involved in political advertising and voter mobilization constitutes a form of free speech. This has opened the floodgates for individual and corporate contributions to campaign-focused, tax-exempt organizations. These are often barely distinguishable from candidates' campaigns. This has had the effect of accelerating the longer term trend toward professionally managed nonprofit organizations' direct involvement in electoral politics at the behest of their wealthy donors. Political action committees (PACs) and so-called "super-PACs"—many of them lavishly funded—now dominate political advertising, organizing, and voter mobilization efforts in US elections.

Effects of these Trends on US Civil Society

Collectively, the relationships between these shifts in civil society and growing societal inequality help to explain how the number and size of nonprofit organizations could consistently grow at the same time as declines are occurring in associational activity in the United States. They also help to account for the persistence (and in some cases worsening) of social issues despite a proliferation of organizations seemingly devoted to addressing them. The nonprofit model has become so popular that it is being thrust on reluctant or even resistant participants.[5] In many cases, this applies to institutions that might have been public in previous eras, such as schools. Silverman (2012), for instance, described the push toward nonprofit charter schools in New York as a "charter school industry system" (p. 5) in which actors at the local, state, and federal levels reinforce trends leading to a proliferation of nonprofit charter schools.

Nonprofits are often thought (and often claim) to be volunteer- and mission-driven organizations working to improve society, but a closer inspection reveals that nonprofits serve a variety of purposes. Drawing on Mills's (1956) notion of the power elite, Domhoff (2009) offered a compelling analysis of the role of US nonprofit organizations as they relate to the interests of the wealthy and powerful. Nonprofits, he demonstrated, play leading roles in both challenging and defending the interests of elites. Although some nonprofits (e.g., National Council of La Raza, NAACP [National Association for the Advancement of Colored People], and some labor unions) have mounted successful and meaningful challenges to the status quo, there are a large number of nonprofit organizations that resist such changes and defend the interests of the elite. For example, Domhoff traced the bounds of a network of nonprofit organizations receiving large contributions from oil companies that exists to create doubts about anthropocentric global warming and limit policy responses to it. A similar but somewhat distinct network of organizations, think tanks, and public relations groups exists to link conservative moral/ family values to support cuts in social services, unemployment benefits, and welfare. When examining organizations, we must therefore ask not only whether particular nonprofit organizations can be contexts for building community power, but also whether they thwart or distort community power building.

Although philanthropy and civil society are sometimes viewed as a compensation for cuts in government services or as alternative vehicles for solving social problems, much of contemporary civil society is either explicitly or implicitly oriented toward preservation of the status quo. Further, some seek to move from the status quo toward even greater inequality through policies that benefit the wealthy while cutting worker protections and the welfare state. It is often necessary for nonprofit groups who would mount challenges to powerful interests to moderate their goals in order to continue obtaining funds. Many organizations walk a tightrope between, on the one hand, providing services for those in need and remaining financially viable, and on the other hand seeking to organize and advocate on behalf of their clients (Stoecker, 1995). The distinctions between the private sector, private wealth, and the philanthropic sector have blurred, sometimes allowing defenders of the status quo to masquerade as challengers (Nickel & Eikenberry, 2009). Moreover, the opportunities for citizens to play meaningful roles in civil society have diminished, as they are increasingly expected to participate at an arm's length, through financial contributions, memberships, and symbolic forms of engagement (e.g., online engagement and social media engagement, bumper stickers) while professionals do the "real" work in the civic sphere.

Implications for Organizational Power and Empowerment

When considering the concepts of community power and empowerment in light of these trends, it becomes clear that we are in need of a framework that allows us to distinguish certain types of organizational settings and interorganizational efforts from civil society as a whole. A framework for organizational empowerment must enable identification, for instance, of the subset of nonprofit organizations that could conceivably achieve social, systemic, and policy changes that run counter to the continued increases in societal inequality and the interests of the power elite. Further, it must distinguish between practices within organizational settings that are more or less conducive to building power.

Consistent with empowerment theory, organizational empowerment refers specifically to processes in organizations and organizational settings that involve groups of people—often nonprofessional volunteers and members—in skill building, civic learning, deliberation, leadership, and capacity building as a means to developing organizational power. In this sense, the settings where organizational empowerment tends to take place have similarities to what other scholars have identified as *tiny publics* (G. A. Fine & Harrington, 2004) or *free spaces* (S. M. Evans & Boyte, 1986; Polletta, 1999). Empowering organizational settings are those that enable residents, particularly those with a stake in pressing public issues, to build power and work toward systemic changes that reduce inequality and enhance well-being.

Examples of empowering organizational settings include neighborhood organizations, community organizing initiatives, and social movement actions that are not driven by PACs. Some labor-organizing efforts create empowering community settings. For example, some labor unions create venues for voluntary activity of their membership, ranging from worksite meetings, to trainings, to collective deliberation, to organizing major actions. They are thus primary drivers, at least for some members, of civic engagement and the development of civic skills (Terriquez, 2011). On the other hand, many labor unions are neither deeply participatory nor capable of achieving changes in policies and practices. So, asking whether labor unions qualify as empowering community settings is not, as it turns out, a sufficiently detailed question. Clearly, there is great utility in a framework that can help us to differentiate not only between organizational types but also between internal and external features of organizations that affect their ability to build community power and foster empowerment processes. The framework for organizational empowerment presented in the next section elaborates on characteristics of organizations and interorganizational efforts that have particularly strong effects on the people who participate in them and their relationships to civil society.

Organizational Empowerment

Reflecting its integration with the ecology of empowerment, organizational empowerment can be understood as the organizational aspects of the processes through which people gain and exercise control over their lives. It is held to be inextricable from the psychological and community-level aspects of empowerment. Zimmerman (2000) made a distinction between *empowering* and *empowered* organizations. In this formulation, empowering organizations create contexts for people to develop psychological empowerment through, for instance, opportunities to participate in decision-making and other organizational responsibilities, while empowered organizations have influence over policies and systems in the community. N. A. Peterson and Zimmerman (2004) therefore defined organizational empowerment as "organizational efforts that generate psychological empowerment among members and organizational effectiveness needed for goal achievement" (p. 130). Drawing on earlier work by ecological theorists such as Barker (1968), they proposed a framework with three distinct components of organizational empowerment (intraorganizational, interorganizational, and extraorganizational) and made distinctions between organizational empowerment processes and outcomes.

In N. A. Peterson and Zimmerman's (2004) three-component framework of organizational empowerment, the three components are held to be interrelated. First, the intraorganizational component of organizational empowerment involves the internal structure and functioning of organizations. Second, the interorganizational component includes relationships (e.g., communications, collaborations, competition) between organizations. Third, the extraorganizational component includes the ways that organizations relate to their broader communities and environments and take actions to influence them (e.g., through advocacy for policy changes or information dissemination). N. A. Peterson and Zimmerman provided this template to guide future research on organizational empowerment, while acknowledging that the framework would likely need to be updated or replaced over time.

Some research has used this three-component structure for studying organizational empowerment (e.g., Griffith et al., 2008), but others have not (e.g., Maton, 2008). Meanwhile, a spate of recent research on organizational development, organizational learning, interorganizational networks, and coalitions has spurred cross-disciplinary conversations in community psychology, public administration, public health, and other related fields. In the remainder of this chapter, I draw on this multidisciplinary literature to construct an updated conceptual framework for organizational empowerment.

The framework that follows builds on N. A. Peterson and Zimmerman's (2004). For example, I adopt their concept of components of organizational empowerment to structure this synthesis, although with some modifications. One modification is that instead of referring to three components, I refer more simply to aspects of empowerment within organizations (internal) and aspects of empowerment between or among organizations (external).[6] In both categories, I draw on recent work and research from several disciplines, and as throughout this book, I emphasize links to community power. What follows can therefore be considered as a critical interdisciplinary analysis intended to update and sharpen existing concepts of empowerment in organizations.

Empowerment Within Organizations

What are the most salient internal features of organizational settings that indicate that empowerment is taking place (empowering organizations) and power is being built (empowered organizations)? This task of identification of specific features of organizational settings is similar to what Seidman (1988) has described as a focus on *social regularities*: consistent patterns in the relationships between individuals and their environments. N. A. Peterson and Zimmerman (2004) catalogued social regularities within organizational settings that are indicators of organizational empowerment processes, including *incentive management, subgroup linkages, opportunity role structure, leadership, social support,* and a *group-based belief system*. Likewise, they identified a related set of outcomes of empowerment processes that can be observed within organizations. These include *viability, resource identification, underpopulated settings, co-empowered subgroups,* and *resolved ideological conflict* (Table 5.1). In what follows, I describe each of these processes and some of the process outcomes that are most closely associated with them, drawing additional insights from the last decade of community psychology research. I then turn to the research literature on organizational development and organizational learning for additional

Table 5.1 **Internal Aspects of Organizational Empowerment, Including Organizational Learning Processes and Outcomes**

Processes		*Process (Intermediate) Outcomes*
• Leadership		• Organizational viability
• Social support	$\longrightarrow$	• Resource identification
• Incentive management		• Sense of community
• Opportunity role structure	$\longrightarrow$	• Underpopulated settings
• Subgroup linkages	$\longrightarrow$	• Co-empowered subgroups
• Group-based belief system	$\longrightarrow$	• Resolved ideological conflict
• Open communication and learning practices	$\longrightarrow$	• Culture of learning and development
• Practices to promote internal and external system alignment	$\longrightarrow$	• Systems thinking capacity and pursuit of systems change
• Analysis of power	$\longrightarrow$	• Strategic action and efforts to shift dominant narratives

Note: N. A. Peterson and Zimmerman (2004) did not explicitly link particular processes to particular outcomes, but some of the research literature that they summarized did. The horizontal lines in this table indicate likely relationships between processes and outcomes. Opportunity role structure, for example, is likely to lead to underpopulated settings. In other cases, several processes may lead to several outcomes, as in the organizational learning domains listed at the bottom of the table.

indicators of empowerment processes and outcomes within organizations. At the outset, I should emphasize that these process and outcome distinctions (as in the treatment of psychological empowerment in Chapter 4) really are referring to process, or intermediate, outcomes rather than to the ultimate intended outcomes and impacts of empowerment processes. These distinctions regarding processes and outcomes are explored in greater detail in Chapter 7.

Features of Settings

Leadership, social support, and *incentive management* are all processes that contribute to organizational *viability* and to success in *resource identification* (N. A. Peterson & Zimmerman, 2004). The concept of *viability* is perhaps the most easily understood of the outcomes of organizational empowerment. It refers simply to the fact that the organization is reliably active as opposed to dormant or inactive (Prestby, Wandersman, Florin, Rich, & Chavis, 1990) and has active participants (D. D. Perkins, Brown, & Taylor, 1996). Many nonprofit and voluntary organizations either cycle between dormancy and viability or become and remain dormant for long periods of time. This fact is highlighted by the difficulty in the United States in regulating and accounting for the activities of smaller nonprofit organizations and voluntary associations, which are often below the threshold for detailed financial reporting to the Internal Revenue Service (Anheier, 2014). Closely related, *resource identification*—a concept that draws on resource mobilization in social movement theory (J. D. McCarthy & Zald, 1977)—refers to an organization's ability to identify resources to support its core functions and achieve its goals.

Leadership and Social Support

Leadership and a system for the provision of *social support* are two social regularities that were identified in Maton and Salem's (1995) study of different types of empowering organizational settings. In this study of leadership in three empowering organizations, leaders in each were described as committed, inspirational, and talented. Yet, across all three different types of empowering organizations in their study, leadership was also found to be shared (rather than cohering in one or only several leaders) and to be open to the involvement of new leaders. Likewise, systems existed in all three organizations that provided members and participants with social support. The support systems were encompassing in the sense that a variety of types (e.g., information, help with daily tasks, emotional support) and sources (i.e., from many different peers and leaders in the organization) of support were available. Furthermore, these support systems were peer-based, meaning that members were giving and receiving social support to and from their peers in the organization. And, social support systems were found (in this study and in others, e.g., Christens & Lin, 2014) to contribute to a psychological sense of community within the organization.

Incentive Management

Incentive management (organizations' efforts to increase benefits to participants while decreasing the costs of participation; Bond & Keys, 1993; Prestby et al., 1990) is an internal organizational process that is held to contribute to organizational viability. Incentives include, for example, skill development and access to information, while costs include transportation, time, and arrangements for child care. Organizations that actively tilt the balance toward incentives and away from costs, it follows, are more likely to become and remain viable.

Opportunity Role Structure and Underpopulated Settings

A key feature of organizational empowerment processes has been termed *opportunity role structure*, first by Maton and Salem (1995).[7] Opportunity role structure refers to the breadth and diversity of roles that members or participants in an organization can play. Or, as N. A. Peterson and Zimmerman (2004) described it: "the amount, accessibility, and arrangement of formal positions or roles within an organization that provides opportunities for members to take control of group tasks and build their skills and competencies" (p. 135). In organizational settings characterized by narrow or limited opportunity role structures, a small and stable cohort of people will consistently play principal roles and assume responsibility for most organizational functions. In contrast, in an organizational setting with a broad or rich opportunity role structure, people will frequently have the opportunity to play new roles, take ownership of processes, and build new skills. The outcome of this sort of opportunity role structure is that the internal organizational environment is characterized by *underpopulated settings*. This means simply that organizational settings routinely have a smaller number of people than the available roles for people to play. In contrast, an overpopulated setting has a higher number of people than the available roles.

This view of settings draws directly on Barker's (1968) work on behavior settings. Barker and colleagues meticulously catalogued the features and patterns that occurred in various social settings, including organizational contexts, and saw these as keys to an ecological understanding of social and psychological phenomena. This work informed Seidman's (1988, 2012) conception of social regularities. Accordingly, the notions of opportunity role structure and underpopulated settings draw attention to the features of specific settings within organizations. They are ratios of setting-level features rather than simpler and more common aggregate indicators of organizational strength (e.g., the total number of employees or volunteers or the annual budget of the organization) (Shinn & Rapkin, 2000). Opportunity role structure and underpopulated settings are therefore observable indicators that efforts are being made to generate meaningful involvement of participants and to integrate this involvement deeply into the structure and culture of an organization.

Subgroup Linkages

Studies of organizational empowerment processes have acknowledged that while collaboration between members of organizations is valuable, it is also common for members to form subgroups. For example, in Bond and Keys's (1993) study of an organization advocating for rights for people with developmental disabilities, parents and community members formed distinct subgroups within the organization and developed their own respective group identities. The formation of these subgroups was seen by Bond and Keys to be a vital contributor to the strength of the organization. Each group was able to build solidarity among constituencies that they represented. They were then able to leverage the contributions of these constituencies toward to the larger goals of the organization. The processes that allow for this type of co-empowerment of different subgroups within the organization has been termed *subgroup linkages*, which refers not only to the people who play boundary spanning roles within the organization between different subgroups but also to the policies and practices within the organization that provide clarity on communication between subgroups, power relationships between subgroups, and representation of subgroups in key positions, such as the board of directors of the organization or other committee roles.

Co-empowered Subgroups

An outcome of the successful establishment of subgroups and effective boundary spanning between subgroups can be termed *co-empowered subgroups*, an indication that the subgroups within the organization are activating the resources of the groups that they represent and bringing the contributions of these subgroups to bear on the goals of the larger group. There are many barriers to the formation of co-empowered subgroups in organizational contexts. These include, for example, organizational actors working to prevent the formation of subgroups in order to foster a greater sense of organizational unity or members of subgroups in an organization whose mistrust of members of other subgroups causes them to take actions that are detrimental to the overall capacity of the organization.

Group-Based Belief System

The final internal aspects of organizational empowerment catalogued by N. A. Peterson and Zimmerman (2004) are a *group-based belief system* (process) and *resolved ideological conflict* (outcome). A belief system in an organization involves its ideology, values, and culture. It allows members and participants to work within a system of goals and norms in their attempts to achieve goals. Certainly, not all belief systems are equally conducive to organizational empowerment. Maton and Salem (1995) identified three specific features of group-based belief systems that characterize empowering processes within organizational settings. First, these belief systems inspired growth by motivating and challenging members and participants to set and achieve goals. Second, the belief systems emphasized the strengths and capabilities of members and participants to achieve goals themselves. Finally, the belief systems encouraged members and participants to think of themselves in terms of a larger, group-based mission.

Organizational settings that have successfully established a group-based belief system can be said to have *resolved ideological conflict*, which indicates successful navigation of some of the key tensions between competing visions for organizational functioning and decision-making processes. This notion was drawn by Zimmerman (2000) from Riger's (1994) work on development and formalization of feminist organizations. Thus, the term should not be mistaken for a squelching of different ideological viewpoints about, for instance, social issues or policy debates. Instead, it indicates general agreement on a particular structure of leadership (e.g., hierarchical or decentralized) and decision-making that can accommodate or mediate between different viewpoints.

This last distinction, however, points toward some of the weaknesses of the existing literature on internal aspects of organizational empowerment. As it stands, there is little that can identify and distinguish the types of organizations that Domhoff (2009) described as challengers of the power elite from those that may be more neutral or even act as defenders of elite interests. As I argued previously in this chapter, trends in civil society make such distinctions essential for a theory of organizational empowerment. There is therefore potential utility in augmenting existing frameworks with concepts of organizational learning and change from organization studies.

Organizational Learning Capacity

As with people, organizations must be able to learn and adapt in order to thrive. The field of organization studies has paid particular attention to this topic, particularly at points of intersection with community psychology.[8] The incorporation of the concepts of organizational learning, learning organizations, and organizational change has been one achievement in this interdisciplinary space. Organizational learning involves the processes by which an organization encourages learning and systems thinking by participants and also extends to the organizational system's ability to "learn" at a systems level (Argyris, 1993). It is unfortunately common for organizational systems to fail to incorporate learning at a collective level and therefore fail to adapt to changes in their broader environments (Crutchfield & Grant, 2012). An organization whose capacities and practices make it adept at this kind of collaborative learning can be termed a *learning organization* (Senge, 1990).

Research on these concepts is shedding light on organizational learning capacity and its relationship to achievement of transformational changes within and beyond organizations. In a comparative case study of three different types of nonprofit organizations, D. D. Perkins et al. (2007) identified organizational learning capacities, such as systems thinking and critical analysis of power, as key drivers of capacity to achieve change. Likewise, in a study of a youth organizing initiative, Dolan, Christens, and Lin (2015) detailed the initiative's use of various forms of participatory research to inform and deepen their collective analysis of social problems and take strategic action in the community. This ability to learn and critically analyze issues is key to differentiating organizations and organizational settings that are building community power and empowerment from those that are not. This is a missing ingredient from previous conceptions of organizational empowerment—one that creates some needed links with the theory of community power outlined in Chapter 2.

Building on work from organization studies (Marsick & Watkins, 2003), recent research has adapted a survey measure for studying dimensions of learning specifically for nonprofit organizations. This Organizational Learning Capacity Scale (OLCS) (Bess, Perkins, & McCown (2011)) is provided in Appendix 5.2. Some subscales, such as open communication practices and practices to promote internal and external alignment, are broadly relevant to organizational empowerment, whereas others, such as practices of supporting staff development and practices of staff empowerment, still likely require some adaptations for use in voluntary or grassroots organizational contexts because they focus only on staff to the exclusion of members or volunteers.

Current and Future Directions

How can we observe, detect, and distinguish between key features of empowerment in organizations and the participatory settings that comprise them? Maton (1988) developed a survey instrument to assess several of the internal aspects of organizational empowerment. Drawing on Maton's scale as well as others (e.g., Quinn & Spreitzer, 1991), N. A. Peterson and Speer (2000) developed survey measures for opportunity role structure, leadership, social support, and group-based belief system (Appendix 5.3). Using this measure alongside indicators of sense of community and psychological empowerment in different organizational contexts has given the field a sense of some of the noteworthy cross-level dynamics between psychological and organizational empowerment processes and outcomes.

One key finding, for example, from N. A. Peterson and Speer's (2000) study of three different types of voluntary associations, concerns the distinction between *ecological commonality* and *ecological specificity* in empowerment processes. Although some relationships between organizational and psychological empowerment were similar across different types of organizations, indicating ecological commonalities, the majority of the relationships that were observed were distinct within the different organizational types. This finding emphasizes the importance of ecological specificity in studies of the organizational contexts of empowerment.

Some of the most meaningful work therefore lies not in seeking universal truths about organizational contexts of empowerment, but in understanding differences that occur in specific contexts. N. A. Peterson and Hughey (2002), for instance, built on the study mentioned by surveying participants in grassroots organizing groups, finding that the organizational characteristics associated with empowering organizations were more important for promoting psychological empowerment among participants with lower socioeconomic status. Research continues to use surveys to examine the mediating relationships between organizational characteristics, sense of community, and psychological empowerment in different organizational contexts and for different subgroups within those contexts (e.g., Speer, Peterson, Armstead, & Allen, 2013; Wilke & Speer, 2011). Moreover, a scale for sense of community in community organizations (Hughey, Speer, & Peterson, 1999) allows measurement of this key outcome in an organizational rather than a neighborhood context (Appendix 5.1).

Survey measures, however, are only one tool—and perhaps not the most effective one—for studying organizational empowerment. Despite the influence of ecological theory (i.e., Barker, 1968) on the study of organizational empowerment and the prominence of setting-level features, most attempts to assess these processes and outcomes so far have used surveys of individual participants in these settings and then aggregated these perceptions up to the organizational or setting level.[9] This method of measurement is an indirect way to assess setting-level phenomena, and it risks introducing a range of subjective and individual-level sources of noise into the assessment. In research on related topics, systematic ways of directly assessing settings are being explored. For instance, scholars have developed a youth program quality assessment tool that allows raters to directly observe youth programs and consistently score various components of program quality (see Akiva, 2005). In similar fashion, sociologists and environmental psychologists have developed ecological observational tools for urban environments and behavior (D. D. Perkins & Taylor, 1996; Sampson, 2012). Developing a set of observation-based indicators for setting-level features of organizational empowerment holds enormous promise to advance our current knowledge of these phenomena.

Finally, the existing conceptions of organizational empowerment do not sufficiently attend to the substantive focus of organizational activities or the ways that organizational efforts seek to challenge or reinforce the status quo. Including the concept of organizational learning capacity and associated empirical assessments in future studies promises to fill a gap in the literature on organizational empowerment. Yet, the work on the topic to date has focused only on the learning capacities of open communication practices and internal and external system alignment. It has not directly assessed the more transformational aspects of organizational practice, such as a critical analysis of power dynamics and the ability to influence ideology among participants and the broader public (Gaventa, 1980; Lukes, 1974).

These features of organizational settings are imperative for more fully integrating the concept of organizational empowerment with a theory of community power. Including them also may help to resist some of the forms of conceptual drift that have plagued empowerment, as discussed in Chapter 3. In a descriptive study of a state-level community-organizing initiative, my colleagues and I identified social regularities that allowed the group to build and exercise community power. These included shared social analysis of power (Christens, Inzeo, & Faust, 2014). The addition of a critical analysis of power and associated outcomes such as strategic actions for systems change and shaping the public's interpretation of issues should be included in future studies of organizational empowerment. Table 5.1 proposes such an integration.

As we continue the search for ways to better understand empowerment *within* organizational contexts, I believe that incorporating organizational learning—*particularly critical analysis of power*—is the chief shift that must occur for the concept to more be more clearly linked with community power. If we neglect these learning processes and outcomes, we risk blurring the lines between empowerment processes and other types of activity in civil society, as discussed in the first part of this chapter. Finally, as Kaiser and Rusch (2015) found in their study of community organizing in Detroit, there are likely trade-offs between some of these aspects of empowerment in organizational settings such that an increased emphasis on one or several may make it more difficult to foster and sustain some others. Future studies could continue this line of investigation within various types of organizations. In some cases, building strength in one or more of these internal organizational processes may come at the expense of others.

Interorganizational Aspects of Empowerment

Just as people rarely make systemic changes by themselves, single organizations rarely act independently to change systems. Furthermore, many settings where empowerment occurs are not the sole purview of a particular organization, but contain representatives from a variety of organizations. The interorganizational aspects of empowerment involve the relationships and interactions between organizations that are needed for power to be built and exercised effectively. N. A. Peterson and Zimmerman (2004) emphasized links between organizations that are needed for organizations to share information, garner legitimacy, procure resources, and achieve goals. Reviewing previous research in community psychology, public health, social work, and other disciplines, they identified *collaborations* (e.g., Bartle, Couchonnal, Canda, & Staker, 2002), *creation of organizational alliances* and *participation in alliance-building activities* (Foster-Fishman, Salem, Allen, & Fahrbach, 2001; Itzhaky & York, 2002), and *accessing the social networks of other organizations* (Gulati & Gargiulo, 1999; Snow, Zurcher, &

Ekland-Olson, 1980) as defining processes and outcomes for organizational empowerment.

Focused attempts by organizations to build alliances and community-wide collaborations are particularly featured in N. A. Peterson and Zimmerman's (2004) framework. This conclusion that collaboration between organizations is key to organizational empowerment should not be surprising given the government shrinkage and outsourcing of services discussed previously in this chapter. These trends in civil society not only have led to growth in the overall number of non-profit organizations but also have heightened the specialization and differentiations between organizations and have helped to create and maintain diffuse and competitive networks between local organizations. Informal collaborations between organizations and more formalized interorganizational initiatives are intended as responses to the fragmentation of organizational ecologies. But, how can we distinguish between collaborations that are conducive to building community power and empowerment and those that are more conducive to other processes and outcomes (e.g., service coordination)?

In the years since N. A. Peterson and Zimmerman's (2004) synthesis, the number of initiatives specifically seeking to encourage interorganizational collaborations as a response to the lack of coordination around persistent social issues has continued to increase. Some of this uptick in enthusiasm for interorganizational collaboration has come from the influence of widely known initiatives like the *Harlem Children's Zone*, an effort that has claimed improvements in educational outcomes among low-income students at least in part by bringing churches, universities, schools, and local other nonprofit organizations together to take a more comprehensive approach to youth development and academic achievement (Tough, 2008). The *Harlem Children's Zone* has influenced the approaches taken by the US Department of Education, which has funded similar local collaborations around the country through the *Promise Neighborhoods Initiative*. Other government agencies, international NGOs such as the World Health Organization, and major foundations such as Annie E. Casey and Robert Wood Johnson similarly have programs specifically designed to encourage community-level collaborations and alliances to tackle specific issues from education to transportation to food and healthcare systems.

Alongside the increasing number of coalition-based change efforts, researchers have examined the specific characteristics and dynamics of coalitions that facilitate power and empowerment. For instance, Zakocs and Edwards (2006) reviewed 26 previous studies of coalition functioning, finding that group cohesion, membership diversity, and formalization of rules and procedures were each found to be associated with coalition effectiveness in five or more of those studies. Longitudinal studies of multiple coalitions continue to add depth and specificity to the evidence on coalition functioning and effectiveness (e.g., Shapiro, Oesterle, Abbott, Arthur, & Hawkins, 2013). Some studies have also provided insights into the effects of coalition participation on organizational development (e.g., Nowell & Foster-Fishman,

2011). Most findings on the characteristics of effective coalitions have served to underscore principles that have emerged from practice-based evidence (e.g., Wolff, 2001).

Findings from this multidisciplinary literature on coalition effectiveness largely dovetail with the features of interorganizational empowerment identified by N. A. Peterson and Zimmerman (2004). In order to update the conceptual framework for organizational empowerment, however, there are several additional current and recent trends in practice and research that are particularly relevant to interorganizational aspects of empowerment.

One trend has been the influence of the *collective impact* model on coalition practice. The model is appealing in terms of its simplicity but contrasts in some ways with empowerment theory. Second, the development and use of *community coalition action theory* (CCAT) by public health researchers has provided both conceptual clarity and insights from empirical research. This framework can augment the literature on organizational empowerment from community psychology, enhancing its specificity. Third, the increasing use of network analytic methods in the study of interorganizational relations is bringing valuable perspectives and findings to the fore. In some cases, these go beyond confirming the more intuitive aspects of interorganizational relations. In the remainder of this section, I examine each of these three topics in turn.

Collective Impact

Momentum for community-level collaborative problem-solving has continued to grow as practitioners and decision-makers have sought to achieve *collective impact,* a term defined as "the commitment of a group of important actors from different sectors to a common agenda for solving a specific social problem" (Kania & Kramer, 2011, p. 36). Initiatives like *Shape Up Somerville* (a community-based obesity prevention initiative in Somerville, MA; see Economos et al., 2007) and *Strive Together* (a community-wide effort to promote positive educational success; see Bornstein, 2011) have been identified as exemplary initiatives for bringing leaders together for sustained and targeted community-level changes. In an article defining collective impact with reference to these two initiatives, Kania and Kramer (2011) pointed out that successful collaborative efforts tend to share features, such as continuous communication between stakeholders, commitment to a shared agenda, and agreement on shared measures that allow the group to gauge their progress over time. One especially noteworthy contribution of the burgeoning literature on collective impact has been the case for "backbone" organizations with dedicated staff to convene, support, guide, and sustain the efforts of participating organizational leaders in collaborative activities (HanleyBrown, Kania, & Kramer, 2012).

Collective impact quickly became a prominent model for thinking about and pursuing intentional interorganizational collaborations for change at the community level (Flood, Minkler, Lavery, Estrada, & Falbe, 2015; Walzer, Weaver, & McGuire, 2016). Yet, it has weaknesses. One pronounced weakness of the collective impact approach is that it seeks primarily to engage established leaders of organizations. In this regard, collective impact and many related interorganizational strategies can be thought of as *grasstops* approaches. This stands in contrast to more truly grassroots approaches to change, such as community organizing, which seeks to engage the people most directly affected by a problem (Christens & Inzeo, 2015). Conversely, collective impact has been called "trickle-down community engagement," and this aspect of the model helps to explain why many communities, particularly communities of color, have become frustrated with it (Le, 2015). In general, strategies that seek primarily to mobilize organizational leaders instead of a broader group of local residents are less likely to pursue more transformative changes because their elite membership is more likely to have vested interests in the status quo.

Another limitation is that compared with other models for organizational collaboration (e.g., *partnership synergy*; Lasker, Weiss, & Miller, 2001), the collective impact model places less emphasis on the ability of coalition partners to think about social problems in holistic ways. In particular, many collective impact initiatives may not have the capacity to analyze community power or be prepared for conflict (Christens & Inzeo, 2015). Many of these weaknesses are underscored by Wolff (2016), who has also led efforts to move beyond collective impact toward collaborations for equity and justice that are more likely to bring about empowerment and change community power structures (Wolff et al., 2016). Nevertheless, the influence of the collective impact model and the highly touted successes of related interorganizational efforts are leading more decision-makers to pursue community collaboration and coalitions as antidotes to social problems. Critiques and refinements may be able to address some of the model's weaknesses (Weaver, 2014); on the other hand, it may be difficult or impossible to reorient or reengineer some efforts that began as more elite-driven collective impact initiatives (Wolff et al., 2016). Collective impact lacks the conceptual grounding in social movements and social change efforts that empowerment has. Nevertheless, understanding the collective impact model, the efforts that are seeking to implement it, and critiques of the model and proposed alternatives is necessary for a full picture of interorganizational aspects of empowerment.

Community Coalition Action Theory

Prior to these discussions of collective impact as such, public health researchers developed a *community coalition action theory* (CCAT; Butterfoss & Kegler, 2002; Butterfoss, Kegler, & Francisco, 2008), and have gone on to use it as a framework for systematic inquiry comparing the efforts of various coalitions. Drawing on Kurt Lewin's (1951) stage model for organizational change, CCAT identifies three developmental stages of coalition functioning. First, it outlines processes and structures such as leadership and staffing in a lead organization, communication, and cohesion, which are especially meaningful indicators during the *formation stage* of a community coalition. As a coalition matures, indicators of collaborative synergy include member engagement in different roles within the coalition, pooling of resources among organizations, and assessment and planning. This is described as the *maintenance stage* of the coalition. During the third stage, the *institutionalization stage* of the coalition, strategies are implemented, community-level outcomes are altered, and community capacity is built. Processes at each stage are hypothesized as predictors of proximal outcomes in the next stage. Further, reflecting an ecological orientation, the model identifies five domains of the local community context that are likely to influence coalition formation and effectiveness: history of collaboration, community politics and history, community norms and values, community demographics and economic conditions, and geography.

The comprehensiveness and conceptual clarity of the CCAT model has allowed public health researchers in recent years to examine coalition dynamics and outcomes in more systematic ways. For example, Kegler, Rigler, and Honeycutt (2010) studied the influences of some of the contextual factors outlined in CCAT on coalition functioning during the formation stage, finding that local history of collaboration influenced the broadest range of coalition factors: "Unless a concerted effort is made to form new relationships or establish new ways of working together, future collaborative efforts will likely exhibit many characteristics of past efforts" (p. 9). Kegler and Swan (2011) tracked changes in coalition functioning among 20 coalitions over 2 years as they moved from the formation to the maintenance stage, finding preliminary support for many of the processes hypothesized in CCAT. In a successive study using data from a third year, Kegler and Swan (2012) assessed key process indicators' influences on community capacity outcomes as mediated by member engagement across 19 coalitions. Findings were again largely supportive of the conceptual relationships predicted by CCAT.

In sum, the conceptual model advanced in CCAT and the findings from studies that have used it are largely consistent with the conclusions of N. A. Peterson and Zimmerman's (2004) synthesis on interorganizational empowerment as well as earlier theories of interorganizational relations. For example, both CCAT and N. A. Peterson and Zimmerman emphasized collaboration, cohesion, alliance building, and procurement or pooling of resources. Even though it is not radically altering what was previously known about interorganizational dynamics and empowerment, the CCAT provides specificity on coalition processes, stages of development, and functioning in different contexts, as well as some tools for assessing these dynamics. For this reason, the CCAT (elements depicted in Figure 5.1) can be valuable for advancing conceptualization and informing future studies on interorganizational empowerment. The developmental processes outlined in CCAT and the model's attention to the relationships between coalition processes and specific aspects of community context are particularly relevant for comparing

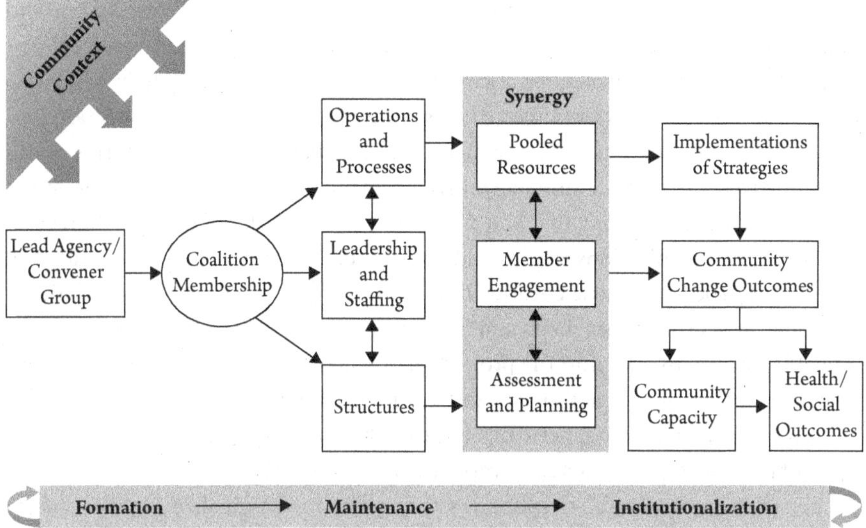

Figure 5.1. Community coalition action theory. *Source:* Butterfoss, Kegler, and Francisco (2008).

different coalitions' functioning and for action research and evaluation in partnership with coalition efforts.

Network Analytic Approaches

One of the most promising avenues for conceptualizing and studying the relationships between organizations that build community power and empowerment is network analysis. Network analytic approaches to understanding organizational linkages allow us to focus on the structural properties and patterns of relationships between people and organizations (J. W. Neal & Christens, 2014; Z. P. Neal, 2014). Studies of interorganizational networks have produced insights into the cohesive and collaborative relationships between organizations that play consequential roles in coalition functioning. They have collectively begun to build our understanding of the specific types and arrangements of relationships that are most advantageous for particular desired outcomes of coalition activities.

Considering relational ties between organizations from a network perspective, it is first critical to distinguish among the many possible varieties of relationships between organizations. Feinberg, Riggs, and Greenberg (2005), for example, compared the social/friendship ties, work-related ties, and social organization ties between participating stakeholders in 23 coalitions. They concluded that work-related ties were the most useful for assessing the relational structure of coalition networks.[10] Nowell (2009) used several different indicators of relationship strength, including communication frequency, trust, and perceptions of shared philosophy with other stakeholders in 48 interorganizational collaboratives. Provan, Nakama, Veazie, Teufel-Shone, and Huddleston (2003) examined the presence of ties among participants in a local network of health and human service organizations in Arizona according to information, referrals, and exchange of resources. They multiplied these forms of connection into an index of collaboration to reflect greater strength of ties when multiple forms of collaboration were taking place simultaneously. Further, Provan and colleagues measured trust between organizations that had ties and their expectations that collaborations with particular organizations would yield specific benefits or drawbacks (as defined by Lasker et al., 2001). Because collaborative relationships can include many relational properties, it is critical that the overarching concept of collaboration be unpacked[11] to enable deeper insights into the properties of collaborative relationships and their effects on participating organizations and whole coalitions.

Studies of organizational networks indicate that although cohesion is vital, some forms of relationships may actually impede coalition functioning. For example, close ties between some central stakeholders may serve to marginalize others. Closely linked stakeholders may have politicized histories or even interpersonal animosity as a result of previous collaborations. In a study of 23 coalitions, for example, Feinberg et al. (2005) found that the average closeness in the interorganizational networks was positively related to coalition readiness (assessed though self-report surveys and external staff ratings of coalition dynamics), and the average level of betweenness (i.e., brokering of indirect relationships) was negatively related to readiness. Moreover, this study found that the variance in closeness and betweenness among individual actors within these interorganizational networks was associated with readiness in similar ways to the mean scores. These findings emphasize that centralization of network ties around relatively few core stakeholders is not likely to lead to effective coalition functioning. The authors surmised that "coalitions seem to benefit from relatively homogenous, non-centralized networks in which closeness to others and brokering is not limited to a few key players" (p. 294). This finding runs counter to some recommendations for practice, including collective impact, which encourages coalitions to form a central backbone entity to guide coalition efforts.

Different properties of relational networks among organizations may be more or less advantageous for attempts to achieve different kinds of outcomes. In her 2009 study mentioned previously, for example, Nowell further examined the relative importance of stakeholder relationships on different outcomes, finding that close stakeholder relationships were more crucial for building capacity for systems change efforts than they were for coordination of services and information across organizations. Thus, depending on the outcomes that a coalition (or a researcher) is targeting, different network structures and properties may be optimal, and closer relationships between organizations are likely to be necessary for empowerment processes (which involve systems change efforts) than for other sorts of outcomes.

Regardless of the form that it takes (more centralized or more distributed), leadership in interorganizational efforts is often a delicate balance. On one hand, there is a clear need for specific individuals to enact and guide collaborative processes; on the other hand, for the coalition to flourish, leaders must avoid becoming central brokers of the relationships between the other organizations involved (Nowell & Harrison, 2011). It appears that inclusive leadership is a more determinative factor in attracting new participants to coalition activities than is a well-coordinated group process (Wells, Ward, Feinberg, & Alexander, 2008). For this reason, empowerment-oriented coalition work should err on the side of inclusive leadership structures.

Longitudinal studies of organizational collaboration networks have also been conducted (e.g., Galaskiewicz, Bielefeld, & Dowell, 2006). These have typically focused only on single networks.[12] Taken together, however, they begin to shed light on how organizational networks tend to change over time in different contexts. For instance, Provan and colleagues' (2003) study (of health and human service organizations in Arizona, described previously) found that although the number of relationships grew in the network over the course of a year, trust among members of the network declined (Provan, et al., 2003). On the whole, however, participants remained very positive about participation in the coalition, suggesting that declines in trust may have been temporary results of newly established collaborations. Much work remains to document and analyze patterns and fluctuations of organizational characteristics, perceptions, relationships, actions, and outcomes as coalitions and organizational networks form and evolve.

Of course, studying only relationships between local organizations may be missing some of the most significant relationships. This is particularly true in the contemporary era of global capitalism. Some studies have sought to capture the links between organizations at different scales. For example, in a longitudinal study of a single organizational network, Kegler, Rigler, and Ravani (2010) found that density of information exchange and joint planning relationships increased over a 9-year period in an environmental health coalition (made up of 21 organizations and a subset of eight tribes surrounding a Superfund site in Oklahoma), concluding that this change was likely associated with greater capacity to address community and environmental issues. Importantly, this study included not only local organizations but also the state and federal agencies with responsibilities relevant to the Superfund site. As might be expected, the evolution of the relationships between local organizations and these extralocal entities yielded key insights into the overall network's structure and functioning.

This raises a critical question regarding the study of interorganizational networks and community power and empowerment: How is it best to bound a relevant network of organizations? Bounding in this context refers to specifically designating those organizations that are part of a network, and should therefore be observed or surveyed, and those that are not. Studies of interorganizational dynamics in local communities have typically focused on the organizations that are participating in coalition activities, even to the detriment of other organizations in those same communities that are not part of the coalition or collaborative initiative. This approach is likely missing many of the most consequential interorganizational dynamics taking place in communities and therefore providing misleading conclusions. Studies by Bess and colleagues (Bess, 2015; Bess, Speer, & Perkins, 2012) on a youth violence prevention coalition in Nashville, Tennessee, are particularly instructive on this issue. These studies assessed relationships among 99 organizations in the city, 30 of which were formal participants in the coalition. Findings indicated that although collaborative activities increased slightly among organizations involved in the formal coalition, collaborative capacity was somewhat reduced in the larger interorganizational system during the 5-year period.

Had Bess only studied the 30 organizations participating in the formal coalition, the conclusion would likely have been that collaborative capacity in the city was increased through the coalition's activities. Taking the larger system of 99 organizations into account, however, she concluded that the coalition initiative only *redistributed* interorganizational collaborative relationships, to the slight detriment of the overall collaborative capacity of organizations in the city. This study clearly has significant implications for the future study of the interorganizational component of organizational empowerment. It demonstrates both the challenges and the immense promise of employing network analytic methods to the study of organizational power and empowerment. Future studies must grapple with these concepts and challenges and their relationships to community empowerment—the topic of the next chapter.

Conclusions

Organizations are truly the lynchpins of empowerment. Certain types of organizational settings enable people to participate and build skills, knowledge, and relationships. Some organizations and interorganizational collaboratives are the vehicles of effective community action and change. Yet, despite the rapid growth in the number of nonprofit and voluntary organizations ostensibly working to serve the public interest, there remain relatively few organizations that can effectively build community power while sustaining settings that facilitate participants' empowerment. Many nonprofits exist to serve elite interests. With the goal of developing a framework for identifying the characteristics of organizations and their relational networks that can build community power, this chapter has synthesized, updated, and extended organizational empowerment theory.

The framework for organizational empowerment, summarized most recently by N. A. Peterson and Zimmerman (2004), can be advanced through including organizational learning as a characteristic of empowering organizations. This capacity complements the notions of group-based belief systems in organizational settings. It is especially crucial as it relates to the critical analysis of power in social issues. Attention to critical organizational learning capacity creates a clear point of intersection between internal aspects of organizational empowerment and the cognitive component of psychological empowerment. It provides stronger links between organizational empowerment and community power, particularly to Lukes's notion of the third dimension of power. This is therefore one modification that can enhance both the transactional–ecological view of empowerment and the concept's connections to a coherent theory of power.

There is much that can be added, moreover, to existing conceptions of interorganizational relations and empowerment, as well as emerging unanswered questions. More widespread use of CCAT and network analytic approaches are two of the most promising directions for research designs and methods in this area of study. Many of the attributes of interorganizational networks that are indicative of empowerment are similar to attributes of empowering/empowered organizations themselves. Leadership, social support, and opportunity role structure, for example, may have analogues at the interorganizational level. Yet, research is still only in the early stages of developing a clear understanding of these dynamics. It is therefore likely that the conceptual framework presented in this chapter will likewise need updating and reworking as research on organizational power and empowerment continues to advance.

Appendix 5.1 Sense of Community in Community Organizations Scale

Stem: *Please rate your agreement or disagreement with the following statements:*

Item	Item Wording
COSOC-R1	People have a real say about what goes on in (organization name).
COSOC-R2	People in (organization name) respond to what I think is important.
COSOC-R3	Being in (organization name) allows me to be around important people.
COSOC-R4	(Organization name) helps me to be a part of other groups in this city.
COSOC-R5	(Organization name) is respected in this city.
COSOC-R6	(Organization name) gets a lot done in this community.
COSOC-R7	I like living in this town; (city name) is the place for me.
COSOC-R8	(City name) is a good place for me to live.

Note: Items 1 and 2 are indicators of the relationship to organization dimension; Items 3 and 4 are indicators of the organization as mediator dimension; Items 5 and 6 are indicators of the influence of the organization dimension; and Items 7 and 8 are indicators of the bond to the community dimension.

Source: N. A. Peterson et al. (2008).

Appendix 5.2 Organizational Learning Capacity Scale (OLCS) (Contains Subscales for Dimensions of Learning Organizations)

Stem: *Thinking about your organization, please state the extent to which you disagree or agree with the following statements:*

Item	Item Wording
OLCS-1	My organization encourages people to think from a community perspective.
OLCS-2	My organization works together with the outside community to meet mutual needs.
OLCS-3	In my organization, leaders ensure that the organization's actions are consistent with its values.
OLCS-4	My organization builds alignment of visions across different levels and work groups.
OLCS-5	My organization considers the impact of decisions on employee morale.
OLCS-6	My organization encourages people to get answers from across the organization when solving problems.
OLCS-7	In my organization, people openly discuss mistakes in order to learn from them.
OLCS-8	In my organization, people give open and honest feedback to each other.
OLCS-9	In my organization, people view problems in their work as an opportunity to learn.
OLCS-10	In my organization, people are rewarded for exploring new ways of working.
OLCS-11	My organization enables people to get needed information at any time quickly and easily.
OLCS-12	My organization recognizes people for taking initiative.
OLCS-13	My organization gives people control over the resources they need to accomplish their work.
OLCS-14	In my organization, leaders generally support requests for learning opportunities and training.
OLCS-15	In my organization, investment in workers' skills and professional development is greater than last year.
OLCS-16	In my organization, the number of individuals learning new skills is greater than last year.

Note: Items 1 through.

Sources: Bess, Perkins, and McCown (2011); Marsick and Watkins (2003).

Appendix 5.3   Organizational Characteristics Survey (OCS) (Contains Subscales for Multiple Internal Aspects of Organizational Empowerment)

Stem: *Thinking about your organization, please state the extent to which you disagree or agree with the following statements:*

Item	Item Wording
OCS-1	Different members of the organization are in charge of different aspects of its functioning.
OCS-2	The members of the organization have responsibility for running many aspects of the organization.
OCS-3	The organization draws upon the talents and abilities of a number of different people to get organizational tasks done.
OCS-4	If a member desires, he/she can take on responsibility for some organization task.
OCS-5	Positions of responsibility are spread among members of the organization.
OCS-6	The leaders are very committed and dedicated to the organization.
OCS-7	The leaders relate and respond well to organization members.
OCS-8	The leaders have strong organizational skills and know-how.
OCS-9	The leadership is very talented as far as organization operations are concerned.
OCS-10	The leaders' own problems and personality get in the way of effective leadership.*
OCS-11	I receive as much support and help as I presently desire from the organization.
OCS-12	I provide as much support and help to the organization as I presently desire.
OCS-13	I provide as much support as I receive at organizational meetings.
OCS-14	I have developed a close friendship with another organization member.
OCS-15	If I stopped coming to the organization, I would continue my friendships developed with organization members.

Item	Item Wording
OCS-16	The organization encourages participation and open discussion.
OCS-17	There is a focus on flexibility and decentralization within this organization.
OCS-18	The leaders in the organization assess member concerns and ideas.
OCS-19	The organization uses creative problem solving processes.
OCS-20	There is a focus on human relations, teamwork, and cohesion within the organization.

Note: Items 1 through 5 are indicators for opportunity role structure; Items 6 through 10 are indicators for leadership; Items 11 through 15 are indicators for social support; and Items 16 through 20 are indicators for group-based belief system.

* Indicates reverse-coded item. Reliability of this scale may improve in future implementation from revising to avoid reverse coding (see N. A. Peterson et al., 2006).

Sources: Maton, 1988; N. A. Peterson and Speer, 2000.

Notes

1. Some observers dispute the notion that labor unions were as powerful in the post–World War II decades leading up to the 1970s as they are now made out to be. Domhoff (2013) and others argued that corporations held just as much power during the postwar years, but that their leadership was more moderate than the corporate leadership that began taking over in the 1970s.
2. Because US corporations increasingly operate at multinational or global scales, their increased organization has exerted influence on national policy environments around the world in similar directions to those described in the United States, as well in more exploitative ways in countries with fewer environmental or labor protections.
3. In order to receive the tax deduction, donors must itemize their income tax deductions, which fewer than half of US households do because their total eligible deductions (which include mortgage interest) do not exceed the standard deduction (Hall, 2013).
4. Philanthropic enterprises tend not to be concerned, for instance, with increases in inequality per se. Despite their focus on social issues, they have been unlikely to identify worsening inequality as a root cause and target for action. This may be changing, however. Prominent foundations have recently shifted their priorities explicitly toward reducing inequality. Examples include the California Endowment, the Ford Foundation, the W. K. Kellogg Foundation, and the William T. Grant Foundation.
5. Invoking Eisenhower's notion of the military–industrial complex, a group of authors has produced an analysis of the *nonprofit–industrial complex* (INCITE! Women of Color Against Violence, 2009). In this view, major funders use the nonprofit model to constrain the scope of what organizational efforts might seek to transform. When community organizations or social movements coalesce, they are urged to incorporate as nonprofit organizations and participate in a funding terrain that is dominated by foundations.
6. The extraorganizational component of organizational empowerment has been the least clearly described in previous treatments. For example, in contrast to the detailed

concepts that exist for characterizing internal features of empowering organizations, only two extraorganizational empowering processes were described by N. A. Peterson and Zimmerman (2004): community action and dissemination of information. Instead of treating it as a distinct component in this chapter, I therefore stick to simpler categories of internal and external aspects of organizational empowerment. Organizations' ability to take action and influence community narratives, for instance, are fundamental to the notion of empowerment but may not require a distinct extraorganizational component when considering organizational development in empowerment processes. I believe this approach also eliminates some potential for confusion when theorizing community empowerment, which is the topic of Chapter 6.

7. Recall that this feature of organizational empowerment was discussed in Chapter 1 in relation to the Wisconsin Uprising.

8. Greater cross-fertilization between organization studies and community psychology has been cultivated through, for instance, special issues of the *Journal of Community Psychology* (N. M. Boyd, 2015; N. M. Boyd & Angelique, 2007) and the *Journal of Prevention & Intervention in the Community* (N. M. Boyd, 2011) on organization studies in community psychology.

9. Confusion exists about these organizational and setting "levels" of analysis. Social network analyses may help both to define settings and illuminate setting-level dynamics (see, for example, J. W. Neal, 2014).

10. This finding is echoed by Wells, Ford, McClure, Holt, and Ward (2007), who identified work relationships as more salient than personal friendships in their multimethod study of two coalitions.

11. Guo and Acar (2005) took a promising step in this direction with their taxonomy of forms of organizational collaboration.

12. The resource intensity of conducting interorganizational network analyses over time makes multisite longitudinal comparisons difficult. Some studies have been conducted, albeit with outcomes less relevant to community power and empowerment (e.g., Valente, Chou, & Pentz, 2007).

6

Community Development

Introduction

The single most glaring inconsistency in contemporary empowerment theory is this: On the one hand, empowerment has been specified according to a multilevel, ecological framework that emphasizes inextricable processes and outcomes at the psychological, organizational, and community levels of analysis. On the other hand, the bulk of the research on empowerment has been on psychological dynamics, with far less attention to group-level processes, particularly at the scale of entire communities. The relative neglect of community empowerment in theory and research colludes with increasingly popular notions of empowerment as an individual process to render work on community empowerment nearly invisible. To the extent that empowerment connotes a feeling rather than a real change in power relationships, this notion is reinforced by the disproportionate attention paid to individuals and psychological processes. The symbolic ideology of empowerment is thereby distorted, and the potential for the concept to act as an orienting framework for action toward social justice is damaged or even lost.

Perhaps this lopsidedness should not be surprising. Looking prospectively at the study of empowerment, Rappaport (1987) pointed to the danger of conceptual imbalance in the study of empowerment: "As a practical matter not all research can be at every level of analysis, but the subject matter, and therefore the theory, and the research community as a collectivity, must address all levels. For psychologists, the largest danger is that we will limit ourselves to the study of individuals" (p. 139). As predicted, the relative overemphasis on psychological empowerment as well as individualistic misuses of the term have contributed to the broad sense that the concept is diluted and poorly defined, as pointed out, for instance, in critical appraisals by Cattaneo et al. (2014) and Woodall et al. (2012). There is a clear need for more emphasis on community empowerment in scholarship and in practice to achieve the balance on which the concept's symbolic ideology depends.

Although there has been some theoretical and empirical work on empowerment as it relates to community development, the concepts and methods are not nearly as far along as their counterparts for human development or even for organizational development. To address this gap, I work toward a new framework for community empowerment in this chapter. This involves a reconstitution of the social and political theory of community power that was scrutinized in Chapter 2. Instead of addressing the ways that community power structures preserve unequal power relationships of domination and oppression, here I ask the reverse: How do community groups develop and exercise social power to foster the conditions for greater pluralism and flourishing? Before outlining the framework, several things should be considered first. For instance, what—for present purposes—is a community? How has community empowerment been studied up to this point? And, which theoretically related concepts are most important to consider in developing a framework for community empowerment?

The Concept of Community

An enduring challenge in discussing empowerment (and other constructs) related to communities is the question: What constitutes a community? To put it mildly, it is a term that has a variety of connotations. A useful broad-brush distinction was made by Newbrough (1973), who demarcated two common social scientific notions of community. The first, more prevalent in sociology and social psychology, is that a community refers to a population of people who share things in common. This often has included living in the same geographic area, but may also encompass shared interests, habits, or characteristics. As societies have become more interconnected across space, this more sociological understanding of community has often stretched beyond geographic commonalities. People who share characteristics, interests, or ideology—but not proximity—are commonly referred to as a community (e.g., the business community, communities of practice, the African American community, or online communities formed through social media). The second concept of community that Newbrough identified is more prevalent in political science. In this case, a community refers to "a set of organizations and interests that interact to pursue their own purposes while being in the same geographic area" (p. 209).

This latter concept of community as a set of local organizations and interests that interact to pursue their own interests is, I believe, more useful when considering a framework for community empowerment. It emphasizes geographic proximity and deemphasizes commonalities and shared interests or characteristics. Not incidentally, this concept of community is similar to those that have been used in studies of community power structure. For example, the studies by the community power theorists examined in Chapter 2 nearly all defined community as a geographic area: a town, a city, or a region. Moreover, they all included various actors and interest groups in their studies of community, not only those who shared characteristics or interests. For example, Flyvbjerg's (1998) study of Aalborg included numerous organizations and interests—from activists, to bureaucrats, to reporters, to the chamber of commerce—as did Gaventa's (1980) study of the Appalachian mining town.[1] These studies do not ignore relevant extralocal actors or groups, but they include them only as they are relevant to the power dynamics in the geographically defined community.

Viewing community in this holistic and geographically delineated way is consistent with a human ecological perspective, bringing the concept into alignment with some of the foundations of empowerment theory. Newbrough (1973) advanced an ecological understand of community as "a habitat for the development of its residents and a support system for improving the quality of life" (p. 210). But, Newbrough also recognized that this ecological view risks consigning the concept of community to a sort of backdrop, or simply an aggregation of other entities (i.e., individuals, organizations, interest groups). He therefore sought to build on these more passive ecological concepts of community by borrowing Long's (1958) metaphor of the local community as an *ecology of games*. This is the idea that there are a variety of interacting games in a locality: the bankers' game, the local leadership and social games, the developers' game, the political game, the news game, the educators' game, the religious leaders' game, and so on. Each of these games has different rules, but players (residents, organizations, institutions) may use other players from other games in pursuit of wins in their respective games. The interaction between these games produces functional systems that go beyond the immediate intentions of the players in each narrow game.

Local issues that arise, such as a debate over the construction of a new highway or a new convention center, tend to affect players in many different games. We might expect a new highway project to primarily concern particular groups, such as road builders, developers, engineers, those in the hotel and tourism games, or residents whose neighborhoods or businesses might be negatively affected. But, the players of many other local games in the community do also tend to take notice. Many consider how they might use new issue debates to improve their chances of achieving their purposes in their particular games. Few of them are acting deliberately on behalf of the whole community in their day-to-day decision making, yet all of them do seek to mobilize the general public and to shape public opinion.

This is a fundamental distinction between local human communities and the ecological systems studied in plant and animal biology, according to Long. The ecology of a forest, for example, also has many games taking place (e.g., the birds' game or the ants' game). These games also interact to produce functional systems beyond the immediate intentions of these particular players or games. Yet, the players in the games that constitute a forest do not seek to mobilize anything like a general public of all participants in that forest, and they do not they have (at least so far as we can tell) any sense of the public's opinion. Participants in local human communities are conscious of the ways that their actions will be viewed and understood by the larger public, and they tend to adjust their strategies accordingly.

Strategies employed in this way can be understood by considering Lukes's (1974) third dimension of power. In other words, the relationships between players in the local ecology of games are partly shaped by their attention to—and anticipation of—the ways their actions will shape public opinion and ideology.

It is imperative not to mistake the metaphor of the local community as an ecology of games for a sort of rational actor theory in the microeconomic sense. The community, in this way of thinking, literally *comprises* the interactions between the games. Yet, it simultaneously structures the rules and roles of the various games that comprise it. Games may have communitarian or liberation-oriented goals. They may have profit motives. It is more likely they have a combination of goals and motivations. So, the point is not that every actor is purely pursuing their own narrow self-interest. The point is that members of different games view the community and the systems that comprise it differently and pursue different ends within it—even if their actions, when taken together, can appear to be choreographed. In this view, the community itself is structuring the games and the roles for game players in ways that surpass the abilities and understanding of any particular leader or set of game players. We can build on this metaphor to theorize a more active ecological conception of community, one that understands it as an adaptive metasystem rather than simply as an aggregation of other entities.

Although it may at first seem strange to define a unit of analysis within human ecology by interactions between entities, rather than by a stable set of intrinsic characteristics, in fact this is consistent with ecological systems theory.[2] For example, J. W. Neal and Neal's (2013) network-based work on ecology defines a macrosystem as "the set of social patterns that govern the formation and dissolution of social interactions between individuals, and thus the relationship among ecological systems" (p. 8). Adapting this definition using insights from studies of local community power and empowerment, as well as Newbrough's (1973) definition of community, we can describe community as the *social patterns shaping interactions between various "games" in a locality (i.e., a city, town, or region) and thus the relationship among ecological systems, including support systems for improving quality of life.*[3]

Taking a holistic view, we realize that there can be no community or organization without individual people, and we struggle to conceive of the psychology of individuals who are entirely distinct from these collectives. Community is therefore a local habitat that is both shaped by its inhabitants' actions and perceptions and, reciprocally, shapes those inhabitants' actions and perceptions. Likewise, structural forces from outside the community, such as history and political economy, exert influences on communities. As M. Fine (2015) wrote, community researchers "have typically under-theorized the impinging forces pressing from outside the community membrane, and ignored the vibrant, sometimes boiling complexities within" (p. 8). The local community, defined geographically and understood as an ecology of games, does provide basic tools for understanding complexities within communities, but connecting local "games" and structural arrangements such as neoliberal globalization and social forces is also critical for understanding power dynamics in contemporary communities. With these ways of defining and understanding "community" in mind, let us look specifically at community empowerment processes.

Community Empowerment

It is true that there has been a relative lack of attention to community empowerment when compared to psychological and organizational empowerment. There have nevertheless been some previous efforts to describe what makes up the concept. The most prominent effort to date has been the "domains" approach to community empowerment (Laverack, 2001, 2006; Laverack & Wallerstein, 2001). This approach was developed for use in health promotion and community development efforts and is particularly focused on programs as drivers of community empowerment. The domains approach to community empowerment built on earlier public health work on community capacity (e.g., Chaskin, 2001; Goodman et al., 1998); community competence (e.g., Eng & Parker, 1994); and community participation (Rifkin, Muller, & Bichman, 1988). In each of these strands of literature, community empowerment was a goal for program staff to aspire to in their collaborative work with residents.

Although the domains approach uses the term *community empowerment*, it is far from the only work relevant to the topic. Social research and community practice have addressed community empowerment processes but have often used different terms. Thus, I examine the domains approach alongside relevant work on components of neighborhood social processes, community mobilization domains from studies of social movements, and principles of grassroots community organizing. The goal is to construct an integrated framework for community empowerment that clearly connects with the dimensions of community power described in Chapter 2.

Domains Approach to Community Empowerment

The nine domains of community empowerment identified by Laverack referred specifically to programs. In this formulation, a program can be expected to enhance community empowerment if it (a) improves participation, (b) develops local leadership, (c) builds empowering organizational structures, (d) increases problem assessment capacities, (e) enhances the ability to "ask why" (critical awareness), (f) improves resource mobilization, (g) strengthens links to other organizations and people, (h) creates an equitable relationship with outside agents, and (i) increases local control over program management. Laverack (2006) provided examples in which he claimed that health promotion practitioners can be thought to be "empowering women living in low income housing" and "empowering the victims of domestic violence in Fiji" (p. 8).

These sorts of claims about one person or group (in this case professional practitioners) "empowering" another are common in the health promotion and community development literature on empowerment. They are also central to the confusion about the roles that different people can play in empowerment processes (as discussed in Chapter 3). To revisit in brief, these notions are at odds with much of the symbolic ideology of empowerment described by Rappaport and other empowerment theorists. The notion contradicts critical assessments of failed attempts by members of more powerful groups seeking to "empower" another less powerful group, such as Gruber and Trickett's (1987) study.

On the other hand, practitioners and programs certainly can make contributions to community empowerment processes. Conversely, when practice is carried out without the intent to build local capacity or reflection on power dynamics, it can distract from or even thwart other local attempts to build community power. So, Laverack's domains approach represents a synthesis of earlier work in applied fields like public health and international development (e.g., Craig & Mayo, 1995) and can be a helpful tool for practitioners to reflect on and improve their work. Like much of the empowerment literature, however, it is limited not only by its potential to create confusion about roles in empowerment processes but also by its lack of clarity on community power structure, its emphasis on professionally driven programs, and corresponding inattention to empowerment outside of programmatic contexts.

A focus on professionally driven programs is a common feature of existing work on community empowerment, even beyond that which has used this particular "domains" approach. Specifically, most work on the topic has been case studies of individual public health and community development programs and initiatives. The public health approach to community empowerment has largely built on or adapted notions of community capacity when theorizing and assessing community empowerment (e.g., Ahmad & Abu Talib, 2014; Heritage & Dooris, 2009; Sudhipongpracha, 2013). Like the domains approach, these community capacity approaches have tended to hinge on the delivery of programs or initiatives rather than on efforts that are driven by local communities and organizations (Crisp, Swerissen, & Duckett, 2000; Freudenberg, 2004; Goodman et al., 1998). In much of this literature, community capacity and community empowerment are used interchangeably or in overlapping ways (i.e., one concept subsuming the other). The risk is that these approaches can dilute the concept of empowerment, which ought to emphasize the agency of local residents. As described in Chapter 3, professional practice and programs can sometimes support locally driven efforts, but should not be the focus of a framework for community empowerment.

What about research on community empowerment beyond programmatic contexts? There has unfortunately been relatively little that has examined these processes while referring to a specific framework for community empowerment.

One example of a case study is Laverack and Whipple's (2010) study that details the processes by which a prostitutes' collective in New Zealand organized and directly influenced public policy. Yet, this study does not use the domains of community empowerment, begging the question of the applicability of the domains approach to such grassroots policy change efforts. Still, studies of community empowerment processes per se outside of program contexts are few and far between, and this represents a major shortcoming of the existing research literature.

Neighborhood Social Processes

The sociological concept of collective efficacy, which includes social cohesion and social control, provides a perspective through which some aspects of community empowerment can be understood. *Collective efficacy* (Sampson, 2004, 2012) refers to shared expectations of engagement and action for the common good in a neighborhood. As described by Sampson and others, collective efficacy has two dimensions: social cohesion and social control. Social cohesion refers to mutual trust and solidarity in a neighborhood. Social control refers to the belief that others in the neighborhood would take action to remedy problems such as public services being cut or youth skipping school and loitering in public spaces. The two aspects of collective efficacy depend on each other since the shared expectations of action and mutual trust reinforce one another (Sampson, Raudenbush, & Earls, 1997) (Appendix 6.1).

In the book *Great American City* (2012), Sampson synthesized decades of research on collective efficacy. In several countries, studies controlling for a number of other structural, economic, and sociodemographic factors have found that neighborhoods that are relatively high in collective efficacy tend to have lower levels of violence. Some research also links collective efficacy with other population health indicators, such as birth weight and mortality (more on this in the next chapter). Neighborhoods with higher levels of collective efficacy have been found to have reductions over time in poverty and crime. Concentrated disadvantage and violence are associated with lower collective efficacy not only in the present, but also into the future. What this cumulative evidence points to are feedback loops of reciprocal influence between neighborhood-level variations in violent crime, neighborhood structural characteristics such as concentrated disadvantage and residential stability, and neighborhood-level social processes such as collective efficacy.

Although collective efficacy is likely related to community empowerment, it is important to make the differences between the two concepts clear. One basic point of distinction is that collective efficacy refers specifically to neighborhoods while community empowerment processes typically are not bound to the neighborhood level. So, gains in collective efficacy across multiple neighborhoods in a city could be indicative of community empowerment processes. Another key difference is that although collective efficacy captures the norms and expectations among neighbors about individual behaviors, it does not assess many other facets of community empowerment processes. For instance, it does not assess the ability of the neighborhood to build powerful organizations that can seek to change policies that maintain inequities. It also does not assess relationships and networks of institutions and organizations. Hence, while collective efficacy is likely related to community empowerment, it is a more domain-specific and geographically bound concept referring specifically to neighbors' expectations of each other. As a neighborhood social process, therefore, it is likely a byproduct or predictor of community empowerment processes.

In fact, some recent work hypothesized collective efficacy as a component of community empowerment. Aiyer, Zimmerman, Morrel-Samuels, and Reischl (2015) conceptualized community empowerment according to three components and specified neighborhood social process indicators for each of the three components. The first component, the intracommunity component, involves collective efficacy, social cohesion, and sense of community. The second component, the interactional component, involves social capital and social control. Third, the behavioral component involves individual and collective actions to influence neighborhood outcomes. According to Aiyer and colleagues, these neighborhood social processes lead to neighborhoods with "busy streets," in which residents feel comfortable being outside and behaving in prosocial ways, which include maintaining the physical appearance of the neighborhood (as per Jacobs, 1961). This phenomenon of busy streets, in turn, is thought to lead to higher levels of safety and health in the neighborhood.

This neighborhood social process approach to community empowerment specified by Aiyer and colleagues (2015) is valuable as a synthesis of other sociological and criminological concepts. It does differ, however, in fundamental ways from studies of community power. First, as mentioned with regard to collective efficacy, the neighborhood-level focus is different from the concept of community in most studies of community power structure. Second, as discussed in the next section, these neighborhood social processes are particularly useful for understanding the first dimension of community power (described in Chapter 2) but are not as well attuned to the second and third dimensions. Collective efficacy and related neighborhood social process indicators are therefore useful concepts for understanding community empowerment processes but are not sufficient by themselves for understanding how social action relates to community power structure.

Social Movements and Mobilization

Social movement activists and scholars have also developed concepts that can help to elucidate aspects of community empowerment. Concepts such as *mobilizing structures* and *repertoires of contention*, for example, have been influential for thinking through and comparing social movements in different places and eras (Tilly & Tarrow, 2015).[4] Repertoires of contention are tools for public enactment of social movements and can include a variety of forms of direct action: demonstrations, rallies, protests, art and performances, public meetings, boycotts, strikes, and media and Internet-based actions, among others. When successful, these tools often spread through movement organizations and are sometimes taken up by other movements.

Social movement studies have also been attentive to the organizational and interorganizational structures that movements construct to create opportunities for change or to take advantage of opportunities that arise due to external factors. Mobilizing structures can include specific organizations as well as organizational networks or even less formalized networks of active participants. These structures have sometimes been compared for their effectiveness at supporting and sustaining social movements (e.g., Walker & McCarthy, 2007). Social network analysts, for instance, have examined heterogeneity versus homogeneity in characteristics of the organizations within the networks that participate in social movements (Diani, 2012). This concept of the mobilizing structures that comprise organizations as well as interorganizational networks and linkages is useful for thinking about power and empowerment across whole communities.

The rhetorical and political–ideological *frames* that movements use to bring greater public awareness to their grievances—and to change the way that others think about issues—are also subjects of social movement studies (e.g., Diani, 1996). This concept of frames was taken from social constructionist theorists like Goffman (1974) and is used by social movement scholars to examine the ways that movement actors and their targets (e.g., elected officials, media, scholars, the public) make meaning out of facts and ongoing events. Alternative frames can play transformative roles in the sense that they can change the ways that people interpret social phenomena, systems, and relationships (Snow, 2013). Critical frames can aid in the development of critical consciousness, which can in turn help fuel sociopolitical action (Watts & Hipolito-Delgado, 2015).[5]

Few have explicitly drawn on social movement concepts to understand local/regional community empowerment processes. One exception is Fedi, Mannarini, and Maton's (2009) study of a resistance movement against construction of a high-speed rail through the Susa Valley in Italy. This study described how the resistance movement created settings that fit the description of empowering community settings (Maton, 2008; i.e., group-based belief system, opportunity role structure, and the other internal features of organizational empowerment described in Chapter 5). Beyond these settings that were created and maintained as part of the movement, however, external linkages were formed between the movement organization and the broader community, as well as to national and international environmental and political groups. The leaders of the movement organization became involved in a variety of other forms of democratic participation and changed the social and political structure of the region, allowing for greater collaboration between localities on a range of other issues. This research underscores the need for attention to the specific kinds of settings that enable community empowerment processes to occur.

One recent effort is noteworthy for pulling together concepts from research on social movements and neighborhood social processes to understand community mobilization. Working in an HIV prevention context, Lippman and colleagues (2013) reviewed and integrated these concepts with the domains approach to community empowerment and several other related concepts from the community development and community capacity literatures. Through this process, they identified six domains of community mobilization: (a) shared concern, (b) critical consciousness, (c) organizational structures and networks, (d) leadership, (e) collective action, and (f) social cohesion.[6] This community mobilization framework represents a conceptual integration of neighborhood social processes and concepts from social movements with the domains approach to community empowerment and community capacity.

Community Organizing

Community organizing is continually devising and refining practical methods for enhancing residents' power in local decision-making. The field has grown steadily in the United States over several recent decades. For example, as mentioned previously in this book, although there were only a handful of institution-based community organizing initiatives in the 1970s, there are now broad-based community organizing initiatives rooted in multiple local institutions in nearly every midsize and large US city (Wood et al., 2013). Although there are variations in the methods employed by organizers in different branches of the field, there are also many commonalities that are expressed in the forms of specific principles and organizing models. These principles and models function as touchstones for people involved in community organizing to learn the practice and experiment with building power to make change in their own communities (Christens & Speer, 2015).

These models often use a basic illustration of community organizing as a recurring cycle with four phases: (a) listening/assessment that informs (b) organizing issue research leading toward (c) action/mobilization, which is followed by (d) reflection and then back to (a) listening and so on (Christens & Dolan, 2011; Speer, Hughey, Gensheimer, & Adams-Leavitt, 1995). The listening phase of this cycle of community organizing hinges on one-to-one or small-group meetings in which residents build relationships and understand each other's concerns and hopes for the community. Intentionality around interpersonal relationship development and the formation of group identities has helped many local organizing groups to forge durable alliances across lines of race, language, class, political ideology, and religion (Christens, 2010; Swarts, 2011). Connecting this process to empowerment, Speer and Hughey (1995) highlight the organizing principle that social power is built on the strength of interpersonal relationships. This is a cardinal point for understanding leadership in community empowerment processes—leaders in powerful community-driven efforts are not necessarily the holders of positions of institutional authority, but are people who have relationships that they can mobilize (Christens, Inzeo, et al., 2014).

The issues that are identified through these listening campaigns then become the subjects of ongoing research carried out collectively by leaders in the organizing process. Leaders hold meetings with experts and public officials to gain a rich understanding of issues and their root causes, to identify potential (typically partial) solutions to the issues, and to understand the community power structure as it relates to the issues at hand. This collective social analysis sometimes involves more formal social scientific research methods (i.e., survey research, geographic analyses) conducted independently or in collaboration with professional researchers in universities or nonprofits (e.g., Dolan et al., 2015; Speer et al., 2003). In this process, participants in organizing are gaining not only in-depth knowledge about the root causes of social issues and the sociopolitical systems that allow them to persist, but they are also gaining insights into the power relationships between individuals and organizations in their communities. They study power relations and identify potential allies and potential targets of action. In other words, they seek not only to achieve progress in addressing persistent social problems in their community, but also to change the structure of power relations between residents and institutions.

In large public actions, they call on decision-makers to make commitments to specific changes in policies and systems that will help to address issues. Afterward, the organizing initiative stays vigilant in holding those decision-makers to account for their public commitments. The successes of some organizing initiatives in implementing these community-driven processes for changes in policies and systems have been scrutinized in case studies using multiple methods, such as interviews and participant observation alongside examinations of archival documents, such as meeting agendas and minutes, local and national news media coverage, and reports and audits of public agencies (e.g., Bezboruah, 2013; Edwards, 2011; Speer & Christens, 2012; Speer, Tesdahl, & Ayers, 2014). In many of these cases, the perspectives and proposed solutions of the organizing initiative were taken up as priorities by other actors, institutions, and coalitions. This points to the influence of the organizing initiatives in setting policy agendas and aligning institutional priorities across sectors. Studying one model for community organizing, Speer and Hughey (1995) defined community empowerment processes as consisting of multisector relationship development, institutional linkages across sectors, and collective attention to common community issues. In other words, these initiatives are building and exercising power by aligning multiple organizations and agencies toward specific actions to address pressing problems facing the community.

Successes in community organizing are typically partial. On one hand, they often result in meaningful progress toward addressing pernicious challenges in communities. On the other hand, they do so in the face of persistent and mounting socioeconomic inequality and the havoc being wreaked on communities by neoliberal policies. This is why organizing models have increasingly emphasized the importance of critical reflection, or as Speer and Hughey (1995) described it, a dialectic of action and reflection. Indeed, there is evidence that this dialectic in community organizing builds critical consciousness among participants (Rogers, Mediratta, & Shah, 2012; Terriquez, 2015). Throughout the cycle of listening, research, action, and reflection, participants not only are building the capacities to assess particular social problems and the specific arrangements that allow those to persist but also are gaining insights into the structural political, economic, and historical forces that shape disparate outcomes between and among communities.

Unsurprisingly, these complex understandings of community issues are often at odds with the ways the issues are discussed by local leaders, decision-makers, and professionals. Community organizers often work with a concept called *public narratives,* which helps leaders consider the discursive practices that can guide others toward action (Ganz, 2011). Organizers seek to alter dominant public narratives (e.g., victim blaming) through strategic actions that promote alternative public narratives focused on shared values and hope for a better future. This concept of public narratives is similar to the frames described by social movement scholars. By introducing new public narratives, community organizers seek to shift public interpretation of community events toward systemic understanding and capacity to imagine more socially just arrangements that allow all residents more opportunities to thrive.

Summary

To briefly recap, the terminology of community empowerment has been applied most often in the context of public health and community development programs. In these contexts, it has sometimes been used interchangeably with community participation and community capacity. The most prominent framework specifically for community empowerment thus far has been the domains approach (Laverack, 2001, 2006; Laverack & Wallerstein, 2001), although this approach is limited by its applicability primarily to professionally driven program delivery contexts. The broader multidisciplinary literature on community organizing and social movements has used the term *community empowerment,* albeit less frequently, but has provided a number of case studies detailing illustrative community empowerment processes. Many of these processes have more in common with Rappaport's view of the symbolic ideology of empowerment than the professionally driven processes that have more often tended to embrace the language of community empowerment. Several recent scholarly efforts have sought to integrate neighborhood social process concepts with the domains approach to community empowerment or social movement concepts.

Clear links between empowerment processes and community power structure have not been made in many of these strands of literature (aside from a few studies of social movements and community organizing). And, although the conceptual contributions described previously do illuminate some aspects of community empowerment processes, none do so in a way that comprehensively addresses the different facets of community power described in Chapter 2, and that could apply to a broad range of community-driven systems change processes. A central goal for advancing empowerment theory, then, is to construct a framework that can integrate concepts from different branches of this literature to describe and assess community empowerment processes and to organize findings and practice-based insights from various efforts to build and exercise community power for systemic change.

Constructing a Framework for Community Empowerment

Theorists initially envisioned empowerment as a guiding orientation for social theory and practice that could address both rights and needs of disadvantaged groups in the process of bringing about more socially just arrangements of resources and power. Guided by a human ecological perspective, they suggested that empowerment processes were necessarily simultaneously psychological, organizational, and community processes (see Chapter 3). In other words, psychological empowerment should be inextricable from community empowerment and vice versa. Psychological empowerment has steadily been defined more specifically and measured more precisely, and the use of the concept and measures has become more geographically widespread (as described in Chapter 4), while work on organizational (Chapter 5) and (especially) community empowerment has lagged further behind. Examining the existing literature on community empowerment reveals conceptual shortcomings, such as ambiguous, weak, or nonexistent links between the concepts of power and empowerment. A new framework for understanding community empowerment is needed.

What are some basic goals that a framework for community empowerment should seek to accomplish? First, as mentioned, it is important that community empowerment processes be understood as inextricably linked to psychological and organizational empowerment processes. Second, it should specify features of community processes that can be operationalized and studied descriptively to guide empirical research and evaluation. In other words, it should allow community empowerment processes to be distinguished from other (even closely related) processes. Third, it should draw on understanding of community and social power from fields of practice such as community-organizing and social movements. Fourth, it should mine existing work from public health and community development where the term *community empowerment* has been most frequently applied. Fifth and finally, it is critical that the framework emphasize and elucidate the links between power and empowerment.

Taking this last point first, a framework for community empowerment ought to have clear relationships to theories of community power. How can the three-dimensional view of power (described in Chapter 2) contribute to understanding community empowerment? Recall that the three dimensions—first described by Lukes (1974) and labeled by Alford and Friedland (1985) as (a) situational, (b) institutional, and (c) systemic—refer respectively to the role of power in (a) determining who wins and who loses in publicly visible conflicts, (b) determining which conflicts emerge in public debate and which do not, and (c) determining public understanding and interpretation of events and issues. We can take the domains of community empowerment identified by Laverack and sort them according to these three dimensions of community power: situational, institutional, and systemic. The frameworks created by Lippman and colleagues (2013) for community mobilization and by Aiyer and colleagues (2015) for community empowerment can be likewise sorted. Finally, principles of grassroots community organizing can be aligned with these three dimensions of power.

As Table 6.1 shows, the operational/programmatic domains, community mobilization domains, and community-organizing principles can be mapped across all three dimensions of power. All three components of community empowerment (intracommunity, interactional, and behavioral) identified by Aiyer and colleagues (2015) are most closely associated with the situational (first) dimension of power. Of the seven community mobilization domains identified by Lippman and colleagues (2013), four can be mapped onto the situational (first dimension), two to the institutional (second dimension), and one to the systemic (third dimension). The organizational/programmatic domains posited by Laverack are similarly attentive to the situational and institutional domains, while paying relatively scant attention to the systemic domain. As the last column in the table shows, principles from community organizing can be identified that map onto each of the three dimensions of power.

Looking horizontally across each of the three dimensions, some commonalities in the frameworks can quickly be identified. For example, participation, leadership, collective efficacy (including social cohesion and social control), and collective action are apparent as commonalities across many of the frameworks/models in the situational (first) dimension. Terminology and emphases are somewhat different in the community-organizing column. For instance, although leadership is described in a variety of ways in the other frameworks, community organizing makes clear that social power is built on the strength of relationships, and leadership is relationally, rather than positionally, determined. Table 6.2 collapses themes from the four frameworks/models across all three of the dimensions of community power to outline an overarching framework for identifying features of community

Table 6.1 **Domains, Components, and Principles From Existing Frameworks Mapped Onto Three Dimensions of Community Power**

Dimensions of Community Power (Alford & Friedland, 1985; Lukes, 1974)	*Operational/Programmatic Domains* (Laverack, 2001, 2006; Laverack & Wallerstein, 2001)	*Neighborhood Social Process Components* (Aiyer, Zimmerman, Morrel-Samuels, & Reischl, 2015)	*Community Mobilization Domains* (Lippman et al., 2013, 2016)	*Community-Organizing Principles* (Alinsky, 1971; Speer & Hughey, 1995)
1. Situational	• Improves participation • Develops local leadership • Improves resource mobilization • Increases control over program management	*Intracommunity component* • Social cohesion • Collective efficacy • Sense of community *Interactional component* • Social capital • Social control *Behavioral component* • Individual and collective action	• Leadership • Collective action • Social cohesion • Social control	• Listening/assessment • Social power and leadership built on strength of interpersonal relationships • Public actions
2. Institutional	• Builds empowering organizational structures • Increases problem assessment capacities • Strengthens links to other organizations and people • Creates an equitable relationship with outside agents		• Shared concerns • Organizations and networks	• Multiple powerful organizations • Organizing research on issues • Power mapping • Institutional linkages and cross-sector alignment
3. Systemic	• Enhances ability to "ask why" (critical awareness)		• Critical consciousness	• Social analysis • Shaping public narratives • Dialectic of action and reflection

Table 6.2 **Features of Community Empowerment Across Three Dimensions of Community Power**

Dimensions of Power	Features of Community Empowerment
1. Situational	• Broad participation and collective action, including contests to the status quo • Collective efficacy (social cohesion and social control) in neighborhoods, towns • Leadership and social power built on strength of relationships
2. Institutional	• Multiple empowering organizations and networks (mobilizing structures), including multiscalar mobilization networks • Issue/problem assessment capacity • Power mapping, ability to align institutional agendas around prioritized community issues
3. Systemic	• Social/collective analysis of the root causes of community issues and inequities • Development of critical consciousness and resistance to hegemony • Shaping public narratives and frames, providing for interpretations that suggest alternatives, transformation

empowerment. Next, I take up each these features of community empowerment alongside concepts from the study of community power. I also consider some structural features (political and economic) that can be conducive or inhibitive of these processes.

Situational

The situational (first) dimension of power involves the factors that influence the determination of outcomes in public debates over policies and resources. Broad participation and collective action are identified in all frameworks and models as important features of community empowerment. In many ways, participation is both a precursor to and an expression of community empowerment. Broad participation is fundamental to democratic functioning (Skocpol & Fiorina, 1999) and to community organizing (Alinsky, 1971), and it stands to reason that it is important for determining outcomes in public debates. Thinking about participation and collective action from the perspective of community power, it is essential that participation not only be in service-oriented modalities but also that it acts as a channel for contention (McAdam, Tarrow, & Tilly, 2008), including expressions of sociopolitical differences and instrumental action to transform sociopolitical systems to address injustices. To the extent that those seeking to oppress communities (or subgroups within geographic communities such as people of color and immigrants) are able to suppress broad participation and contentious collective action at the community level, this tends to serve their purposes. Oligarchs, however, may allow or even encourage forms of participation that do not challenge the status quo, such as volunteering for charities or participation in demonstrations of national-istic/patriotic pride.[7] Broad participation and action at an aggregate level, however, particularly that which evidences dynamics of contention and contestation of the interests of those in power, is one indicator that community empowerment is likely taking place.

Collective efficacy (Sampson, 2004, 2012) is specifically identified in both the neighborhood social process approach to community empowerment (Aiyer et al., 2015) and the community mobilization domains (Lippman et al., 2013). It extends beyond participation and collective action to the shared norms and expectations of neighbors or members of a community. If collective action and broad participa-tion are behavioral manifestations of community empowerment, collective efficacy, which involves perceptions of social cohesion and norms of informal social control, can be more of a collective gauge of a community's or neighborhood's emotional disposition toward collective action to address community issues. High levels of collective efficacy in a community are therefore another situational indicator that community empowerment processes are likely taking place and having effects on the beliefs and expectations of residents.

Local leadership is identified as a domain in many of the frameworks and models (in all but the neighborhood social process approach). Considering leadership in the context of community power, we must avoid connotations often associated with the term. Leadership is often represented as a set of personality traits or practices of individuals within an organizational hierarchy. In the context of struggles for social justice, leadership is instead often a set of collective or shared leadership practices (S. Kelly, 2014; P. M. Miller, Brown, & Hopson, 2011; Preskill & Brookfield, 2009). In fact, some of the most successful community change initiatives have broadly distrib-uted leadership to the point that they might appear "leaderless" to observers with more conventional expectations for what leadership looks like. Instead of looking for prominent individual leaders, then, observers of community empowerment processes should look for "leaderful" communities, movements, and organizations (Raelin, 2011). This notion is akin to the community-organizing principle that social power is built on the strength (and breadth) of interpersonal relationships (Speer & Hughey, 1995) rather than on positional authority, charisma, or other individual characteristics. Communities where empowerment processes are taking place, then, are communities where we expect to find a large number of leaders, as defined by their relational networks, and their ability to mobilize those networks for greater par-ticipation and collective action.

Of course, for the features of community empowerment to be manifested in the situational (first) dimension, it is helpful if certain basic needs are met and rights are protected in societies. In instances of total domination and oppression, basic democratic participation can be difficult or dangerous, much less outright contentious (Prilleltensky, 2008). In some contexts (i.e., in countries with recent violent interethnic conflicts), traditions of participation and collective action may have different meanings and not be representative of community empowerment (e.g., Belloni, 2001). As empowerment theorists have long emphasized, context likely determines differences in empowerment processes. Nevertheless, the situational features identified here are common to many community empowerment processes, although they may be less publicly visible in political contexts with weak protections for democratic participation. Comparing manifestations of community empowerment processes in different societies or cultures therefore requires understanding of the historical and sociopolitical context.

Institutional

The institutional (second) dimension of power is focused on agenda-setting that enables or prevents specific community issues and grievances from emerging in public debates. One indicator of community empowerment in the institutional dimension is the presence of multiple organizations, interorganizational networks, or less formally constituted social networks in a community that can act as mobilizing structures (Tilly & Tarrow, 2015). When community empowerment processes take place, numerous organizations and community settings may begin to foster the features of community empowerment in the situational (first) dimension: broad participation and collective action, collective efficacy, and local leadership. At an aggregate level, these organizations and networks could be described as the presence of a robust civil society (C. A. Flanagan, Martínez, & Cumsille, 2011). Organizations and networks that create empowering community settings (Maton, 2008) can cumulatively contribute to diffuse and inclusive—pluralistic rather than elite driven—community power structures.

Observing and comparing these institutional infrastructures across places, however, is no simple task. Counting the numbers or size of voluntary organizations in a community, or even identifying the prevalence of particular roles for volunteers, examining interorganizational networks, or estimating the frequency of volunteer activity among residents, would still omit crucial features of community empowerment. As discussed in Chapter 5, nonprofits can act as defenders of the status quo as well as challengers (Domhoff, 2009). In contemporary societies facing persistent injustices, it is necessary to place particular emphasis on the organizations and interorganizational networks that can effectively act as challengers to elite interests, domination, and oligarchy. In the context of globalization, this increasingly means the ability to operate not only at the local level, but also at the regional, national, and international scales. Therefore, a complete picture of the institutional dimension of community empowerment requires attention to the prevalence of particular types of organizations (i.e., those mounting challenges to the interests of elites) and the presence of multiscalar mobilization networks (see Bosco, 2001; Case & Caragata, 2009; Kaiser & Rusch, 2015; Nicholls, Miller, & Beaumont, 2016; Sarmiento & Beard, 2013). These networks and their ability to exercise power at multiple scales are key aspects of a community's capacity to resist domination and to mount and sustain challenges to elite interests in an increasingly globalized era.

A second feature of community empowerment in the institutional dimension is the ability of organizations and networks to assess and understand community problems. Laverack (2001, 2006), for example, identified increases in problem assessment capacity as a domain of community empowerment. Likewise, participant–leaders in community organizing initiatives assess their fellow residents' concerns through one-to-one conversations and conduct research on the issues that surface as themes through these listening campaigns (Christens, 2010). Community empowerment processes both depend on and enhance the ability of community groups and networks to identify and strategically prioritize issues and to determine possibilities for changes that will help to address these issues.

Participants and organizations engaged in community empowerment processes also need the ability to understand the makeup of the local power structures that wield influence in local decision-making. Understanding local power structures enables those pursuing systemic changes to employ strategy in relationship development, collaborations, and direct action. It stands to reason that understanding the power structures operating in a community is requisite for transforming them, yet the reverse is also true. "If you want to understand something, try to change it" (Bronfenbrenner, 1977, p. 211), a quotation often attributed to Kurt Lewin, is also applicable here. A nuanced understanding of local power structures is often gained through experiential learning that takes place during the course of collective efforts to achieve transformative changes.[8] In grassroots community-organizing and social movements, for instance, this is often cultivated through "power-mapping" processes (see Noy, 2008), in which participants map a constellation of actors in a community, locating each actor or entity according to their relative power and interest in pursuing particular policy and systems changes. Thus, when community empowerment processes are taking place, we can observe organizations and networks working to understand and reorient the agendas of local institutions and decision-makers. When these efforts are successful, we can also detect institutional realignments (Speer & Hughey, 1995) and changes in community power relations enabling greater influence by groups that were previously less powerful, excluded from, or marginalized within important "games" and decision-making processes.

As with the situational (first) dimension, there are political conditions that can constrain and enable community empowerment processes in the institutional (second) dimension. At the most basic level, the freedom to form private, nongovernmental organizations that can take social action without fear of reprisal or repression is of great importance. In order for these types of organizations to serve as effective vehicles for community empowerment, however, there must be many of them, creating a wide range of opportunities for civic participation for residents. The ability of these civic organizations to form multiscalar networks for mobilization depends in part on their sustainability and the stability of their funding and membership structures. It also depends on the range of possible or feasible mechanisms for citizens to hold powerful decision-makers accountable. Policies like those that have been recently implemented in Wisconsin, discussed in the first chapter of this book (e.g., curtailing of collective bargaining rights, restrictions on how unions or other civic organizations can raise funds), can make it more difficult for civic organizations to persist and access resources. Political regimes can also impair community empowerment processes by making government less transparent and accountable (e.g., weakening or eliminating regulatory and government oversight agencies, weakening or eliminating open records laws); creating easier inroads for elite interests to influence decision-making (e.g., eliminating restrictions on campaign financing); and diminishing or eradicating established avenues for resident engagement in decision-making, or what Campbell, Cornish, Gibbs, and Scott (2010) called "receptive social environments" (p. 964) in which decision-makers listen to residents with fewer resources.

Systemic

The systemic (third) dimension of community power is the most foundational of the three dimensions. It represents the ways that power operates to shape people's beliefs, desires, and perceptions of community issues. This dimension of power has received the least attention in existing theoretical frameworks for community empowerment (see Table 6.1), perhaps because it is, in many cases, the least easily observable dimension. Yet, by building on theory and research on this dimension of community power, as well as on community-organizing and social mobilization efforts, it is possible to identify some salient, observable features of community empowerment processes in this systemic dimension. Recall the definition of a community, developed previously in this chapter, as the social patterns shaping interactions between various "games" in a locality. The systemic dimension of power is where many of the conflicts are waged that ultimately result in restructuring of the various games and the roles and rules for game players. The systemic dimension of community power is therefore indispensable for a complete understanding of community empowerment. Game players' attention to and anticipation of how their actions might shape ideology (i.e., public opinion) is a primary point of interest for uncovering dynamics in this dimension.

One feature of community empowerment processes in the systemic dimension is collective analysis of the root causes of community issues and inequities. This is akin to what Rogers and Oakes (2005), drawing on Dewey, called "public social inquiry" (p. 2178). It is related to problem assessment capacities as discussed in the institutional (second) dimension, but goes beyond assessment of issues to more detailed analysis of the often-complex sets of factors that create and sustain inequities. An example of this type of collective analysis is a group of residents conducting participatory inquiry to determine causal factors at the root of disproportionate levels of exposure to violence and unequal access to educational opportunities (Dolan et al., 2015). These collective analyses hinge on (and develop) critical understanding of the cycles that privilege certain groups and oppress or dispossess others (M. Fine & Ruglis, 2009). Many organizations and networks have repertoires that facilitate collective analysis and develop critical awareness of the ways that power is operating to create and sustain inequities (Christens, Inzeo, et al., 2014; McCarthy & Walker, 2004). These analyses not only can deepen participants' own understanding of social systems but also can influence the broader public's values, beliefs, desires, and interpretation of community issues and current events.

A second feature of community empowerment processes in the systemic dimension is the development of critical consciousness and resistance to hegemony. This extends beyond understanding root causes of problems in a community and into the ideological realm. For instance, in the current era of global capitalism, neoliberal ideology attempts to justify increasing inequality and decreased social security. It is advanced through numerous channels from education to mass media and entertainment. In order to resist hegemonic forces such as neoliberal ideology, groups need tools to foster critical consciousness, both among their own members and in the broader public. Popular education is an example of a model that has been used in many contexts for the development of critical consciousness (Freire, 1973; Kane, 2010). Identity, difference, and culture can be effective tools for resisting dominant ideology (Barnes, 2005; Escobar, 2006) and culture can also facilitate resistance in multiscalar networks (Perreault, 2003).[9]

Communities where empowerment processes are taking place are therefore those that are able to identify and resist these hegemonic ideologies through promotion of critical consciousness. In the United States, one example of this would be the ability to identify and resist hegemonic white supremacy as it manifests in policies, institutional practices, and cultural production. A hypothesis that flows from this is that we would expect to see processes akin to popular education taking place, resulting, for example, in relatively low levels of system justification (Jost, Banaji, & Nosek, 2004; Kay & Jost, 2003; van der Toorn et al., 2015) in communities where empowerment processes are achieving success (a measure for system justification is provided in Appendix 6.2) and building critical consciousness.

Finally, a third feature of community empowerment processes in the systemic dimension involves shaping public narratives or frames and providing for interpretations that suggest alternatives and transformative possibilities. Action to shape public narratives and alternative frames can take many forms, including protests and demonstrations, arts-based activism, media advocacy, or work to change values and principles within institutions such as workplaces, schools, government agencies, and places of worship. This feature of community empowerment goes beyond resistance to ideological systems that serve the interests of dominant groups and extends to the promotion of different ways of understanding the contemporary world and of imagining alternative futures. Examples include alterations to urban policies that would promote greater equity (Imbroscio, 2013; Sarmiento & Sims, 2015), alternatives to mass incarceration (Davis, 2003; Western, 2014), and alternatives to social institutions and capitalist economic structures that would be more just and expand possibilities for human flourishing (Coates, 2014; Wright, 2013). Organizers might describe this process as shifting public narratives (Ganz, 2011), whereas activists might describe it in terms of alternative frames (Diani, 1996; Snow, 2013). Regardless, in communities where power relations are truly being transformed, we are able to observe organizations and networks reshaping the public's values such that their interpretation of current events changes, as do their preferences for how sociopolitical systems evolve. We can also observe the effectiveness of these efforts in the reciprocal effects that they produce: Powerful actors adapt their framing and narratives in order to continue to pursue their interests using new forms of justification.

Political systems can encourage or suppress community empowerment in the systemic dimension, although actions tend to be subtler in this dimension than in the other two. Some governments seek to preserve the status quo through concerted action in the systemic dimension, such as banning and discouraging particular forms of media, debate, and sociopolitical expression. Paradoxically, these repressive efforts often serve to increase the visibility of those who challenge the status quo because they are doing so in open defiance of authoritarian pressures (e.g., Gessen, 2014). At the other end of the spectrum, governments can open up structures designed to encourage a wide range of perspectives by, for instance, providing public funding for community-run media (Sirianni & Friedland, 2001) or mandating a range of public deliberation processes (Rusch & Swarts, 2015). Participatory budgeting processes, for instance, after originating in Brazil (de Souza Santos, 1998), are now being implemented throughout the world.[10] Educational institutions are likewise important sites for advancing or contesting ideology, so it is no surprise that educational policies, curricula, and pedagogical practices are often the focus both of efforts to preserve and to challenge the status quo (Hope & Jagers, 2014; McAvoy & Hess, 2013).

Example: Philadelphia Student Union

We have now taken deep dives into theory on empowerment processes in human development (Chapter 4), organizational development (Chapter 5), and community development (Chapter 6) and drawn those threads together into a holistic model for empowerment, emphasizing community power structure and transactions across ecological systems. Examples of empowerment processes have been cited and mentioned throughout these chapters, but with this chapter's integrated model of empowerment in view (Table 6.3), it may be useful to now consider an additional example, of the Philadelphia Student Union (PSU) to explore how a specific process might be mapped onto it.

The PSU is a community-driven systems change effort that can be considered as an exemplar of empowerment.[11] Founded in 1995, the mission of PSU is as follows:

> To build the power of young people to demand a high quality education in the Philadelphia public school system. We are a youth led organization and we make positive changes in the short term by learning how to organize to build power. We also work toward becoming life-long learners and leaders who can bring diverse groups of people together to address the problems that our communities face. (PSU, 2017)

Initially comprising a small group of students (~12), PSU quickly expanded in the late 1990s as a result of many students' passion for addressing urgent needs in the Philadelphia schools. It established chapters in a number of public high schools and magnet schools and began training and supporting students to bring people together to solve problems related to public education in the city. The overarching idea was that although the teachers had a union that could exert influence on schools and the education system, there was no equivalent entity representing the interests of students.

The PSU has pursued policy and systems changes on numerous issues affecting students, including resistance to privatization of public schools, changes in punitive school discipline policies, advocacy for the creation of student success centers in Philadelphia schools, increased funding and resources for education, and accountability mechanisms for police working in schools. Their actions have taken place during a turbulent time for urban public education in the United States—one that has been characterized by cuts, closures, privatization, harsh discipline, and a lack of trust and safety—that has translated into a lack of opportunity for students in public city schools, who are disproportionately youth of color (Kirshner, Hipolito-Delgado, & Zion, 2015). In this context, PSU's efforts have garnered widespread attention. For example, it has helped to inspire similar student-led school improvement efforts in other United States cities (Burns, 2013), it has generated media coverage, and education researchers have sought to document and understand PSU's effects, both on the individuals who have participated in it and on the broader policy environment in Philadelphia (e.g., J. Conner, 2014; J. Conner & Rosen, 2013; J. Conner & Zaino, 2014; J. Conner, Zaino, & Scarola, 2013; J. O. Conner & Rosen, 2015; Dzurinko, McCants, & Stith, 2011; Rosen, 2012, 2016; Suess & Lewis, 2007).

Table 6.3 **The Ecology of Empowerment Across Three Dimensions of Community Power**

Dimensions of Power		*Ecology of Empowerment*	
	Psychological	*Organizational*	*Community*
1. Situational	• Behavioral component— ⟷ community and organizational participation • Emotional component— sociopolitical control	• Organizational viability ⟷ and leadership • Social support, sense of community in organizations • Opportunity role structure	• Broad participation and collective action • Collective efficacy • Leadership and social power
2. Institutional	• Relational component— ⟷ nurturing leaders, facilitating, collaborating, mobilizing, bridging	• Co-empowered ⟷ subgroups and subgroup linkages • Organizational learning and systems thinking • Networks and coalitions, systems alignment	• Mobilization structures/ networks • Issue/problem assessment capacity • Power mapping, institutional alignment
3. Systemic	• Cognitive component— ⟷ understanding of the source, nature, and instruments of social power • Critical reflection	• Group-based ⟷ belief system • Critical analysis of power • Strategy for systemic transformations and shaping public understanding	• Social/collective analysis of root causes of community issues • Critical consciousness and resistance to hegemony • Shifting public narratives and frames

Because many of PSU's activities and their effects have been documented and studied over a number of years, it is possible to layer some of the reports and findings regarding PSU onto the model for empowerment processes in Table 6.3. The goal here is not a rigorous analysis,[12] but an example of some of the ways that major features of empowerment processes are manifesting in one specific case. To that end, each of the next three subsections layers some selected aspects of PSU's work onto the three rows shown in Table 6.3, which correspond to the three dimensions of community power: situational, institutional, and systemic. Throughout, the italicized terms designate the links to the model.

Situational

Over its history, PSU has spurred and sustained participation and collective action among successive groups of students. In 2013, J. Conner and Rosen estimated that PSU had between 125 and 150 core members who were attending monthly meetings and participating in other forms of action. Their participation has taken many forms: Youth involved in PSU have organized listening campaigns and initiated petition drives; they have held press conferences, rallies, and marches. In other words, the organization is creating multiple contexts and settings that foster the *behavioral component* of psychological empowerment. Moreover, PSU's leadership development program has graduated more than 3,500 participants (PSU, 2017). Interviews with former participants indicate that many of them attribute their development as community leaders to their involvement in PSU. The following quotation provides just one example that appears to indicate the development of sociopolitical control, or the *emotional component* of psychological empowerment: "Student Union really showed me how I can use my strengths to be a part of something bigger and how I can contribute myself to making this world a better place, not off in some distant future, but now in the present" (J. Conner, 2014, p. 464). Similarly, another alumnus said: "It's given me the confidence that I can take the lead on pretty much any issue that I find important" (J. O. Conner, 2011, p. 936). PSU can therefore be seen as an organization that is providing opportunities for participation and the development of new civic leaders.

Organizationally, PSU provides an example of a diverse *opportunity role structure*, with chapters formed in different high schools in the city (six schools as of 2013, per Conner and Rosen). These school-based chapters organize on school-specific issues, in addition to driving and participating in citywide campaigns. This multilevel organizational structure creates many different settings that contain opportunities for meaningful participation and leadership development. The group as a whole and the chapters remain youth-led, and youth make the key decisions (e.g., regarding which issues to prioritize and which mobilization strategies to select), but older people, including paid staff, support the organization in a variety of ways. Some of the adults who are involved are themselves alumni of PSU, meaning that they became leaders in the organization when they were in high school. In the situational dimension, then, the growth of the organization, its persistence over two decades, and its ability to develop numerous leaders in the community provides indications that organizational empowerment processes (*leadership development, organizational viability*) are taking place.

Moreover, alumni of PSU have indicated that the organization served a context that fostered *social support* and a *sense of community* within the organization. For example, one former participant, describing their experiences, highlighted "the importance of friendship. In order to be a part of a group and be friends is a major thing. You can't really do work with someone you don't get along with. So having friends and being friends in an organization like Student Union makes it more powerful" (J. Conner, 2014, p. 466).

The mobilization efforts of PSU have often proven effective in exerting influence in education policy in Philadelphia. For example, interviews with a range of stakeholders in education policy in the city credited PSU with having played key roles in blocking the takeover of the city schools by a private company in 2002, with having successfully advocated for increased funding for Philadelphia education in the 2008 state budget, and with the creation of student success centers in Philadelphia city schools. PSU's actions are therefore often effective in shifting the outcomes of publicly visible policy debates, and this is reflected in their reputation as a powerful group among other stakeholders in the education policy arena in Philadelphia (J. Conner et al., 2013). Furthermore, although studies have not specifically addressed *collective efficacy* in regard to PSU,[13] it is likely that by shifting adults' attitudes about youth, they are contributing to collective efficacy in Philadelphia neighborhoods. This can be glimpsed in anecdotes, such as when the chief school safety officer in the Philadelphia schools went from telling students that they needed to "know their place" and "submit to authority" to supporting student-led trainings for school police officers (Dzurinko et al., 2011). By demonstrating that students can help to maintain safe environments, therefore, PSU is likely contributing to collective efficacy in schools and surrounding neighborhoods.

Institutional

Students participating in PSU build networks of relationships within their schools and throughout the city. These relationships are essential to how PSU selects and prioritizes issues, potential solutions, and strategies for action. For example, in the aftermath of an incident at one high school in Philadelphia, in which police placed the school on "lockdown" and an altercation took place between police and students, PSU members were critical of the city and school responses, as well as how the incident was being represented in local media. PSU held a listening campaign with fellow students and discovered two major concerns that many students shared: (a) Ninth graders did not feel adequately supported in their transition to high school, and (b) students repeatedly cited negative interactions with particular police officers. After the listening campaign, a press conference was held to draw attention to student perspectives. This was followed by a facilitated dialogue with security staff, which led to better understanding and improved relationships between students and police at the school (Dzurinko et al., 2011).

Many other examples of *relational* and organizational empowerment processes can be seen in PSU's work. For instance, deeply ingrained group norms help to develop collectivist leadership within PSU. For example, Rosen (2012) described the groups' emphasis on "stepping up" and then "stepping back" to create room for newer members to take visible roles and to take responsibility and ownership of the group's work. One participant expressed the understanding that underpins this practice: "A leader is only defined by the leaders he helps to build" (p. 226). Furthermore, in the aftermath of violent conflicts taking place between Asian and African American students in one school, students representing both groups held meetings to build relationships and common purpose (*co-empowered subgroups*; Dzurinko et al., 2011). As in many other community organizing initiatives, these relationships are the foundation of the social power that PSU exercises. The networks that PSU weaves also enable the organization to identify pressing issues and potential solutions. These priorities often differ from the concerns of school leaders, the police, or the media. PSU's actions have created bridges between students in different schools across the city, between students identifying with different racial/ethnic groups, and between students, school staff, and local decision-makers.

Also, PSU has been active in forming collaborations with other organizations. For example, PSU has worked with another local youth-organizing group, Youth United for Change (YUC), "to define and advocate for a citywide high school equity agenda" (S. Shah & Mediratta, 2008, p. 55). PSU and YUC also worked with seven other youth-organizing and youth development organizations to launch the Campaign for Nonviolent Schools in 2010, a coalition effort that explicitly seeks changes at the systemic, school, and individual levels (Dzurinko et al., 2011). Moreover, PSU is active in multiscalar networks, playing prominent roles in national *networks and coalitions* like the Journey for Justice[14] alliance, which exists to strengthen community-led resistance to dismantling of public education systems in 24 cities across the United States and in Johannesburg, South Africa.

Clearly, PSU is operating in community power's second (institutional) dimension by bringing attention to issues and perspectives that might otherwise be ignored (*issue/problem assessment capacity*) and by influencing the terms of public debates regarding education (J. Conner & Zaino, 2014). J. Conner et al. (2013) highlighted this theme of agenda setting and problem framing in their interviews with education policy stakeholders in Philadelphia:

> By constantly drawing policymakers' attention back to the ways in which
> these students are impacted by their schools' practices and policies, a

journalist believed that PSU "forced the terms of the debate to change somewhat, and the focus of the debate to keep on the students." Similarly, an academic who attended several SRC [School Reform Commission] and reform committee meetings observed: "The adults could be blabbering and arguing [about] their ridiculous agendas . . . and then they [PSU youth] could kind of bring you back to reality—back to what really was important." (p. 575–6)

It is likely, therefore, that PSU is exercising power not only when it prevails in publicly visible disputes over education policies and practices, but also, through its ability to influence agenda-setting, when it is changing the terrain on which those disputes take place, ensuring that students' concerns are reflected in education policy debates.

Systemic

Through their involvement, PSU members learn about how systemic change happens, and that it requires collective, rather than individual, action to make change (knowledge of the *source* of social power, an aspect of the *cognitive* component of psychological empowerment). J. Conner (2014) quoted an alumnus of PSU, who explained that "everyone can play a part and everybody can contribute to something. And your part is not enough on its own, but when joined in with everyone else playing their part, it's a powerful force. . . . The sum of all our parts is greater than the whole" (p. 474). It is also evident that PSU participants understand that achieving systemic changes requires both collaboration and conflict (or the *nature* of social power). For example, J. Conner and Zaino (2014) described PSU's status as both an insider and an outsider in education policymaking in the city, and J. Conner et al. (2013) reported that stakeholders in the city's education system perceived PSU to be both an adversary and an ally. For example, although many respect PSU as a collaborator,

> Respondents within the district explained how PSU protests and actions "freak people out" and make administrators think, "Oh my God! They're not going to go away. What do we do? . . . or What can we do to make that never happen again?" Because journalists "pay attention" to the students' voices, take them seriously, and "quote them extensively," PSU has been able to build political capital, which has helped it to become a force to be reckoned with inside the district. (p. 578)

Considering these descriptions of PSU's ability to pursue change using conflict alongside the descriptions of their collaborative change efforts, it is clear that participants are capable of strategically pursuing change using collaboration or conflict as the situation requires.

It is also evident that PSU members engage in *critical analysis* of power and the root causes of issues in the Philadelphia education system (or *critical reflection*). For instance, J. Conner (2014) quoted a recent graduate of PSU's leadership development program: "We were learning about oppression, racism, sexism, capitalism, globalization, all these different kinds of things. That's political education. That's enhancing your mind to learn about the world and it's just really cool" (p. 461). Through her interviews of other PSU alumni, Conner found that PSU participants were able to connect problems faced in their educational environments to specific sociopolitical forces at the city and national levels. For example, one alumnus said: "I learned about everything that was going on systemically with my education and in relation to the city of Philadelphia and the country—why my school didn't have certain resources and other schools across the city border did" (p. 461).

These critical analyses of power inform many of PSU's actions, from the selection of issues to strategies for collective action. Some of the actions taken by PSU are specifically intended to *reshape public understanding of issues* and of the roles that different groups play in education systems. For example, PSU has rejected the dominant narrative indicating that there is a problem of "youth violence" in Philadelphia schools and has instead "flipped the script" by drawing attention to some of the root causes of lack of safety in school environments, including overpolicing, lack of trust between teachers and students, and prison-like school environments (Dzurinko et al., 2011). Moreover, they are intentional in their public messaging to connect these issues to social forces such as poverty and neoliberalism (J. Conner & Rosen, 2013). They have thus been able to *shift public narratives* in the city—as evinced by changes in the ways that other stakeholders and decision-makers think about issues such as educational equity, investments in public schools, and the roles that young people can play in the sociopolitical arena (J. Conner & Rosen, 2013; J. Conner et al., 2013).

Conclusions

When successful at achieving their aims, empowerment processes can alter community power structures. To understand these ecological dynamics, we can think of communities as the sets of social patterns shaping interactions between various local "games," and thus the relationships among systems, including support systems for improving quality of life. Changing these patterns involves the development and exercise of social power through cyclical processes that, when successful, tend to have certain distinguishing features in common. A lack of clarity on what these common processes might be has long been a major hindrance to overall understanding of community power and empowerment. For example, in studies that have sought to empirically examine community empowerment processes, there has been little conceptual consistency, limiting comparability and the accumulation of knowledge.

Drawing on theory and existing research, as well as on models for grassroots community-organizing and social movements, this chapter has presented a set of features of community empowerment processes (Table 6.2) that can be understood in relationship to psychological and organizational empowerment processes (Table 6.3) and according to the three-dimensional view of community power. This multifeature framework can be used to understand complex empowerment processes, which may exhibit strengths in some dimensions of community power while exhibiting weaknesses in others (e.g., Gotham & Campanella, 2011). Taken together with the frameworks presented in the other chapters in this section, this represents a new take on the ecology of empowerment—one that emphasizes its relationship to community power and the inextricability of different "levels" of human ecology. Although this framework will certainly benefit from future refinements, it nevertheless has potential to move empowerment theory and empowerment-oriented practice forward past some long-standing hurdles and toward greater clarity and effectiveness. In the next section of this book, I first explore how these processes operate holistically to drive outcomes and impacts (Chapter 7) and then explore how this reworking of empowerment theory can inform future designs for research and systems change efforts.

Appendix 6.1   Neighborhood Collective Efficacy: Informal Social Control and Social Cohesion and Trust

Item	Item Wording
Stem: *Please rate the likelihood that neighbors could be counted on to intervene if:*	
CE-1	Children were skipping school and hanging out on a street corner
CE-2	Children were spray-painting graffiti on a local building
CE-3	Children were showing disrespect to an adult
CE-4	A fight broke out in front of their house
CE-5	The fire station closest to their home was threatened with budget cuts
Stem: *Please rate your agreement or disagreement with the following statements:*	
CE-6	People around here are willing to help their neighbors
CE-7	This is a close-knit neighborhood
CE-8	People in this neighborhood can be trusted
CE-9	People in this neighborhood generally don't get along with each other*
CE-10	People in this neighborhood do not share the same values*

Note: Items CE1 through CE5 are indicators for informal social control, while Items CE6 through CE10 are indicators for social cohesion and trust.

* Indicates reverse-coded item.

Source: Sampson, Raudenbush, and Earls (1997).

Appendix 6.2   System Justification Scale: Fairness, Legitimacy, and Justifiability of the Prevailing Social System

Stem: *Please rate your agreement or disagreement with the following statements:*

Item	Item Wording
SJ-1	In general, you find society to be fair.
SJ-2	In general, the [*American*] political system operates as it should.
SJ-3	[*American*] society needs to be radically restructured.*
SJ-4	[*The United States*] is the best country to live in.
SJ-5	Most policies serve the greater good.
SJ-6	Everyone has a fair shot at wealth and happiness.
SJ-7	Our society is getting worse every year.*
SJ-8	Society is set up so that people usually get what they deserve.

Note: Bracketed terms refer specifically to the United States but could be modified for other countries or levels of analysis (e.g., cities or states instead of nation states) as relevant.

* Indicates reverse-coded item.

Source: Kay and Jost (2003).

Notes

1. In Gaventa's (1980) study, for example, the company, the union, the miners, the news media, and other organizations and interests are all included in the study of community power structure. This is in keeping with the earlier methods of studying community power structure.

2. This relational concept of community is consistent with how I believe we should be viewing psychology and organizations in a transactional–ecological framework that best serves inquiry on community empowerment.

3. Referring to "games" in this definition of community is of course Norton Long's (1958) terminology. If we were to follow Bronfenbrenner's ecological systems theory, we might replace games with "exosystems," for instance, in an example provided by J. W. Neal and Neal (2013).

4. Here, I necessarily draw only very selectively on concepts from social movement studies. For instance, resource mobilization theories and political process theories, which seek to describe social movements in ways that mirror rational actor approaches to economics, are not addressed. As we saw in Chapters 2 and 3, rational actor approaches are of limited value for understanding community power. Although new social movements (NSMs) are (debatably) useful as a descriptive category in social movement studies, I have not encountered concepts that have emerged uniquely from studies of NSMs that seem particularly relevant to a framework for community empowerment.

5. However, as Watts and Hipolito-Delgado (2015) pointed out, critical consciousness is unlikely to lead to sustained sociopolitical action in the absence of other conditions in group settings, such as leadership and mobilizing skills.

6. In a subsequent publication, Lippman and colleagues (2016) developed a measure for community mobilization with items that mapped onto each of these domains, as well as a seventh: social control (complementing the social cohesion domain for fuller understanding of collective efficacy). This Community Mobilization Measure was developed and tested in a rural South African context. The shared-concern domain was geared specifically toward concerns around HIV prevention, but the other six domains were not. Social control and social cohesion are adaptations of the measure by Sampson et al. (1997). The remaining domains refer to opinions of the village/community or frequencies or likelihoods of particular forms of action. Scrutinizing many of the items in the measure, it is clear that while the conceptual synthesis that preceded it is valuable, work remains to identify specific indicators that map onto the identified conceptual domains.

7. For example, the Chinese government encourages many forms of volunteering and participation in civil society, while suppressing forms of civic engagement that challenge governmental authority (Zhao, Haste, Selman, & Luan, 2014). In the United States, government-sanctioned violence has been used to suppress movements that threatened oligarchic control or racial hierarchies, such as the Black Power movement (Brewer & Heitzeg, 2008), while promoting many other forms of civic expression that are less challenging to the status quo.

8. This is as described in the experiential learning praxis mechanism for psychological empowerment in Chapter 4.

9. Although culture and difference can be useful in resistance to domination, in highly diverse communities, they can also limit the degree of solidarity and therefore the potential to resist larger forces such as global corporations (Sites, 2007).

10. Yet, in many cases participatory budgeting's implementation has suffered from being disconnected from actual local power structures and decision-making. As Baiocchi and Ganuza (2014) argued, for efforts like these to reach their true emancipatory potential, they must combine a communicative dimension (defined as active and inclusive public deliberation) with an empowerment dimension (defined as the degree of actual power that participants in the process have over the budget, as well as over the rules of participation).

11. Although it has some similarities to groups that I have worked with, I have not had any involvement with PSU. I use it as an example here in part because it has been active for more than 20 years. During that time, it has been prominently featured in both research and media accounts, providing enough published secondary material to at least touch on every aspect of the model for empowerment processes presented in this chapter.

12. One limitation of such a secondary source analysis, for instance, is that it likely glosses over much of the complexity and dynamism that characterize most youth-organizing initiatives. PSU's organization and power have undoubtedly ebbed and flowed over the years, and some of the observations cited here may be capturing particular periods of strength and effectiveness while devoting less attention to time periods when the group was less effective.

13. Although no studies that I have encountered have specifically addressed PSU's role in building collective efficacy, there are studies that suggest it. For example, Suess and Lewis (2007) indicated that the persistence of PSU youth organizers has reminded adults not to give up in their efforts for school and neighborhood improvements and has thereby strengthened civic capacity.

14. As of 2018, PSU was one of nine local organizations on the coordinating committee of Journey for Justice (https://www.j4jalliance.com/members/)

7

Health and Well-Being

Introduction

Community power structures shape the policies and institutional practices that create or destroy opportunities for people to survive and to thrive. The ecological definition of empowerment, prominently advanced by Rappaport (1981, 1987) and adopted by many others, is a process by which people, organizations, and communities gain greater control over their lives; it is premised on the belief that such enhanced control helps those gaining it to realize their full potential. By changing community power structures, policies, and institutions, they may also influence others' well-being. The ultimate intended outcome of empowerment processes is therefore greater human flourishing, including improvements in health and enhanced well-being across life domains (i.e., beyond the sociopolitical domain). In much of the literature on empowerment, the links between empowerment processes and these impacts on health and well-being are implicit or mentioned briefly but have not been specified in detail. In this chapter, I examine the multiple pathways through which empowerment processes have impacts on health and well-being.

Ecological theories of empowerment have often made distinctions between processes and outcomes (Zimmerman, 2000). For instance, the framework for organizational empowerment by N. A. Peterson and Zimmerman (2004) identifies features of empowerment processes within and between organizations that lead to empowered organizational outcomes. These frameworks have sought specific observable indicators of the effects of empowerment processes within the same domains and settings. For example, enhancing the opportunity role structure within organizational settings is likely to lead to the outcome of more underpopulated settings and so on.

Like the example, however, many of the proposed outcomes of empowerment processes are themselves process indicators (such as underpopulated settings). In some cases, they are very closely conceptually related to the processes whose effects they are intended to indicate. For example, the formation of subgroup linkages (process) is indicated by co-empowered subgroups (outcome). Outcomes like these do not designate the ultimate intended impacts of empowerment processes but are instead designated as clear indicators that processes are occurring and resulting in changes in patterns of behaviors and social relations (or social regularities) within settings. This is why I labeled them as process indicators in previous chapters.

Many have pointed to a need to distinguish more clearly between process indicators, longer term outcomes, and impacts of empoerment processes (e.g., Jason et al., 2016). One way to discuss these distinctions is to use concepts from logic modeling and theories of change (e.g., Kellogg Foundation, 2004) to designate some observable phenomena as outputs of processes, some as direct outcomes of processes, some as intermediate outcomes of processes, along the way toward ultimate impacts of these chains of cause and effect. In proceeding down this path, it is worth acknowledging and seeking to avoid some of the conceptual and terminological confusion that sometimes accompanies some of these terms associated with logic models of this sort (see Krieger, 2008).[1] Furthermore, there are limits to how specific empowerment theory can productively be in an overarching sense. Empowerment processes vary considerably in different contexts. In a broad sense, however, many of the outcomes that have been identified in existing research on empowerment can best be thought of as outputs or process indicators, while others are longer term cumulative outcomes of those processes, and still others are best considered as intermediate outcomes between these two ends of the spectrum. There is a need for greater clarity on how processes and observable outputs of processes are linked to power and, ultimately, to health and well-being.

It may be helpful here to once again revisit a widely accepted definition of empowerment as a *process* through which people, organizations, and communities gain greater control over their lives and environments. Empowerment is defined as a process, not as a set of processes and outcomes. Of course, processes have numerous outcomes as they unfold, but their outcomes are not the same as the processes, although the two are closely related. Even though they represented an useful theoretical distinction that continues to be widely used (e.g., Christens, Peterson, et al., 2014), I have come to believe that the terms *empowering processes* and *empowered outcomes* can be subtly misleading in their connotations. If successful empowerment processes result in participants having greater control over their lives and environments, then the most imminent outcome of empowerment processes could better be referred to as *social power*. Recall Wright's definition of social power (cited in Chapter 2) as "power rooted in voluntary cooperation through collective action" (2013, p. 19).

Fixing our sights on social power as a *primary* outcome of empowerment processes helps to maintain a focus on transformational change. As Speer (2008) pointed out, the goal of empowerment theory and practice should be restructuring of social and structural systems, rather than other types of social change. Restructuring can be differentiated from two other categories of social changes: tuning and incremental changes (Seidman, 1988). Restructuring refers to changes involving subgroups gaining or losing resources relative to the sociopolitical whole through "a fundamental alteration of the existing social regularities or the creation of new sociostructural regularities" (p. 20). In contrast, tuning describes adaptive changes on the part of individuals, groups, and settings. Incremental change, in turn, involves gradual changes across whole populations through, for instance, improved services that have beneficial effects across whole populations but do not alter the disparities between groups. Changes in each of these categories can result in effects that we would likely consider beneficial, but because empowerment is about changes in social power and power relations, outcomes of empowerment processes should involve at least some element of restructuring (Speer, 2008). An emphasis on social power as the primary outcome of empowerment processes helps to maintain and strengthen empowerment theory's emphasis on transformational or liberatory change (Prilleltensky, 2008).

What have been referred to as "empowered outcomes" in some research and theory can, I believe, be usefully sorted into several categories of outcomes along hypothesized causal pathways. Some are best thought of as process indicators, or observable outputs from empowerment processes. For instance, increases in meeting participation or underpopulated settings within voluntary organizations are indications that empowerment processes are taking place in specific settings within an organization or community. These process indicators are necessary but insufficient conditions for the development and exercise of social power.

Other outcomes such as interorganizational network mobilization, collective action, pursuit of systems change, and strategic action to shift narratives/frames are more direct indicators that social power is being built and exercised. These indicators of social power go beyond indications that empowerment processes are taking place and suggest that they are having an effect through the development and exercise of social power. Further, some "empowered outcomes" are best thought of as neither process outputs nor direct indicators of social power. This other category of phenomena, ranging from some of the observable changes associated with psychological empowerment processes to the policy and systems changes that result from the exercise of social power, can be thought of as intermediate outcomes between the exercise of social power and the ultimate *impacts* of empowerment processes: improvements in health and well-being. These intermediate outcomes do not occur immediately (or, often, solely) as a result of the empowerment processes taking place in the community. But, they are causally, cumulatively, and bidirectionally related. Finally, when social power is exercised to change policies and systems, the explicit hypothesized impacts of these chains of events and influences are improvements in the health and well-being of communities, particularly among more marginalized or disadvantaged groups.

This is not a single, linear causal chain. Empowerment theory, however, has not yet clearly distinguished among the various mechanisms or causal pathways through which these impacts on the health and well-being of communities are occurring. For instance, some beneficial effects accrue primarily to participants in empowerment processes, whereas others are likely radiating out or spilling over to others in the broader community. As a step toward clarifying some of these distinctions, Figure 7.1 provides a concept map of some of the categories of outcomes described thus far and introduces a distinction between three pathways through which empowerment processes have impacts on health and well-being through the development and exercise of social power. On the left side of the figure are empowerment processes, which can be conceptualized as a cycle (Cattaneo & Chapman, 2010). Moving to the right are intermediate outcomes and impacts on health and well-being grouped into three categories of pathways.

These three categories I term (a) participant pathways, (b) ecological pathways, and (c) pluralist pathways. In each category, the term *pathways* is plural to indicate that there are multiple pathways within each of these categories. Participant pathways refer to the category of effects primarily or solely on those residents who are themselves participating in and leading systems change efforts. Ecological pathways refer to the category of impacts on health and well-being that result from successful efforts to change to policies, systems, and environments. Finally, pluralist pathways refer to the beneficial effects of living in a community with a more balanced or egalitarian power structure.

These three sets of pathways are not entirely distinct from each other. Many times, there are interrelationships between them. Separating them conceptually, however, serves a heuristic purpose. In much of the empowerment literature, it has been difficult to discern whether effects are being described as part of one, several, or all three of these sets of pathways. Distinguishing them from each other can

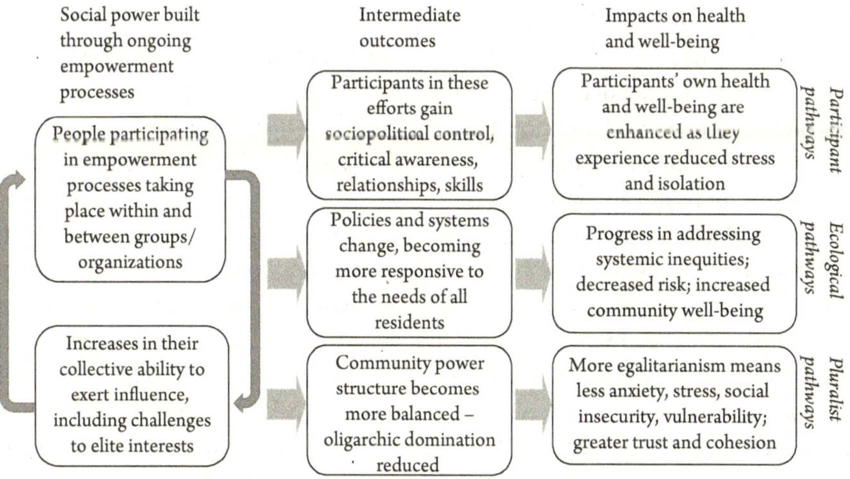

Figure 7.1. Pathways from empowerment processes to outcomes and impacts.

help achieve greater clarity and precision in interpreting and assessing existing evidence and designing future research and evaluation of empowerment processes. To be clear, processes that are building and exercising social power and achieving social changes that involve restructuring are likely influencing health and well-being through all three of these sets of pathways simultaneously. When studying empowerment processes, sometimes we are only able to account for effects along one, or maybe two, of these pathways, typically due to time and other resource constraints. Distinguishing participant, ecological, and pluralist pathways from each other allows us to more clearly identify and examine the chains of cause and effect that promote health and well-being and to more clearly situate specific lines of inquiry and research findings within a holistic framework.

These three sets of pathways can be understood, in some cases, along a continuum of scale. The effects described in the participant pathway, for instance, tend to involve only a relatively small subset of the total population in a community. Effects along this pathway are likely to precede any changes in the broader community's health and well-being, and gains are likely to be more pronounced among participants. Ecological effects, in contrast, can vary in scale but can be as small as a setting or neighborhood. Improvements in a school or creation of a new community center, park, or farmers' market, for instance, are likely contributing to gradual, diffuse improvements in health and well-being in neighborhoods. Other changes to policies and systems—housing and transportation policy, for instance—can have effects on whole cities or even larger geographies. Together, these smaller and larger scale ecological changes exert cumulative influences on the health and well-being of residents, whether or not those residents are participating directly in the empowerment processes driving those changes.

Finally, the pluralist pathway describes effects that tend to operate on the level of whole communities or even larger geographies. There is mounting evidence suggesting that the political ecology (or power structure) of a community exerts an influence on health and well-being that is distinct from, but of course related to, other ecological influences. To the extent that empowerment processes are truly restructuring power relations and creating more egalitarian political economies and ecologies, therefore, this suggests that they are, in the process, improving the conditions for health and well-being.

The model represented in Figure 7.1 is a high-level concept map, and it is inevitably oversimplifying some very complicated chains of influence and causation. There are bidirectional influences, cycles, and feedback loops operating in each of these three sets of pathways that are not depicted. The intent is not to suggest that these three sets of pathways operate in a linear and parallel fashion or that their causes and effects are entirely distinct. Instead, the goal is to clarify what I believe are some important categorical distinctions that can help to disentangle the various mechanisms through which empowerment processes are simultaneously promoting health and well-being. Clearly distinguishing categories of causal mechanisms that have often been conflated enables us to strategically situate lines of inquiry more specifically within one or across several of these hypothesized causal mechanisms. In the remainder of this chapter, therefore, I delve more deeply into each of these three sets of pathways in turn. Before doing that, however, the impacts designated by this model, health and well-being, merit a closer look.

What Is Meant by Health and Well-Being?

Health and well-being: these two terms are often used together. In health sciences, policy, and fields of practice (i.e., medicine, public health, health promotion), this pairing is often intended to indicate a broadening of the definition of health from the traditional biomedical model (in which health is defined more narrowly as the absence of diseases) toward a biopsychosocial model of health, in which health is viewed as encompassing the social and psychological factors that interact with and influence physical health. For instance, the World Health Organization's (WHO's) definition of health is "a state of complete physical, mental, and social well-being and not merely the absence of disease or infirmity" (Commission on the Social Determinants of Health [CSDH], 2008, p. 33).

This broader definition of health is consistent with evidence on the interrelatedness of physical health with social and psychological dynamics. Definitions of health like the those of WHO are therefore important for influencing attempts to promote public health because they encompass the wider array of modifiable influences (from behaviors to economics and the social and physical environment) without unduly emphasizing the potential of clinical or behavioral services to improve health. At population levels in the United States, for instance, access to healthcare and the quality of healthcare together account for only around 20% of the variance in life expectancy and quality of life, according to the County Health Rankings model (Remington, Catlin, & Gennuso, 2015).[2]

More expansive definitions of health, however, rarely provide specificity on the social and psychological factors that comprise well-being. An interdisciplinary literature review by de Chavez, Backett-Milburn, Parry, and Platt (2005), for instance, concluded that although well-being functions as a unifying concept for researchers and practitioners, different disciplines tend to emphasize different aspects of it, and few have offered comprehensive definitions. In other words, much like empowerment, the strategic attraction to "well-being" has not been matched with conceptual clarity and precision.

Perhaps the most prevalent misconception is that well-being simply means happiness. This is common in the economics literature in particular but can also be found in psychology. Some psychologists have indicated, for instance, that prevention programs should seek to increase kindness, forgiveness, positive expectancies and attributions, optimism, and other so-called positive psychological characteristics, despite evidence that the relationships between these characteristics and processes and indicators of well-being (including happiness) are highly contingent on contexts (McNulty & Fincham, 2012). Others have sought to clearly define well-being in ways that go beyond happiness. Diener, for instance, defined subjective well-being as "an umbrella term for different valuations that people make regarding their lives, the events happening to them, their bodies and minds, and the circumstances in which they live" (Diener, 2006, p. 400). Yet, others have pointed out that this broad definition mixes elements of life satisfaction, psychological well-being, and subjective well-being in a way that makes it virtually conceptually indistinguishable from earlier work on quality of life (Camfield & Skevington, 2008).

In fact, these concepts are all quite closely related, and a good case can be made for combining them as constituent dimensions of overall well-being. For instance, Prilleltensky et al. (2015) defined overall well-being in a way that subsumes elements of quality of life, life satisfaction, and subjective well-being yet has separate subscales for different life domains. Their measure of overall well-being contains six factors corresponding to interpersonal, community, occupational, physical, psychological, and economic well-being. In each of these domains, survey respondents are asked to rate their status (e.g., their physical health and wellness, their economic situation, the community where they live) along a scale from the worst to the best that their life could be, as well as to indicate where they think they will stand along this scale 1 year from that moment. The strength of this approach is that it is both a holistic and a domain-specific way of assessing overall well-being.

It also bears mentioning that some scholars have sought to develop more expansive contextual understanding of *community well-being* to avoid both the individualism inherent in subjective assessments of well-being as well and the generality of national indicators. Wiseman and Brasher (2008), for instance, defined community well-being as "the combination of social, economic, environmental, cultural, and political conditions identified by individuals and their communities as essential for them to flourish and fulfil their potential" (p. 358). And, some research is seeking to assess elements of community well-being. For instance, a study of older adults in Spain identified three dimensions of community well-being: community services, community attachment, and the physical and social environment (Forjaz et al., 2011). These efforts seek to locate community well-being in the systems and structures that affect people's daily lives, rather than solely relying on people's subjective assessments or satisfaction. These contributions represent a distinct strand in the literature on well-being that has more in common with concepts such as livability (Badland et al., 2014) than it does with most other efforts to define well-being. In Figure 7.1, for example, these conditions are indicated as intermediate outcomes in the ecological pathway rather than as impacts on health and well-being.

For present purposes, therefore, the concept of overall well-being developed by Prilleltensky and colleagues (2015) provides a definition of well-being that is consonant with WHO's definition of health as "a state of complete physical, mental, and social well-being and not merely the absence of disease or infirmity" (p. 33). When theorizing the links between empowerment processes and health and well-being, then, my claim here is that the development and exercise of social power is positively—through multiple pathways—influencing both people's assessment of their own quality of life across various life domains (e.g., interpersonal, community, economic) and their aggregate health behaviors and health outcomes, which are likely improving as a result. The order or timing of these improvements and the levels at which they are occurring vary, and understanding these differences is a benefit of disentangling some of these causal pathways.

Damaging Effects of Stress

Within each of the three categories of pathways identified in Figure 7.1 (participant, ecological, and pluralist), there are multiple mechanisms in effect. Many of these mechanisms have to do with disrupting, mediating, or buffering the effects of stress on health and well-being. Through advancements across multiple fields of study, we are rapidly gaining better understanding of how stress inflicts damage on people's health and well-being. Summarizing decades of research evidence, Thoits (2010) offered five major overarching findings: (a) stress, defined comprehensively to include negative events, chronic stress, and trauma, exerts substantial negative influence on physical and mental health; (b) differential exposure to stressors maintains disparities between demographic groups (e.g., racial/ethnic, gender) in health and well-being; (c) discrimination stress experienced by members of marginalized groups exerts an additional negative influence on health and well-being; (d) the differential cumulative impacts of stressors across the life span of individuals and across generations operate to widen disparities between groups; and finally (e) the negative effects of stress on health and well-being can be reduced or "buffered" when people have high levels of mastery, self-esteem, or social support.

The damaging effects of stress are being uncovered across a range of diseases and physical and mental health outcomes. For example, recent advances have been made in understanding the relationships between stressors earlier in life and a range of outcomes later in life, such as cardiovascular disease (Steptoe & Kivimäki, 2013); depression (Hammen, 2005); suicide ideation (Thompson et al., 2012); cancer (Reiche, Nunes, & Morimoto, 2004); obesity (Foss & Dyrstad, 2011); Type 2 diabetes; and other age-related diseases (Danese & McEwen, 2012). Rates of prematurity and poor birth outcomes are linked to stress not only during pregnancy but also throughout the life-course of the mother (Livingood et al., 2010; Lu & Halfon, 2003).

The physiological mechanisms of these effects of stress on poor health outcomes across the life course are still being discovered, but it is clear that they have to do with the body's inflammatory responses to stress, the immune and endocrine systems, and priming of neural circuitry (Shonkoff, Boyce, & McEwen, 2009;

Wilkinson & Pickett, 2010). Some of these responses to stress may have served humans well in other evolutionary eras, enabling us, for instance, to respond well to short-term environmental stressors and threats, but they are not well adapted to the chronic stressors often experienced in modern life (Raison & Miller, 2013), particularly for those living in poverty, who tend to experience disproportionate levels of chronic stress (Santiago, Wadsworth, & Stump, 2011; Underlid, 2007). In each of the hypothesized pathways through which empowerment affects health and well-being, reducing or buffering the deleterious and compounding effects of stress plays crucial roles.

Participant Pathways

This first set of pathways, participant pathways, refers to effects on participants in empowerment processes. As Chapter 4 detailed, participating in community change efforts leads to psychological empowerment among participants. Yet, gains across some components of psychological empowerment (i.e., cognitive, emotional) do not tend to unfold evenly, even among participants in relatively successful empowerment processes. Furthermore, characteristics of participants—their racial, ethnic, and gender identities and their levels of income and education—play mediating and moderating roles in how psychological empowerment tends to progress, on average. And, not all systems change efforts in which people participate are successful, particularly over shorter time periods. It stands to reason, then, that participants in unsuccessful efforts (i.e., disempowering processes) would not benefit to the same degree or might even experience deleterious effects—the inverse of these participant pathways. Nevertheless, mounting research does point to beneficial effects of psychological empowerment processes on health and well-being. These effects can be grouped into three related pathways: connectedness and support, purpose and control, and critical awareness.

Connectedness and Support

In empowering community and organizational settings, participants give and receive social support to other members (Maton, 2008; Maton & Salem, 1995). Receiving and (especially) giving social support in organizational contexts has been found to be positively related to self-appraisals of psychological well-being (Maton, 1988). There are numerous mental health benefits to social ties and connectedness (Kawachi & Berkman, 2001). Thoits (2011), for example, described a variety of functions of social support in promoting health and well-being. These functions include emotional, informational, and instrumental forms of help, expression, and influence. The benefits of giving and receiving (and perceiving) social support include a sense of belonging and companionship, of purpose and meaning, and of self-esteem and social control. Participants in empowerment processes are therefore contributing to their own well-being by providing social support to others and gaining greater assurance that aid and companionship is available when they themselves are in need.

Considering this, it is unsurprising that social support also plays several key roles in buffering the effects of stress (Zimmerman, Ramírez-Valles, Zapert, & Maton, 2000), particularly in cases of acute stress. There are the direct ways that social support kicks in when people are experiencing stress. Social connections directly provide emotional sustenance and active coping assistance. These forms of support tend to manifest differently among primary social support networks (close friends and significant others) than among secondary networks of others who share similar experiences (e.g., other participants in community and organizational change processes) (Thoits, 2011), and both forms of support appear to be uniquely important. Empowerment processes enable participants to build these secondary connections in community settings, and this increases their available stock of social support and also creates expectations that they, in turn, will provide social support to others. This reciprocal giving and receiving provides boosts to people's sense of purpose and meaning, belonging and companionship, self-esteem, and social control. These, in turn, act as key components of resilience in the face chronic and acute stress, providing short- and long-term benefits to well-being and health.[3]

Purpose and Control

Being involved in community change processes is also a form of meaningful instrumental activity that has been linked to improved subjective well-being (Klar & Kasser, 2009). Across many contexts, involvement in activities that people find instrumentally meaningful has been found to be positively associated with well-being. In a study of two samples of young people in the United States, for example, engagement in meaningful instrumental activity exerted a beneficial influence on psychological well-being that was distinct from the influence of social support (Maton, 1990). Involvement in meaningful instrumental activities linked to community change has also been linked to a sense of personal mastery, which Thoits (2010) identified as one of the primary mediators of the effects of stress on health and well-being. In the Chicago Community Adult Health study, Gilster (2012) found that those who had engaged in community activism reported higher levels of neighborhood and personal mastery than those who had only volunteered in the previous year. These activists reported higher levels of psychological well-being and connectedness than among other residents. Although activism was a stronger predictor of indicators of well-being than volunteerism, those who both volunteered and participated in community activism had the highest levels of self-reported well-being. These findings on mastery and meaningful instrumental activity speak to the value of a sense of purpose for promoting well-being among those involved in community change efforts.

In addition to a sense of purpose, participants in empowerment processes often gain a sense of control. Sociopolitical control, which has often been used as an indicator for the emotional component of psychological empowerment (N. A. Peterson et al., 2011; Zimmerman & Zahniser, 1991), is likely a key stress-buffering mechanism. Unlike personal mastery or self-esteem, which are global self-concepts, sociopolitical control refers specifically to a person's perceived leadership competence and ability to exert control in sociopolitical decision-making processes. Particularly for those who are experiencing stresses related to sociopolitical systems (i.e., poverty, oppression, marginalization, and discrimination), therefore, sociopolitical control is likely to be of particular importance since it specifically involves control over the same life domain responsible for the disproportionate exposure to stressors (Christens, 2012a).

Evidence indeed indicates that sociopolitical control may play a stress-buffering role (Christens & Peterson, 2012; Zimmerman et al., 1999), and that these effects may be most pronounced among participants who identify as members of more marginalized or minority racial or ethnic groups (Israel et al., 1994; Molix & Bettencourt, 2010). Yet, the evidence for this key assertion of empowerment theory is not nearly as advanced as it should be. In other domains, the buffering effects of perceived control on the negative health impacts of stress have been more rigorously scrutinized and are therefore better understood. In occupational environments, for example, it has been well established that when high demands are coupled with low control, and when there is an imbalance in effort and rewards, this produces increases in occupational stress that are deleterious to both shorter term self-rated health and longer term health outcomes, such as cardiovascular disease (Kivimäki et al., 2004; Siegrist & Marmot, 2004). We can extrapolate from these findings that there is a likelihood that sociopolitical control plays a similarly unique stress-buffering role in the effects of sociopolitical stressors on short- and longer term health, but there is a need for longitudinal and population representative studies to examine this hypothesis in greater detail. In addition to buffering the effects of chronic stressors, empowerment is closely conceptually related to resilience (Brodsky & Cattaneo, 2013), which involves the ability to adapt to, withstand, and resist both chronic and acute stressors.[4]

Yet, there is an inherent "dark side" risk that has also not been sufficiently addressed in empowerment research to date. Many resident-driven efforts are unsuccessful at achieving their goals for policy and systems change. Social change organizations fail to achieve transformative goals, and many go dormant or dissolve after succumbing to internal and external pressures (Chetkovich & Kunreuther, 2006). In some cases, participants may experience disempowerment resulting in progressive diminishment in sociopolitical control (e.g., Cornish, Campbell, Shukla, & Banerji, 2012; Gaventa, 1980). We may surmise that this has negative effects on health and well-being. In fact, sociopolitical control was initially theorized as "learned hopefulness" (Zimmerman, 1990b), influenced by the concept of learned helplessness, which has well-established negative effects on health and well-being (Seligman, 1975). Certainly not everyone who participates in change efforts that do not succeed in their often-ambitious transformative goals experiences sustained helplessness, but a goal for future research should be to discover which community and organizational processes do in fact produce short- and longer term deficits in sociopolitical control and the relationship between these forms of disempowerment and health and well-being.

Critical Awareness

Participants in empowerment processes often gain insights into how society works, including the roles that various structural forces play in shaping individual circumstances and outcomes. Recall that the cognitive component of psychological empowerment, described in greater detail in Chapter 4, involves critical understanding of systems, environments, and the forces that shape them, as well as strategic understanding of what is required to make change. For the sake of brevity here, I refer to these psychological processes and outcomes involving critical consciousness and the cognitive component of psychological empowerment simply by the shorthand of "critical awareness." We have some evidence that critical awareness is associated with higher levels of mental well-being (e.g., Christens et al., 2013), yet the relationships between gains in critical awareness and health and well-being are likely more complex than the two other participant pathways described thus far.

As an example, awareness of neighborhood problems not only can spark participation but also can exert a dampening effect on the neighborhood sense of community (N. A. Peterson & Reid, 2003). Moreover, there is some evidence of a positive relationship between people's critical understanding of social power and a sense of alienation (Christens, Speer, et al., 2011), which is in turn negatively related to sociopolitical control and some indicators of mental well-being. Yet, some of the complexity in this multivariate puzzle has to do with the disparate ways that psychological empowerment may unfold in members of different demographic groups. In brief, members of more marginalized groups tend on average to have higher levels of critical awareness and also tend to gain critical awareness more readily through community and organizational participation than do members of more privileged groups (Christens et al., 2013; Christens, Speer, et al., 2011; N. A. Peterson et al., 2002).

There may be particularly pronounced benefits of critical awareness for those who experience oppression or identify as part of marginalized groups. Learning about the structural conditions that create disadvantages and systems of oppression may be a part of healing from traumas and developing hope for transformation (Ginwright, 2010). Indeed, there is stronger evidence of the benefits of critical awareness specifically among less advantaged groups. This is partly because the development of critical consciousness has most often been studied among racial/ethnic minority youth in urban areas (e.g., Diemer & Blustein, 2006; Diemer & Li, 2011). From these studies, there is evidence that development of critical consciousness promotes civic engagement and educational and career aspirations. The other participant pathways discussed previously (connectedness and support, purpose and control) may be of greater relative value to members of societies who are experiencing greater sociopolitical stress, but they are almost certainly also valuable stress-buffering mechanisms for members of more privileged groups. The roles that critical awareness plays for more privileged people is less well understood and perhaps more complex but is also a key topic for ongoing and future research (Wernick, 2016).

Summary: Participant Pathways

These three participant pathways—social support, purpose and control, and critical awareness—are related. For instance, social support and perceived control are positively related (Christens & Lin, 2014), and critical awareness and sociopolitical control have a complex relationship that varies among different groups (Christens et al., 2013). Community and developmental psychologists are making progress in understanding these participant pathways and their relationships to each other. Studies from other contexts and life domains offer insights that should be examined in further investigations of empowerment processes. For instance, in a recent study of technical and administrative workers, Blanch (2016) found that social support mediated the relationship between occupational control and work-related stress. The analogous multivariate mechanisms should continue to be studied and understood more clearly in community change processes.

Understanding the specific nature of the relationships between empowerment and health and well-being along participant pathways—and how these differ across contexts and among different groups—must remain a central goal of empowerment theory and empirical research. Yet, this is only one of the three sets of pathways described previously through which empowerment has an impact on health and well-being. The other two pathways—ecological and pluralist—have effects on a larger number of community residents, although their effects may be less immediate and more diffuse.

Ecological Pathways

The settings and environments in which we live our daily lives (e.g., neighborhoods, schools, homes, workplaces) exert influences on our health outcomes to a degree that is often underestimated (Earls & Carlson, 2001; Sampson, 2013). There are blatant and profound disparities manifested in these settings and environments. Take, for example, differences between schools in wealthier neighborhoods and many schools in poorer neighborhoods in the United States that struggle to meet what are often much greater needs of their students (i.e., for safety or food security), typically with fewer resources (Silverman, 2014) and politically driven reforms that are hampering their efforts (Levine & Levine, 2012). Similarly, while many people live in neighborhoods, towns, and cities where they do not fear violence on a regular basis, others regularly experience or observe violence and fear for their safety (Aber, Gershoff, Ware, & Kotler, 2004; Qouta, Punamäki, & El Sarraj, 2008). The roles that these settings play in either promoting or inhibiting human flourishing account for a large portion of the longer term inequities in outcomes (for example, racial disparities in the United States in education attainment and employment) (CSDH, 2008; Helliwell & Putnam, 2004; Nkansah-Amankra et al., 2013; Sampson, 2003).

The social ecological model of health promotion (Green, Richard, & Potvin, 1996; Stokols, 1992) provides some useful perspectives for understanding these relationships between health, well-being, and characteristics of the various environments that affect living conditions. This is parallel to (but distinct from) the ways that ecology has provided a useful metaphor for empowerment theory (D. D. Perkins et al., 1996; Rappaport, 1987). Empowerment processes, as we have seen, can be understood ecologically. The outcomes pursued by participants in empowerment processes (restructuring of policies and systems to provide improvements in daily living conditions) can likewise be viewed as changes in human ecology. Improvements in conditions can create opportunities for broader groups of people in a geographic area (beyond those who participate directly in the empowerment processes) to lead healthier lives and experience gains in well-being. It is beyond the scope of this book to comprehensively review the vast and continually growing research literature on how settings and environments influence health and well-being. Instead, in the remainder of this section, I simply highlight some of this literature that I believe provides particularly noteworthy insights that relate to community power and empowerment.

Neighborhood characteristics, for example, are consequential determinants in the distribution of human health and well-being. For instance, a variety of physical environmental factors—from transportation systems and parks and trails to the types and locations of restaurants and food vendors—have impacts on obesity-related outcomes such as nutrition and physical activity (Mayne, Auchincloss, & Michael, 2015; R. Yan, Bastian, & Griffin, 2015). School and neighborhood characteristics can lead to differential perceptions of social support, cohesion, and belonging and thereby affect mental health outcomes (Hurd, Stoddard, & Zimmerman, 2013; Maurizi, Ceballo, Epstein-Ngo, & Cortina, 2013). The density of alcohol outlets in neighborhoods has consistently been found to exert an influence on alcohol use (Cederbaum et al., 2015). Many other features of places are demonstrably influential on a variety of population-level outcomes.[5] Moreover, environmental influences and (dis)advantages have effects on human development that affect trajectories of health and well-being over the longer term (Umberson, Williams, Thomas, Liu, & Thomeer, 2014) and even across generations (Turney, 2014).

This wide variety of social and structural determinants of health has led some researchers, practitioners, and advocates to propose integrative models for organizing the various domains through which ecological conditions of places are influencing the health and well-being of residents. Badland and colleagues (2014), for example, identified a variety of domains of urban livability, including crime and safety, education, employment and income, health and social services, housing, leisure and culture, local food and other goods, public open space, and transportation. Taking an even broader view, the CSDH (2008) of WHO has issued recommendations for achieving health equity by improving living conditions across the life span. These include increasing early childhood education and development programs; creating of accessible transportation options; preventing crime through environmental design; providing safe drinking water and clean air; limiting the number of alcohol outlets; providing accessible public open spaces for leisure and recreation; promoting sustainable agriculture and rural infrastructure; creating fair employment and decent work; providing a healthy living wage; building and expanding social security (including unemployment and disability benefits) and social services systems; providing maternity leave, paid leave, and childcare; and providing universal healthcare. Because of such wide-ranging ecological influences on health and well-being, many have concluded that health and health equity should be considered in all policy decisions and have advocated and implemented this approach under the banner of "health in all policies" (Bacigalupe, Esnaola, Martín, & Zuazagoitia, 2010, p. 505).

Policy, economic, and other structural or systems changes affect health and well-being through settings and spatial effects; yet, influences on health and well-being also spread ecologically through social networks, which in turn have complicated relationships with geographic space. Describing the overlaps and differences in neighborhoods and social networks, Sampson (2003) wrote:

> The traditional perspective in urban research is premised on the notion that networks of personal ties and associations map neatly onto the geographic boundaries of spatially defined neighborhoods (e.g., census tracts), such that neighborhoods can be analyzed as indepeddent social entities. By contrast, modern neighborhoods are less distinctly defined and have permeable borders. Social networks in this setting are more likely to traverse traditional ecological boundaries, implying that social processes are not neatly contained in geographic enclaves. Social behavior is also potentially contagious and can have diffusion effects represented in spatial interdependence. (p. S60)

Some researchers are modeling processes of spatial and relational transmission of health behaviors (e.g., Frerichs, Araz, & Huang, 2013) and seeking to understand how creating new settings for healthy behaviors, social services, education, and community building can develop new networks of relationships (Alia, Freedman, Brandt, & Browne, 2014).

Some of the most compelling work on long-term human ecological impacts of policy and systems change has been done by Wallace and Wallace (R. Wallace & Wallace, 1990; D. Wallace & Wallace, 1998a, 1998b, 2000, 2008) on the effects of fires in the Bronx and Upper Manhattan in the 1970s. Wallace and Wallace empirically examined how discriminatory "policy-driven process of contagious fire and building abandonment" (D. Wallace & Wallace, 2000, p. 1245) led to dehousing and dislocation of some of New York City's poorest communities and how these dislocations were associated with longer term increases in the low-weight birth rate, in the rate of homicide, in rates of substance abuse, and in the spread of tuberculosis and AIDS (Freudenberg, Fahs, Galea, Greenberg, 2006).

These epidemics spread through the city through spatial and social networks and may have even spread to other US cities through interurban networks. This is a vivid demonstration of the ways in which disparate parts of human ecological systems are connected through space and social relationships, particularly when a longer term view is taken. The structural violence of the policy of "benign neglect" (D. Wallace & Wallace, 1998a, p. 21) that led to the destruction of housing in the Bronx and other such dislocations are continuously reverberating through US urban systems (Fullilove & Wallace, 2011). Halting these cycles and reverberations of ill effects will require more equitable power structures, enabling communities to resist and avoid these forms of policy-driven structural violence. This example and others (e.g., Timmermans, Orrico, & Smith, 2014) also demonstrate a central insight from the social ecological model: that when one portion of a human ecological system is oppressed or damaged, it can also result in harm to other segments of the society in less direct ways. We truly are all interconnected in ways that are sometimes obscured by individualist orientations.

Yet, even as we gain clarity on the longer term social ecological effects of past injustices such as the burning of the Bronx in the 1970s, new pernicious structures and systems continue to prey on more vulnerable populations. For example, over the past few decades in the United States, rates of incarceration and involvement in the criminal justice system have rapidly increased in an unprecedented way, with people of color much more likely to spend time in prison (Alexander, 2010; Davis, 2003). This phenomenon of mass incarceration, as should be expected, has ill effects that ripple through families, communities, and generations (Freudenberg, 2002; Freudenberg, Daniels, Crum, Perkins, & Richie, 2005; Turney, 2014). The system of mass incarceration can be considered a "predatory formation," which Sassen (2014) described as assemblages of knowledge, interests, and outcomes that go beyond the project of particular companies or governments. The system acts to expel people from livelihoods, lands, and even from the conditions that make life possible (e.g., drinkable water). Many of the constituents of these predatory formations have profit motives, which speaks to the connections between their emergence and neoliberal political economy. These connections are explored in greater depth in the next section on pluralist pathways.

In summary, when empowerment processes are successful, communities are better able to defend and improve the multiple aspects of their environments and settings that are capable of promoting health and well-being. Although these ecological pathways are different from the participant pathways described in the preceding section, they are not entirely unrelated. For example, aspects of the physical environment (i.e., housing, neighborhood characteristics) may influence participatory behaviors and psychological empowerment processes (J. W. Nelson, Hall, & Walsh-Bowers, 1998; D. D. Perkins et al., 1996). Yet, the ecological effects of empowerment are not limited to those directly participating in the process. Instead, they radiate out to influence larger numbers of people through effects on neighborhoods, settings, and social networks.

Pluralist Pathways

When empowerment processes are successful in building and exercising social power, they not only influence health and well-being through the participant and ecological pathways described, but also are likely contributing to health and well-being simply by bringing about more equitable power structures. In other words, it appears that living in more egalitarian societies is better for people. In their book, *The Spirit Level*, for instance, Wilkinson and Pickett (2010) knit together a bevy of studies to make this argument as it relates to socioeconomic inequality. As they described in detail, although there are notable and consistent boosts to life expectancy and happiness between countries at the lower end of the spectrum of national income per person, these effects are less and less discernible as countries become wealthier. This suggests that while economic growth in poor countries will likely benefit population health and well-being, most of the wealthier industrialized nations are gaining little in the way of population health and well-being from additional economic growth.

Yet, within industrialized countries, there are clear and consistent differences in health and well-being between poorer and richer residents. Issues like violence, mental illness, educational failures, obesity, and teenage births are more common among poorer populations than richer populations within countries, yet there is little or no relation between the overall prevalence of these conditions and national levels of income. This suggests that socioeconomic status is more important in relative than in absolute terms as it relates to these determinants and outcomes. At an aggregate level, moreover, more unequal countries (and more unequal states within the United States) more often have higher levels of health and social problems. In other words, greater socioeconomic inequality creates ill effects for residents across a range of health and outcomes, regardless of whether the state or country as a whole is richer or poorer. And, as indicated in Figure 7.1, inequality is associated with higher levels of stress and anxiety, as people feel less socially secure. As Wilkinson and Pickett (2010) summarized, "Inequality seems to make countries socially dysfunctional across a wide range of outcomes" (p. 174).

Increasing levels of inequality are related to the rise of neoliberalism, which is now the dominant political–economic philosophy reflected in the actions of many global institutions (e.g., World Trade Organization, World Bank) and governments around the world. We increasingly implement social policy at every level that is consistent with neoliberalism. Mooney (2012) argued that neoliberalism itself is a force that is negatively affecting our health because it amplifies socioeconomic inequalities and leaves the public out of decision-making in favor of market-based solutions to social issues. His proposed solution for improving health and tackling inequities (other than a broader recognition of the central role of neoliberalism in creating these inequities and the need for alternatives) is consonant with the goals of empowerment: for people to "have a real say in what kind of social institutions they have and how these are run" (p. 397). In other words, there is a need for a more pluralist distribution of power.

Of course, neoliberal policies and practices can often serve only to deepen longer-standing societal cleavages and forms of oppression. Structural racism, for example, has been further entrenched through widening inequality in the neoliberal era (Nkansah-Amankra et al., 2013). Race plays multiple important roles in the relationships between inequality and health, particularly in countries like the United States and South Africa, where legacies of race-based oppression are deeply ingrained and racial inequities persist. Regardless of individual and family socioeconomic status, for instance, US Blacks are more likely to experience some of the contextual effects of poverty than are whites or Latinos (K. L. Perkins & Sampson, 2015). Moreover, the experience of discrimination likely mediates the relationship between poverty and health (Fuller-Rowell, Evans, & Ong, 2012).

Racial disparities in health exist to varying degrees in different countries, even in countries as similar as the United States and Canada (Ramraj et al., 2016). However, forms of structural discrimination exist in nearly every country. What differs is the extent to which they are pronounced along lines of race, ethnicity, indigenous status, immigrant status, age, gender, sexual orientation, or other characteristics. In all cases, discrimination is not just something that is experienced by individuals in interpersonal contexts; structural discrimination is embedded in societal institutions norms and therefore exacerbates health inequity through multiple pathways, from structural violence, to exclusion from opportunity and deprivation, to psychological stress and trauma (Krieger, 2014). Of course, these oppressive and exploitative relationships between racial, ethnic, or other social groups must be contested for a number of reasons, not just for their influence on health and well-being. Nevertheless, combatting inequities in power relationships between groups in society is likely to enhance health and well-being, not only particularly for oppressed and marginalized populations, but also for whole communities and societies that succeed in becoming more egalitarian.

This is certainly not to claim that empowerment processes in local communities—either alone or in aggregate—can fully address or eliminate social, political, and economic forces as pervasive and long-standing as structural racism and neoliberalism. It is, however, a claim that pushing back directly against these intertwined forces and legacies and loosening their grip on local, regional, and national power structures is an inherent and necessary aim for empowerment theory and practice. Because these macrolevel phenomena are operating to skew the distribution of power and resources, concentrating them in the hands of a privileged minority, they are working in direct opposition to empowerment processes' goals. Moreover, structural racism and neoliberalism are often among the primary drivers of the social issues and conditions that most empowerment processes are seeking to improve. They create and sustain unjust and needless suffering and exclusion from the opportunities that can lead to thriving. Therefore, any progress toward lessening or restricting their influence and impacts is likely to produce gains in health and well-being, not only through improved material conditions, but also through the very creation of a more equitable distribution of power.

Despite the evidence for the pluralist pathways' influence on health and well-being, it is somewhat of a conceptual challenge to disentangle the effects of more equitable distributions of power from the conditions that such arrangements make possible or more likely (the latter being the ecological pathways described in the preceding section). How does pluralism enhance health and well-being? As Figure 7.1 depicts, hypothesized impacts of more pluralist or egalitarian power structures include greater social cohesion and trust and reduced anxiety, vulnerability, social insecurity, and stress. Indeed, collective efficacy, which is an indicator of social cohesion and trust, does appear to contribute to health.

For instance, in a sample of women in Ontario, Canada, neighborhood collective efficacy was found to moderate the influence of maternal adverse childhood experiences on later marital conflict (Madigan, Wade, Plamondon, & Jenkins, 2016). Likewise, a study of British children found that neighborhood collective efficacy had protective effects on children's development, particularly for those living in disadvantaged areas (Odgers et al., 2009). But, collective efficacy also appears to have effects at the level of whole neighborhoods. For instance, collective efficacy has been associated with lower rates of youth violence while controlling for neighborhood socioeconomic status (Morenoff, Sampson, & Raudenbush, 2001; Sampson et al., 1997). Greater levels of interorganizational collaboration within communities may have effects on sensitive health indicators, such as the rate of change in population rates of low birthweight (Darnell et al., 2013). Trust and cohesion, then, which are thought to be outcomes of greater pluralism and egalitarianism, are likely to promote health and well-being at the level of the individual and at the neighborhood and population levels. Learning more about how these pluralist pathways in empowerment processes contribute to health and well-being, as well as their relationships with participant and ecological pathways, should be a priority for public and community health research.

Conclusion: Empowerment and Health Equity

Calls to address health disparities and to achieve greater health equity are increasing from leading health sciences and (non)governmental organizations (e.g., Marmot, Friel, Bell, Houweling, & Taylor, 2008; Ottersen et al., 2014). These calls most often focus on action on the social determinants of health, which are most often limited to what have been described here as ecological pathways (e.g., open spaces for leisure and recreation, accessible child care, affordable housing, etc.). However, as community development and health promotion efforts continue to seek to modify such policies, systems, and environments, they often run up against obstacles due to uneven power relationships and concentrations of power that are motivated to defend the status quo—or that seek to change policies in systems in the opposite direction (e.g., through neoliberal reforms that leave goods such as child care and housing entirely to the free market). In many cases, community development and public health professionals refrain from action on these structural determinants of health and well-being out of reluctance to create controversy or outright inability to take political action as part of their professional roles.

Increasingly, however, it is being recognized that for population health to be improved and to achieve greater health equity, changes in policies and power relations are precisely what is required. For example, the CSDH (2008) of WHO issued three principles for action, one of which is to "tackle the inequitable distributions of power, money, and resources—the structural drivers of the conditions of daily life—globally, nationally, and locally" (p. 109). In addition to a number of recommendations that relate to the ecological pathways described in this chapter, they called for holding government accountable for action on health equity across all policies; institutionalizing health equity impact statements for trade agreements and tax policies; reinforcing the primary role of the state (as opposed to the private market) in providing for basic needs such as water and regulating goods such as food, alcohol, and tobacco and services such as health insurance; giving fair representation to workers in developing national policy agendas; addressing gender biases in societal structures; and enabling all groups in society fair representation in decision-making.

These recommendations are noteworthy because they address drivers of health and well-being along the pluralist pathway that are often ignored or believed to be beyond the purview of public health and allied disciplines (Marmot & Allen, 2014). Yet, it is not enough to acknowledge or argue that societal decision-making processes should be open and inclusive, that workers should be represented in these processes as well as corporations and their owners, or that equity should be considered in all policymaking processes. These recommendations are difficult or impossible to achieve without community empowerment processes that are building and exercising social power to exert pressure on societal institutions and decision-makers and hold them accountable to such commitments. And, in fact, many who study disparities in health and well-being and advocate for policy and systems changes to achieve health equity either do not adequately understand or do not fully embrace community power and empowerment processes (Sibal, 2006). Quite simply, this must change in order for these professions to help catalyze more momentum toward achieving equity.

Notes

1. Krieger (2008) argued persuasively that the notions of "proximal" and "distal" have been used in public health in ways that have prioritized a focus on so-called proximal determinants of health outcomes, which are held to be more modifiable, rather than so-called distal social determinants, and that causal "distance" has been conflated with causal strength, among other points of confusion. Among the alternatives that she suggested is an emphasis on "pathways," which is the term I use in this chapter to describe causal relationships between empowerment processes, direct outcomes, intermediate outcomes, and ultimate impacts on health and well-being.
2. In this County Health Rankings model, the remaining 80% is explained by social and economic factors (40%), health behaviors (30%), and the physical environment (10%). Social and economic factors include education, employment, income, family and social support, and community safety. Health behaviors include tobacco use, diet and exercise, alcohol and drug use, and sexual activity. And, physical environmental factors include air and water quality, housing, and transit.
3. Social ties are not always beneficial, and there is a dark side to social connectedness that can produce stress through an inverse of the processes identified in this section. However, Thoits (2011) argued that it is much more common for the benefits of social ties to be reaped than for them to cause increases in stress.
4. Brodsky and Cattaneo (2013) made clear that although they are closely related, the distinction between resilience and empowerment involves the change goals. Empowerment, which is focused on transformation, is focused on changing the conditions that create stress, while resilience is more internally focused on strengths that allow individuals to succeed in the status quo.
5. Some portion of the relationships between place and population-level outcomes is likely due to selection effects, with those who are able to reside in healthier neighborhoods moving to them. Yet, when neighborhood stressors increase or decrease over time, corresponding changes in mental well-being have been observed (Mair et al., 2015). Some research is therefore adopting a reciprocal framework, seeking to account for both the ways that neighborhood characteristics influence the health of residents and their locational decisions, and the ways that health and locational decisions influence neighborhood characteristics (Dunn, Winning, Zaika, & Subramanian, 2014).

8

Designing Research and Action

Introduction

At the beginning of this book, I claimed that in order to better understand, compare, and enhance the effectiveness of community-driven policy and systems change efforts, we need some advances in theory, research design, and measurement. For example, there is a need to be able to more clearly differentiate among different forms of engagement at the local level and to compare and analyze them so that innovations spread and missteps are less often repeated. In particular, I have suggested that to achieve these goals, what is needed is a stronger understanding of *community power*. The three-dimensional view of community power structure offers a foundation, encompassing not only publicly visible conflicts, but also the agenda-setting and gatekeeping processes that determine which conflicts emerge in public debate and the ways that power operates to shape interpretations of information and events. Chapter 2 explored the application of this framework to contemporary communities in an era of global capitalism, arguing that particular attention should be paid to forces such as structural racism and neoliberal ideology and policies.

Although the term has often been used ambiguously, strands of scholarly work on *empowerment* have provided a set of conceptual tools and measures that can be useful for understanding collective action and systems change efforts. Chapter 3 traced the origins of this term and the evolution of empowerment theory up to its current crisis of meaning. The concept has been plagued by a set of interrelated issues: a lack of definitional clarity; the tendency for the concept to be understood individualistically; weak links between community power and empowerment; a lack of clarity on roles for participants, leaders, practitioners, and researchers in empowerment processes; and tensions between collaboration and conflict. Despite these issues, the concept has enduring appeal due to its promise of a holistic framework capable of guiding research and action, one that can balance rights and needs, structure and agency, and micro- and macrolevel processes and outcomes. What is needed now is for the concept to be reviewed holistically and in some cases reclaimed and reworked with an eye toward fulfillment of its initial potential.

177

I have therefore sought to more coherently link theories of community power and empowerment across different human ecological systems, confronting these long-standing conceptual issues (described in Chapter 3) in the process. Empowerment can be observed in behavioral and psychological development processes (Chapter 4), in group settings and organizational development processes (Chapter 5), and in changes in community systems (Chapter 6). Importantly, empowerment in each of these ecological systems is linked with the others. The bulk of the empirical research has focused on psychological empowerment, understood as a set of change processes that occur as people grow and develop through their participation in systems and policy change efforts in community and organizational contexts. This concept has been measured using a multicomponent framework with behavioral, cognitive, and emotional components, with some recent discussions centering on possibilities of alternative conceptual frameworks that might incorporate additional indicators such as a relational component or other process indicators (N. A. Peterson, 2014). Chapter 4 synthesized the research to date and advanced a developmental process model for understanding psychological empowerment.

Empowerment processes tend to occur within and among nonprofits and voluntary associations. Some previous work has sought to identify the social regularities that characterize empowering settings within organizational contexts and the interactions between organizations that are most conducive to empowerment processes. In Chapter 5, I first examined the paradox of a rapidly growing nonprofit sector in an era of declining civic participation and associational membership. These trends are reflective of, and in some ways contributors to, increasing inequality. Situating organizational empowerment in this context and identifying links to community power structure, I proposed some modifications and additions to existing frameworks. One of these is the inclusion of organizational learning as a feature of organizational empowerment processes, including learning to critically analyze power and the roles it plays in social issues. For understanding the relationships and interactions between organizations that take place in empowerment processes, I also advocate for more widespread use and further development of community coalition action theory (Butterfoss et al., 2008) and, when possible, contextually sensitive analytic approaches such as network analysis that can illuminate structural characteristics of organizations and coalitions.

Theory and measurement of community empowerment have lagged behind psychological and organizational empowerment. The work that has been done on the topic has tended to focus on programs geared toward health promotion or community development or on social movements. In Chapter 6, I augmented this work with concepts from grassroots community organizing and studies of community power to develop a new framework for community empowerment with situational, institutional, and systemic dimensions. In order to integrate these concepts with the frameworks discussed in Chapters 4 and 5, I then mapped the ecology of empowerment across psychological, organizational, and community systems according to these same three dimensions of community power structure. Although future work will, with any luck, advance beyond and revise this framework, this represents the most integrated framework that has yet been developed. Importantly, it also links the concepts of empowerment and community power throughout.

This framework for empowerment, however, is primarily concerned with *processes* rather than outcomes and ultimate impacts. In Chapter 7, therefore, I distinguished between the process indicators that have sometimes been referred to as "empowered outcomes" and what I argue should be the primary *outcome* of empowerment processes: development and exercise of social power. Through multiple pathways, the development and exercise of social power can contribute to health and well-being, which I describe as *impacts* of empowerment processes. I distinguish between three interrelated sets of *pathways*—participant, ecological, and pluralist—through which these impacts on health and well-being occur. These distinctions may be helpful for situating various forms of empowerment and health-related inquiry within a holistic framework. The main project of this book has therefore been to link concepts together from various disciplines and build toward a holistic framework for community power and empowerment that can be applied, tested, and refined through ongoing multi-disciplinary research and practice.

Rather than developing distinct sets of recommendations for practice and research, however, in this chapter I instead toggle back and forth between the two. This is in part because there are similarities and parallels in the implications for practice and research. For instance, in many cases, research and evaluation should be designed to be sensitive to the same phenomena that practitioners and participants should be seeking to cultivate or modify. By considering them in tandem, I also hope to identify and highlight opportunities for bridging research and practice. Action research, community-based participatory research, and related forms of community research partnerships are often optimal arrangements for advancing both knowledge and practical effectiveness of systems change efforts (Minkler & Wallerstein, 2008; Snyder, 2009). And, in innovative community change initiatives, efforts are often made to design and plan action and evaluation synchronously (e.g., S. D. Evans, Rosen, Kesten, & Moore, 2014). Yet, there are also some durable differences between empowerment research and practice and the insights and instincts needed to do each effectively. Moreover, there are differences in the language used to describe processes and phenomena.

Empowerment Research and Practice

The terms *empowerment research* and *empowerment practice* could connote many different types of work, so clarity is needed about what sorts of activities are specifically implicated by the use of these terms for present purposes. Empowerment practice is a term that is likely to resonate with a variety of professionals in social and human services, the helping professions, and perhaps beyond these arenas (i.e., in private-sector enterprises). Much of this identification with the term *empowerment* is of course a response to the terminological dilution described in Chapter 3. For purposes here, empowerment practice should not be taken to mean the whole universe of activities that might claim to be empowering in some way or another. Rather, it specifically means those practices seeking to build and exercise social power so that people and organizations gain greater control over their lives and affairs. This distinction may be helpful for understanding the specific contexts where use of theory and research presented in this book will be most relevant.

Activities such as community organizing and grassroots advocacy are therefore clearly engaged in this sort of practice. These are the archetypal varieties of empowerment practice. Many other fields have strains of empowerment in their practice. For instance, some forms of practice in social work, public health, psychology, community development, youth development, public administration, education, and nonprofit/philanthropic work support, catalyze, or seek to amplify the effects of empowerment processes. As this wide variety of "hybrid" types indicate, some practitioners are employed primarily to contribute to empowerment processes in various ways, some have this type of work as only one part of their multifaceted roles, still others manage to engage with empowerment processes as part of their professional work despite competing demands or other institutional barriers and constraints, and many others are not paid for their contributions to empowerment practice.

This last group merits particular attention. Many who encounter empowerment processes tend to overemphasize the contributions of those who are engaged in the efforts as part of their professional roles and to underappreciate the importance of those leading or participating as volunteers. In grassroots organizing initiatives, for instance, there are often hundreds of community leaders involved on a voluntary basis for every one individual who is employed as a full-time organizer by the initiative. Yet, those who are unfamiliar with these forms of practice (and perhaps socialized into identifying people primarily in terms of professional roles) will frequently mistake the paid organizers for uniquely influential leaders deserving credit or blame for the effort's successes and failures. This is common in media accounts of organizing processes, for example, as well as in some research. By pointing this out, I am not intending to diminish the critical contributions of professional community organizers, but rather to emphasize that the notion of empowerment practice must actively counter the frequent overemphasis on professional practice over volunteer leadership and include a much broader array of actors than simply those who are paid to support empowerment processes.

As with many forms of practice, a spectrum exists in terms of scale. At one end of this spectrum are those directly engaged in day-to-day practice in specific community and organizational settings. This is an intensive or direct form of practice. At the other end are those who are less directly engaged in this day-to-day action, yet those engaged at this more extensive end of the spectrum nevertheless can make many meaningful contributions. These include decision-makers and program officers in foundations and government agencies; those paid to provide technical assistance and training to local community groups; professionals in think tanks, networks, and consultancies; and some academics who are engaged in more extensive forms of work on community change.

Although there are similarities across this entire spectrum, there are also unique challenges and opportunities at each end, which are discussed a bit further in this chapter. To summarize for now, empowerment practice includes volunteer leaders and professionals in a variety of roles and from a variety of fields. A staff member at the community center who is working with young people to press for changes to address student concerns in their school is involved in empowerment practice, as of course are the young people themselves. Alternatively, a youth worker whose role is to deliver training on life skills is not. A local health department staff person working with a neighborhood group to address environmental concerns is likely engaging in empowerment practice, as are the neighborhood residents who are involved in such an effort. In contrast, a health department staff person whose role is preventive health education or clinical services is not necessarily engaged in empowerment practice, unless that work is strategically connected with efforts to improve broader community conditions. Furthermore, a foundation staffer who works with many local communities on strategy around mobilization and collective action is engaged in a different form of extensive (rather than intensive) empowerment practice.

Being this specific in defining empowerment practice poses a risk of rigidity, but given the terminological dilution discussed previously, I believe it is necessary to be as clear as possible about what empowerment practice is and is not. Having greater clarity on a definition of empowerment practice can also help to draw parallel lines of distinction around empowerment research and evaluation. Categorically, it is research and evaluation that is conducted on or alongside empowerment processes, often with some level of collaboration (or at a minimum, coordination) with those engaged in empowerment practice. There are, of course, many types of work under this umbrella, just as there are with practice. For example, a sociologist or anthropologist using ethnographic methods to study a particular collective action process may be engaged in an intensive form of empowerment research. A scholar in public health, social welfare, or policy analysis who is involved in a multisite comparative study or evaluation of local coalition-building capacity to change local systems is involved in a more extensive form of empowerment research. Evaluations can likewise be conducted in more intensive ways within particular sites and in more extensive ways across multiple sites.

Empowerment Evaluation?

One potential point of confusion concerns periodic discussions of the concept of "empowerment evaluation." Fetterman (1994), in a presidential address to the

American Evaluation Association, defined the concept of empowerment evaluation as "the use of evaluation concepts and techniques to foster self-determination" (p. 1) and later clarified that "it is designed to help people help themselves and improve their programs using a form of self-evaluation and reflection" (Fetterman, 2002, p. 89). Other evaluators, however, have questioned the usefulness of the concept. Patton (2005), for instance, has faulted proponents of empowerment evaluation for its substantive overlap with other modes of evaluation that had been developed earlier or synchronously, including "participatory, collaborative, stakeholder-involving, and aspects of utilization-focused approaches to evaluation . . . [which also emphasize] attending to such issues as ownership, relevance, understandability, access, and involvement" (p. 409). Patton also faulted the proponents of empowerment evaluation for weak empirical documentation and verification of the claims for the outcomes of their evaluation practices.

Assessments of evaluations that have sought to employ empowerment evaluation largely lend credence to these critiques. For example, in a systematic review of 47 published accounts of empowerment evaluations, R. L. Miller and Campbell (2006) found that there not only was little consistency in the practices that were employed by evaluators, but also the approaches seldom engaged with citizens as stakeholders in the process. Most often, evaluators only extended involvement to those involved in running programs or other staff and managers in community and organizational settings. Moreover, few of the evaluations actually assessed the outcomes that are claimed by the promoters of empowerment evaluation. Describing the results of their review in a follow-up piece, R. L. Miller and Campbell (2007) concluded that there was "little warrant for claims that the specific empowerment evaluation process used provides, of itself, any additional positive benefits beyond the general benefits of having conducted an evaluation" (p. 580). Hence, although empowerment theory has had some degree of influence in the field of evaluation, its application in evaluation practice has been uneven and remains relatively untested. Claims that empowerment evaluation is being carried out should therefore (like claims of empowerment in many other domains) be considered skeptically (Patton, 2015).

These notions of empowerment evaluation represent one common misstep among researchers and evaluators who are interested in empowerment processes or share their values and goals. Broadly, there is a tendency to overestimate and over-emphasize the role of research and evaluation in empowerment processes. In the extreme, some researchers believe that their contributions ought to be central to community change processes. Accordingly, they seek to structure groups' practices and processes around their research (often while claiming that participants' involvement in research or evaluation is "empowering"). In its most blatant forms, this is driven by researchers' inflated sense of the value of the skills and credentials that they uniquely possess. There are many other common missteps, such as the tendency to structure evaluations of community processes primarily around accountability to funders rather than orienting them to the questions that would be most useful and interesting to the participants themselves and to the broader field. Researchers and evaluators interested in empowerment processes must think more critically and strategically about the inherent assumptions in how they connect their interests with the efforts of groups seeking community change.[1]

The Need for Design

For theory and research on community power and empowerment to be useful, it must be considered in the design of initiatives, campaigns, and capacity- and movement-building efforts, as well as in the design of research and evaluation conducted in conjunction with those efforts. In practice, this means that organizations, settings, roles and responsibilities, and strategies for changing policies and systems should be carefully considered from the perspective of community power and empowerment, applying insights provided by practice and research in this area when feasible and relevant. Likewise, research and evaluation must be designed to more consistently document empowerment processes and assess progress toward organizations' desired outcomes and impacts. Researchers and practitioners—and those whose work spans both research and practice—should seek to become ever more systematic and experimental in approaches to assessing and describing various systems change efforts. Creative design is required to tailor work in local contexts so that it is both informed by research and capable of yielding insights that can advance what is currently known.

By advocating for design (rather than, say, implementation fidelity), my intent is to emphasize that applying a framework for community power and empowerment is complicated and often challenging, requiring creativity and adaptation within complex systems (Hawe, 2015). Although more systematic approaches to action and inquiry are needed, this should not imply that there are prepackaged or formulaic approaches that will work in most circumstances. Instead, concepts and measures (such as those provided in the appendices) must be unpacked, considered critically, and adapted for use in various contexts, ideally by, or in collaboration with, those most familiar with the settings in which empowerment processes are taking place.

This last point bears special emphasis. These design principles are intended as a complement to the experience and expertise that leaders and practitioners possess, not as an alternative to or replacement for them. Many who are engaged in empowerment practice creatively improvise daily and rely on their experience and instincts. This grounded knowledge and improvisational ability are often more valuable than anything we could learn from a general model, framework, or specific research finding (Flyvbjerg, 2002). Nevertheless, it is possible to draw on theory and empirical research to identify some broad principles to consider when strategizing approaches to building and exercising social power, as well as when tailoring research and evaluation to understand, compare, and perhaps ultimately bolster the

Table 8.1 **Design Principles for Community Empowerment Praxis**

1. Build organizations and social anchors
2. Settings are primary leverage points
3. Analyze and map community power
4. Think in terms of networks and relationships
5. Mount challenges and sustain pressure
6. Convert nonissues into issues
7. Balance attention to psychology and systems
8. Take a critical developmental approach
9. Disrupt consciousness of powerlessness
10. Emphasize imagination
11. Contend with issues of scale
12. Establish cycles of inquiry and action

effectiveness of these efforts at changing systems. In what follows, I describe some of these broad principles for applying and adapting theory and research on community power and empowerment to ongoing and future work (Table 8.1).

Design Principles

Build Organizations and Social Anchors

Empowerment processes almost always have organizational contexts, with varying levels of organizational formality. To alter community power structures, there need to be many different types of organizations providing opportunities for different forms of engagement and participation. People should feel membership in these organizations, and feel (or, indeed have) collective ownership of organizations and physical (i.e., bricks-and-mortar) institutions in their communities. Community and neighborhood centers, clubs, union halls, schools, cultural and faith-based institutions, and other nonprofit and voluntary organizations function as social anchors. They comprise the building blocks for empowerment processes. Social anchors build social capital and collective identity (Clopton & Finch, 2011) and thereby build capacity to take collective action. Many communities lack a sufficient number of these types of organizations. In other communities, the most pressing need may not be to increase the number of social anchors, but to provide more opportunities for resident engagement and ownership of existing organizations and institutions.

Research needs to be attentive to the organizational ecologies of communities from the perspective of community power and empowerment. In Gaventa's (1980) study of an Appalachian mining town, the opening of a community center that residents felt that they owned was likely a precursor to social action on long-held grievances (p. 162). There are many examples of similar connections between social anchors and empowerment processes, both historically (e.g., McAdam et al., 1996; Morris, 1986) and in contemporary cities (e.g., Lamore, Link, & Blackmond, 2006; M. C. Yan & Sin, 2011). Yet, there are often trade-offs in organizations' approaches to building their capacity (Kaiser & Rusch, 2015), and relatively little research has rigorously investigated and compared the organizational and institutional contexts and networks that likely help to explain varying outcomes of community-driven change efforts. Better understanding of these relationships would help determine more strategic priorities for efforts in local communities.

Settings Are Primary Leverage Points

Ecological/systems perspectives can be valuable, but one inherent risk is that aiming to pay attention to every part of a system at once can lead to losing sight of the best avenues for action. In many cases, the optimal leverage points for empowerment are in organizational and setting design, rather than, for instance, individually focused interventions, such as curricular design for psychological development of participants, or more comprehensive community-wide work. In other words, strategic modifications of existing organizational settings, systems, and networks or creation of new settings is often more efficacious than attempts to alter psychological (micro-) or community (macro-) systems. Practitioners should focus particular attention on designing settings to foster organizational aspects of empowerment (Maton, Seidman, & Aber, 2011), which are addressed in detail in Chapter 5.

For practitioners and researchers, a central question should be the following: How can organizations and interorganizational change efforts create more settings that produce more of the features of organizational empowerment (e.g., opportunity role structure, underpopulated settings, culture of organizational learning)? Although some of these features of settings can be designed, many of them are conceptual aspirations that depend not only on design but also on the skill and improvisation of practitioners. The combination of design and skilled improvisation that creates empowering community settings is likely to radiate out from these settings in terms of both systems changes and psychological changes among participants (Maton & Brodsky, 2011).

Researchers likewise must continue to innovate in order to develop better tools for assessing setting-level phenomena and dynamics to yield new insights into empowerment processes. The concepts and measurement tools described in Chapter 5 provide a good starting point, but new breakthroughs are badly needed in this area (Trickett, 2011). For one thing, most settings can be directly observed. In many cases, researchers and evaluators should be participating and observing or otherwise systematically documenting processes within and across settings rather than relying on aggregated survey measures for data. This will require the development of new methods for systematically assessing social regularities within and between the settings that comprise empowerment processes (Hawe, Shiell, & Riley, 2009; Seidman, 2012). Although much of this work is complex and difficult, it promises to yield valuable insights into empowerment processes and increase the effectiveness of efforts to change community power structures.

Analyze and Map Community Power

Leaders of empowerment processes become astute about their own community's power structures in order to understand opportunities for changing them. In order to enhance understanding of power dynamics, many effective empowerment processes analyze power in participatory ways. For instance (as noted in Chapter 6), many grassroots community-organizing groups carry out power-mapping processes in their communities (Christens, Inzeo, et al., 2014; McAlevey, 2016). In these processes, groups of participants will gather information on decision-makers and other influential institutional actors and locate and depict their relative positions in terms of power and their support for, or opposition to, policy or systemic changes of particular interest. Through these processes, participants reflect on potential strategies for altering power maps, as well as how their own group fits into the map. Which people or organizations represented on the power map could—if moved either in terms of their stance on an issue or in terms of their relative power—make meaningful changes in the systems that affect issues of concern? Processes like power mapping can both develop critical consciousness among participants and clarify the group's strategies for action to change systems and power structures. When community power structures—through their "inevitable limits and contradictions" (Wright, 2010, p. 297)—do provide opportunities and openings for change, groups that have been studiously attentive to power will be well positioned to take strategic transformative action.

Researchers can likewise benefit from engaging in power analysis. This might take shape in several ways. For one thing, researchers can engage in either formal or informal power mapping in order to be more strategic in their engagement with community organizations and initiatives (see Speer & Christens, 2013). Furthermore, they can design research and evaluation in order to shed more light on changes in power structures. For example, Gaventa (2006) and Noy (2008) provided some conceptual and analytical tools for understanding and mapping power that can inform design of empirical research.[2] Through participatory research modalities, there is potential for researchers and evaluators to encourage participatory power-mapping processes in the community groups they are working with. Furthermore, these processes and the data that they produce can be analyzed to answer evaluative questions for process improvement, and they also may be designed so that they have the potential to provide insights into broader social scientific research questions about community power and change processes.

Think in Terms of Relationships and Networks

Scholars have long viewed community power in terms of power relationships between groups (see Chapter 2). Community-organizing efforts likewise understand power in terms of relationships, rather than as something that an individual or institution inherently possesses. Those seeking to build power and to change community power structures should therefore think more in terms of relationships and networks than in terms of positions or fixed traits. Social networks are constantly formed, expanded, and reshaped in meetings and other participatory settings. Effective practitioners often think of their interpersonal and interorganizational work in terms of networks (Westoby & Owen, 2010). Of course, this differs in important ways from the concept of "networking" that is a hallmark of corporate culture and from social media networks. To build and exercise social power, the goal is not simply to grow social networks for social capital or communications, but to strategically build common purpose between people and groups that comprise networks and to mobilize key ties within these networks (Christens, Inzeo, et al., 2014). In societies characterized by high levels of inequality, many relationships between community groups are lopsided in terms of power. The goal of empowerment is to change not only the quantity of ties but also, at an intergroup level, the distribution of power across them.

As practitioners increasingly think in these terms, scholars and evaluators can amplify the effect by providing empirical insights into social or interorganizational networks. By collecting data on relationships and networks, they can compare leaders' grounded understanding of their relational contexts with data on the structural characteristics of networks of people and organizations. Network analysis is thus an especially promising method for yielding insights into context, but it should not necessarily be a default mode for research design. Collecting whole-network data can be onerous, especially because missing data pose such a problem for network analysis. Researchers, evaluators, and their community partners should therefore think carefully about whether the information yielded will justify the effort. There are often alternatives that can yield insights through less intensive data collection processes. In some cases, for example, two-mode network data can be extracted from participation records, organizations' records, media coverage, and other sources (e.g., Todd, Houston, & Suffrin, 2015). Researchers may therefore consider numerous potential sources of network data that can illuminate empowerment processes and changes in community power structures. Regardless of the specific methodologies used, however, research and evaluation should be designed with the understanding that relationships and networks—interpersonal and interorganizational—constitute a crux of empowerment processes.

Mount Challenges and Sustain Pressure

Achieving more equitable societal arrangements requires changes to the status quo, and many of the necessary changes provoke resistance from power holders and create controversies. It is therefore necessary for practitioners and leaders to be prepared to challenge the status quo and to sustain pressure amid contentious public debate and backlash. If efforts to build and exercise social power remain noncontroversial over long periods of time, it begs the question of whether these organizations and initiatives are truly capable of exercising social power for transformative change. Have they instead simply adapted to be able to work within the status quo, without posing the necessary challenges for real systemic changes?

This is of course not to say that organizations, coalitions, or social movement organizations should pursue conflict and controversy haphazardly. Many first seek collaborative solutions (Wolff, 2010) and only resort to strategies that involve conflict or controversy when collaboration proves ineffective at producing meaningful systemic changes. Yet, people and organizations must prepare for the likelihood that conflict will occur as challenges to the status quo are mounted (Speer, 2008) and carefully plan strategies for applying and sustaining pressure accordingly. Setbacks are inevitable, so groups must be prepared to be resilient and resolute in the face of opposition.

In order to link their work to community power, researchers and evaluators must likewise clearly distinguish between community change efforts that produce public contention and debate and those that do not. It is especially critical to understand when and how conflict avoidance results in groups shying away from the contention necessary to air their grievances and demand change. In this way, researchers and evaluators can help community practitioners reflect on their efforts. But, this can happen only when the researchers themselves are not predisposed toward conflict avoidance and pursuit of ameliorative rather than transformative changes (Prilleltensky, 2008). Researchers should therefore critically assess their assumptions, roles, theories, methods, and the advice they give as it relates to collaboration and conflict. The goal should be to bolster groups' abilities to take strategic action on behalf of their interests in the public arena, even when those actions might prove controversial. Researchers and evaluators must be clear that although it is unlikely to be quickly understood by some of their professional-class colleagues, conflict and controversy are in fact often positive indicators that empowerment processes are making progress.

Convert Nonissues Into Issues

Empowerment processes must aim to shift and expand the scope of what is up for public debate. This can be thought of as operating within the second dimension of power. As discussed in Chapter 2, common grievances are often kept out of public contention by powerful individuals and groups who want elements of the status quo not only preserved, but also unquestioned. Community power theorists have referred to this as *mobilization of bias*. When it persists over time, it can be misread as tacit acceptance or acquiescence on the part of groups who are less advantaged by existing structural arrangements. Empowerment practice must be perpetually anchored in the concerns of participants and should build capacity to draw attention to the ways that people's real concerns are not being considered in public debates over issues. This often involves shifting the focus of debates from the symptoms to the root causes of social issues. For example, instead of debating policing responses to violent crime (a symptom), groups might draw attention to the need for educational and employment opportunities and other supports necessary for young people in the community to succeed and thrive (Christens & Dolan, 2011). The lack of such opportunities and supports is a root cause of elevated crime levels, but defenders of the status quo will likely resist debating policy responses to violence on these terms.

Research can help illuminate links between different issues of concern and draw attention to root causes of social problems. Sometimes, this is as simple as identifying relevant research that can inform and buttress community action. For example, recent evidence indeed supported a link between opportunities for youth and rates of violent crime (e.g., Heller, 2014). Those conducting research as part of, or in partnerships with, groups building and exercising social power can also design action research on community issues that helps to illuminate such interconnections. Moreover, evaluation of community change efforts can track organizations' and initiatives' influence in converting nonissues into issues. How have groups' actions changed which issues are on the public agenda, both formally (e.g., in city council meetings) and informally (e.g., in media discussions)? Researchers and evaluators of empowerment processes need to continue to refine methods for case studies that involve often-complex processes of change in public debates (Speer & Christens, 2012). Methods for inquiry must go beyond simply monitoring media because it is often the case that community groups that have been responsible for the conversion of nonissues to issues are not publicly credited for their roles.

Balance Attention to Psychology and Systems

In many areas of practice and research, the last decade saw a growing emphasis on systems thinking (Leischow et al., 2008; Peters, 2014) and on policy, system-level, and environmental changes (Peirson, Boydell, Ferguson, & Ferris, 2011). This emphasis is important, but it sometimes comes at the expense of attention to participatory processes and the psychology of participants. In contrast, some strands of empowerment practice have continued to emphasize participatory and developmental processes (Wong, Zimmerman, & Parker, 2010). Although no less important, practice that is overly reliant on psychological perspectives can likewise become lopsided and fail to change policies, systems, and environments. In fact, these two perspectives can be understood as endpoints of a continuum, and an overemphasis at one of these two ends of the continuum is sometimes intended as correctives to each other. For instance, Dokecki, Scanlan, and Strain (1972) noted that over time there tends to be a pendulum effect between a preponderance of approaches favoring one end of this spectrum or the other. They argued that the pendulum swing should be halted in favor of approaches that stress "the interdependent and transactional relationship between the psychological (person) and the sociological (environment) perspectives" (p. 184). Practitioners and leaders should critically assess their work and seek greater balance between the influences of, and emphasis on, psychological and systemic perspectives.

Scholars should likewise seek to balance these perspectives by investigating both systems change processes and the patterns of behavioral and psychological changes among participants in these same systems change efforts. As noted, there has been a long-standing imbalance in favor of research on psychological processes and outcomes. This is often related to more conservative views of society, which tend to favor individualistic explanations for social problems over systemic and structural explanations (Levine & Levine, 1970). The emergence of systems science (Green, 2006; Luke & Stamatakis, 2012) and the encouragement from entities that fund research to pursue and investigate systemic changes (e.g., National Association of County and City Health Officials [NACCHO, 2011]) have helped to begin addressing this imbalance and to push back against individualist conceptions of social problems. But, there is a risk of a pendulum effect in research as well. There is a great need for researchers and evaluators to design research that is more holistic and capable of capturing and accounting for interdependence and transactions between psychological and systems changes. To this end, researchers should prioritize design of multilevel studies (Shinn & Rapkin, 2000) and, when possible, gather data on interconnected psychological and systems-level characteristics and processes.

Take a Critical Developmental Approach

Efforts focused on younger people are most likely to emphasize development, but as detailed in Chapter 4, grassroots community change initiatives can also be excellent developmental contexts for adults. Developing members' skills, confidence, knowledge, and relationships is also fundamental to the groups' power. Leadership development for community change requires development of critical capacities, akin to what Freire (1973) termed *conscientization*. Critical consciousness can be developed naturally in the course of systems change efforts, but specific intention around group discussions and reflection can further support conscientization processes (Ledwith, 2011).

Learning from social movement history and the stories of leaders who exemplify aspects of empowerment is one example of such an approach. Preskill and Brookfield, in their book *Learning as a Way of Leading* (2009), described processes and concrete strategies for learning and practicing radical openness, critical reflection, questioning, collective leadership, supporting the growth of others, and sustaining hope in the face of struggle. They rooted these "learning tasks" in the life stories of leaders in struggles for social justice (e.g., Ella Baker, Nelson Mandela, Myles Horton). Specific curricular tools may be helpful in some forms of empowerment practice for guiding reflection and critical development, while others may guide and scaffold these developmental processes more organically through cycles of action and reflection. Regardless, it should be a fundamental goal of empowerment practice to cultivate these capacities among participants. Forms of civic action that have been less attentive to critical consciousness and sociopolitical development should study these concepts and seek to embed them more intentionally in their practice.

Research on empowerment should evaluate practical strategies like the ones mentioned for their ability to promote growth of the cognitive component of psychological empowerment and critical consciousness among different groups of participants (see Chapter 4 and appendices). However, research and evaluation should also take a critical developmental approach to organizational development and the study of empowering community settings. Why do some groups establish the features of organizational empowerment described in Chapter 5 while others fail or neglect to establish them? And, when do organizational networks and their actions catalyze empowerment processes in the broader community that are described in Chapter 6? Although it is an ambitious type of multilevel study, there is a great need for integrated, critical accounts of human, organizational, and community development.

Disrupt Consciousness of Powerlessness

A sense of powerlessness can create paralysis as well as greater susceptibility to manipulation. For instance, Gaventa (1980) demonstrated how the vulnerability and dependency of miners in an Appalachian town was instilled and continuously reinforced in order to maintain uncritical loyalty to the mining company. Empowerment processes are full of paradoxes (Rappaport, 1981), and this is one of them. On the one hand, as we map and gain insights into power relationships, we tend to become more acutely aware of injustices and the challenges of changing entrenched structures. On the other hand, we cannot allow those insights to so deeply alienate us and our collaborators that we fail to take action. Many have described this paradox of the need to build critical consciousness (Friere, 1973) while avoiding rational nihilism (West, 2001) and/or radical pessimism (Wright, 2010, p. 290) and the associated loss of hope and meaning. In practice, this means working to build strong systems of social support within community settings so that participants can collectively process the inevitable setbacks and disappointments in mutually supportive contexts. Group cultures and leadership that encourages participants to sustain action and maintain a vision of what is possible can be bulwarks against alienation and burnout. It may also be helpful, especially early on during empowerment processes, to pursue changes on smaller "winnable" issues to build momentum (Foster-Fishman et al., 2006; Weick, 1984).

Research should more thoroughly examine the intricacies of simultaneously empowering and disempowering processes. Retrospective accounts tend to oversimplify these processes into stories of overall success or failure, rather than providing more nuanced understanding of the reality of multiplex and nonlinear empowerment processes. Longitudinal and comparative studies are needed to yield insights into rhythms of empowerment and disempowerment, including the alienation and burnout that can result from participation in often-frustrating systems change efforts. Over time, most community change efforts are losing some participants altogether, while those who continue to participate are experiencing uneven gains across different components of psychological empowerment (Christens & Speer, 2011; Christens, Speer, et al., 2011). Future research and evaluation of empowerment processes should seek to move beyond simple findings, like whether participants scored higher, on average, on a single measure of psychological empowerment over time. They should instead delve into the complexity of diverging indicators and disparate outcomes across subgroups of participants as they participate in a variety of forms of community and organizational action.[3] The types of empirical insights that this can produce will be more useful for informing both theory and practice.

Emphasize Imagination

Those seeking change must resist confusing the status quo with the natural or inevitable. Lukes's (1974) third dimension of power directs our attention to the ways that power can be used to constrain our ability to imagine alternatives to current systems and structural arrangements. Participants in change efforts often interrogate the roles that power plays in shaping their own conceptions of what is possible or desirable, as well as the broader public's conceptions. Accordingly, they should seek to develop capacity—their own and others'—to imagine alternatives. This may involve thought exercises, such as noting the unnatural features of contemporary arrangements, but could also involve experiments with alternatives. For instance, Wright (2013) pointed to initiatives such as worker-owned cooperatives, participatory budgeting processes, and urban agriculture with community land trusts as potential local demonstrations of the viability and desirability of more democratic and egalitarian social and economic relations than are often deemed possible within contemporary global capitalism. Creating more such structures, he suggested, can both "prefigure more comprehensive alternatives and move us in the direction of those alternatives" (p. 21).

Research and evaluation efforts should seek to understand and compare the imagined alternatives of participants in empowerment processes. Many have noted that a central task of change efforts involves moving the world as it is closer to the world as it should be (e.g., Chambers, 2006). Researchers and evaluators could facilitate processes in which participants articulate their perspectives on these two worlds. For example, Boyte and Fretz (2010) described a process for doing this with college students, which can also serve the purpose of encouraging them to "live on the tension lines" (p. 75) between the world as it is and the world as it should be. In other words, processes like these could simultaneously contribute to participants' own clarity while providing systematic documentation of the imagined alternatives of participants. Research should also pay particular attention to efforts to achieve aspects of these alternatives through prefigurative practices (Lin, Pykett, Flanagan, & Chávez, 2016). Furthermore, action research can be a tool for highlighting the contradictions and extreme injustices of current social arrangements. Analyzing patterns in local systems can be key to identifying points of leverage for change. Research can also be a tool for exposing the ways that powerful individuals and groups are seeking to shape public understanding and ideology (Domhoff, 2009; Sirota, 2014), providing helpful insights for resisting hegemony.

Contend With Issues of Scale

In the contemporary era of global capitalism, businesses and the groups that represent their interests have become extremely powerful. Part of this is due to their ever-expanding scale. Large corporations are increasingly able to evade or overcome challenges to their interests from local and even national governments (Sassen, 1996). Even the smaller ones, however, often have more of a free hand to pursue their interests due to neoliberal policies and interlocking of corporations' material interests with those of the broader society's. Neoliberal policies remove legal obligations to workers, to the environment, to taxation, and to public accountability (Harvey, 2007). When other rationales for advancing neoliberal policies fail, interlocking material interests—the fact that nearly every variety of societal institution has become dependent on the ability of businesses to constantly grow their profits—further enhance the bargaining power of corporations (Wright, 2010). Of course, many of the policy and systems changes that would improve residents', workers', and consumers' health and well-being are at odds with the interests of businesses or industries (see, e.g., Biglan, 2011; Mialon, Swinburn, & Sacks, 2015), whose decision-making operates at an increasingly extralocal scale. This presents profound dilemmas for grassroots groups, whose locally-driven structures are among their defining characteristics. Increasingly, the changes necessary to improve local conditions not only are not local, but also are unaccountable to representative bodies in any locality.

This political–economic context undoubtedly calls for ever more sophisticated national and transnational alliances and mobilization networks. Ideally, these networks can serve multiple functions. They can act as clearinghouses for local issues and strategies, they can provide training and support to local initiatives, and they can operate as vehicles for local groups to exercise their power in aggregate to influence national and international policymaking. Because powerful interests are large scale and well networked, there are often patterns to their attempts to exploit local resources and populations. Accordingly, networks may help local groups to spot these "predatory formations" (Sassen, 2014) and resist them before they take root. Building the capacity of these types of strategic mobilization networks, however, is difficult because the resources and sophistication required to move policy at state and national levels risks creating top-down structures that can exploit or stifle local efforts, rather than enhancing and extending them. For those who are committed to meaningful changes, however, there really is no choice but to experiment with building networks and alliances and seek to find the balance in this more extensive end of the spectrum of empowerment practice.

Research can contribute to these network-building efforts in many ways. Action research could be designed, for example, to help networks monitor and improve their effectiveness in striking the balance described. It is also important for researchers to study and learn from past empowerment processes that have had impacts beyond the local level. For example, Chaplin (2010) traced the activities of local social organization of *campesino* (rural laborers) unions in Bolivia in the 1990s leading to a networked movement capable of resisting neoliberal reforms and changing national policies and eventually to the 2005 election of an indigenous campesino, Evo Morales, to the presidency. Although the groups that propelled this historic victory still often protest the actions of the government under Morales, it is clear that many of the country's political and economic systems have shifted during the last decade in ways that enable indigenous residents greater control over their lives. To gain insights, researchers should scrutinize cases like these and contrast them with efforts that have achieved fewer of their goals or have failed to translate local capacity into power at regional or national scales.

Establish Cycles of Inquiry and Action

As I hope that this chapter underscores through its development of design principles that apply to both research and practices, there are numerous opportunities for interweaving inquiry and action within empowerment processes that can yield insights that are both valuable for practical purposes and informative to multiple academic disciplines. Yet, there are also obstacles, including some discussed previously in this chapter regarding common missteps of researchers and evaluators. Additional challenges include the training and socialization that occurs within some social science disciplines and leads to reluctance to design and conduct research in settings that the researcher does not control. There is also reticence in some community groups and nonprofit organizations to have their work scrutinized empirically. One thing that is therefore needed is more long-term intentional relationship development between action-oriented researchers and groups that are dedicated to exercising social power and changing power structures. There is great potential for synergies between the two, but the ability to realize these possibilities often depends on trust and mutual understanding.

Another need is more clarity and precision in both research and practice. In many community change initiatives, for instance, there is some degree of uncertainty around the intended outputs and impacts and a lack of clear articulation of how the processes under way are likely to lead to them. Those involved in empowerment processes should strive to make implicit theories of change more explicit. Yet, they must not allow such efforts to achieve clarity and precision to infringe on their ability to improvise and adapt. Community power dynamics are fluid and often unpredictable. Groups leading community change efforts often modify their strategies to operate more and more effectively in their local contexts. Some features of empowerment processes and the goals they are seeking to achieve, however, are likely to be relatively constant, and these should be identified and, to the extent possible, periodically assessed.

Similar challenges exist in research and evaluation. Many community researchers and evaluators are not well versed enough to design multilevel research that can yield new insights into empowerment processes, and some are not well equipped to report results in ways that advance collective understanding in the field. As noted in Chapter 3, empowerment research has not been confined to one discipline or field of study, but spans multiple subfields within psychology, social sciences, and applied/ professional fields, including education, public health, social work, evaluation, and community development. Differences in terminology and measures across these disciplines pose challenges for researchers attempting to stay current in their knowledge of others' research and relate their findings to existing work. Researchers and evaluators must therefore attempt to coalesce around more common terminology and shared metrics for studying community and systems change efforts. We need to be discerning in selecting and developing suitable baseline and process indicators and determined in our efforts to identify influential mechanisms and meaningful comparisons. Yet, we must also be creative in assessing the complex contexts in which community actions are occurring and tailor our research efforts to reflect the uniqueness of the various contexts where we are working.

Across the disciplines concerned with empowerment processes, there is as yet little consistency and therefore limited comparability. This is a major hindrance for an area of study—one that I hope that this book will be a step toward overcoming. Yet, no amount of conceptual consensus or methodological innovation can obviate the need for contextually sensitive design. Those facing design challenges in action and research may therefore find value in critically reflecting on the principles described in this chapter.

Notes

1. See Speer and Christens (2013) for more discussion of these common missteps by researchers and possibilities for strategic engagement in community-based research.
2. Gaventa (2006) elaborated on the three-dimensional model of community power by developing a "power cube" that also accounts for differences in participatory spaces and the places and levels (local, national, global) at which participatory action can occur. This framework can help guide power analysis and is intended especially for practitioners of community/international development. Meanwhile, Noy (2008) described power mapping as a potential model for conducting public sociology.
3. At the group and community levels, narrative methods may be useful for uncovering the shift from consciousness of powerlessness to collective narratives that embrace the goals of empowerment (Yoshikawa & Ramos Olazagasti, 2011).

9

Conclusion

Most of this book was written before the 2016 US election, in which Donald Trump defied most predictions and preelection polls to win the Electoral College. His campaign was replete with vows—both implicit and explicit—to restore or reinforce racial, ethnic, and religious hierarchies within the country and to flex the nation's power around the globe through more belligerent rhetoric and more vigorous use of military force. His campaign slogan, "Make America Great Again," channeled the longing that many of his supporters—especially older white residents—have to return to a time when their status and access to resources was more secure, at least relative to other groups' (Bouie, 2016). Trump's disparagement of women also provided clear evidence of his devotion to patriarchal gender hierarchy. Throughout the long campaign, he unleashed disdain, mockery, and vindictiveness toward people or institutions that criticized or contradicted him. He has also routinely distorted or invented facts to support a simplistic worldview that nurtures his core constituency's resentments and blames various out-groups for problems, both real and imagined (Stanley, 2016). These authoritarian tendencies raise troubling questions about how he and his followers may seek to reshape institutions in the country, such as the press and the judiciary.

As I write now, in the early days of a Trump presidency, it is impossible to predict what the outcomes of this reality TV presidency will be. Perhaps this administration will be unable to enact many of its policy preferences and will exhaust its limited political capital or become hopelessly mired in scandal. To the extent that a Trump administration is able to reshape institutions and democratic processes in accordance with its campaign promises, however, it will compound suffering in vulnerable groups and create much stronger headwinds for empowerment processes in the United States. It could even reshape the national power structure in ways that might take decades of progress or a cataclysm to reverse. At the very least, this election has provided a pointed reminder that sociopolitical systems are constantly changing, and that the past is not always a good predictor of the future. Many had assumed that for all of its faults and injustices, the US democratic system fundamentally operated within certain boundaries of acceptable political behavior and policy ideology and are now scrambling to adjust their thinking to the new reality (e.g., E. Klein, 2016).

I had planned for this concluding chapter to emphasize what I understand to be a central challenge for empowerment theory and practice. That is the need to navigate a perennial paradox: On the one hand, there is great *urgency* to address the issues currently facing communities; on the other hand, there is need for diligent (and often painfully slow) pursuit of better frameworks and tools that can help advance praxis and make it more effective.

In his presidential address to the Society for Community Research and Action (discussed in Chapter 3), Rappaport (1981) suggested that *"we need to find a renewed symbolic and ideational goal and a renewed sense of urgency"* (emphasis in original, p. 15). It is likely that this statement was at least to some extent a reflection of the conservatism of that era and a desire to revive some of the urgency that animated social change efforts in the preceding decades.[1] In the current sociopolitical context, however, it does not seem nearly as necessary to stress this need for urgency. The urgency should be readily apparent! The Black Lives Matter movement, for example, has taken an issue that has been urgent in poor communities of color for many decades (disproportionate police brutality and murder) and put it front and center in much of the nation's consciousness (Taylor, 2016).

Some who share this acute sense of urgency may view some of the conceptual work in this book as tedious or as unnecessary hair-splitting. Why should we spend time designing research and refining theory on community power and empowerment when there are such urgent needs that demand immediate action? In response to this excellent question, I would first say that theory and research on community power and empowerment should not stand in the way of action or ever seem to encourage a "go slow" approach to change. It is my view that the needs for action are urgent, and the action is therefore primary: Research must seek to grow symbiotically and strategically alongside it where possible. Recall that in Kieffer's (1984) study of the development of psychological empowerment among leaders (described in Chapter 4), none began their involvement because of intellectual analyses or consciousness-raising efforts. They all were people who had some type of personal stake in changing community systems. Researchers should keep this in mind and be sure that attempts to improve understanding and bolster effectiveness of systems change efforts do not act as a sedative to the urgent need for systemic changes. To the contrary, research and evaluation should be used to yield new insights into urgent issues and the processes that are under way to create needed community and social change.

It is of course often easier for a graduate student, a professor, or someone in professional practice—those of us who may have some type of distance or insulation from the most pernicious effects of systemic injustices—to get excited about ideas like long-term studies, improved measures, and better understanding of the links between processes and outcomes. When we ourselves, or the people close to us, are bearing the brunt of systemic injustices in direct and painful ways, these abstractions can seem quite impotent and disconnected from more immediate struggles. Nevertheless, I also believe that the urgency of the issues currently facing communities requires that we apply every available tool at our disposal, including our best attempts to understand systems change efforts using action research. To the extent that we fail to do this, we risk simply reproducing, reenacting, and researching what should be defunct theories for how to achieve change.[2]

The first weekend after Trump's inauguration, millions took to the streets in a set of loosely coordinated protests headlined by the Women's March on Washington, DC (Figure 9.1). In aggregate, it is estimated that between 3.3 and 4.6 million Americans marched in hundreds of cities and towns, making it likely the largest coordinated protest event in US history, not to mention an additional 300,000 marchers in other cities around the world (Broomfield, 2017). In Madison, Wisconsin, a city of about a quarter of a million residents, it is estimated that between 75,000 and 100,000 people took part in the march (Mesch, 2017).

Walking up State Street toward the Wisconsin capitol in the midst of this crowd had a familiar feel. In fact, it was the largest protest in Madison since the peak of the Wisconsin Uprising of 2011, described in Chapter 1 of this book. Many of the same chants that were mainstays of the uprising were repurposed for this Women's March, but new signs and chants were also devised to channel the shock and dismay

Figure 9.1. Women's March on Madison, Wisconsin, January 2017. *Source: The Badger Herald.* https://badgerherald.com/media/2017/01/IMG_8505.jpg

that marchers felt about the outcome of the US election, the new direction of the country, and the misogyny, nativism, and white supremacy of the new president and administration. As with the protests of 2011, I felt extremely heartened on the one hand to stand shoulder to shoulder with so many fellow residents who were creatively and passionately expressing their commitment to values such as diversity and social justice. On the other hand, the question "So what next?" seemed to be on everyone's mind (Hamer, 2017; White, 2017).

When I think about this question, many of the design principles outlined in the last chapter do seem pertinent. It is critical that we build local organizations and grassroots leadership and not to wait for direction from national organizations and movements. We should continue to create new organizations and settings (and enhance existing organizations) that can provide opportunities for broad engagement. We should prioritize leadership by nonprofessionals, particularly by people most directly affected by pressing issues. If there is a single key principle that should be taken from this book, it is that these organizations and mobilization efforts must provide many meaningful opportunities for residents and volunteers to become leaders and not just ask for their signatures on petitions, their likes and re-posts on social media, their time to make phone calls or knock on doors, their money, or their presence at occasional marches.

The crises of the current political situation are also an opportunity to broaden and deepen the civic capacities and commitments of local residents across the United States and beyond.[3] To the extent that we are able to do this, we will stand the best chance of building sufficient community power to withstand the ever-present attempts to cement and strengthen hierarchies based on gender, religion, race/ethnicity, national origin, and wealth. Furthermore, these processes will have many benefits in the long run. They will contribute to the health and well-being of participants, their broader communities, and to a democratic society. And, action research can help to illuminate key elements of these processes so that we learn as much as possible from our successes, as well as from our mistakes or strategic miscalculations.

Notes

1. More recently, in fact, Rappaport (2011) has pointed out that social scientific theories have tended to be congruent with the sociopolitical climate of their times.
2. For instance, King (2006), in a discussion of the importance of the contributions of Ida B. Wells to theory and ideology, reiterated the view of John Maynard Keynes to describe this phenomenon of principally practical people unknowingly embracing tacit theories: "Those cursed with too granitic a conviction of being fully and certainly possessed of knowledge of the truth are those most likely oblivious to being 'the slaves of some defunct' theory" (p. 122).
3. Crises may also present unusual political opportunities. For instance, scholars of social movements emphasize the importance of historical events such as realignments and rifts among elites and institutions for understanding the emergence and outcomes of various movements (McAdam, McCarthy, & Zald, 1996).

ABOUT THE AUTHOR

Brian D. Christens is an associate professor of human and organizational development at Vanderbilt University's Peabody College of Education and Human Development in Nashville, Tennessee. He is a graduate of the PhD program in Community Research and Action at Vanderbilt. From 2009 to 2017, he was on the faculty of the University of Wisconsin–Madison's School of Human Ecology and served as associate director, then faculty director of the Center for Community and Nonprofit Studies. His research on community and systems change processes has been recognized by early career awards from the Society for Community Research and Action, the Society for the Psychological Study of Social Issues, and the American Psychological Association; he is currently an associate editor of the *American Journal of Community Psychology*.

ACKNOWLEDGMENTS

I am convinced that we never really think alone. The ideas in this book are products of numerous conversations, collaborations, and shared contexts. I am grateful to the University of Wisconsin–Madison for providing an environment for investigating the topics addressed in this book, as well as sabbatical leave during the 2015–2016 academic year, when most of the writing was accomplished. Collaborations with faculty, staff, students, and community partners through the University of Wisconsin's School of Human Ecology and Center for Community and Nonprofit Studies have been influential. I am also grateful to collaborators in Vanderbilt University's Department of Human and Organizational Development, where I both completed graduate studies and returned as a faculty member in 2017.

Visits to other universities have also provided venues for discussing and advancing this work. I am grateful to the Instituto Superior de Psicologia Aplicada (Lisbon, Portugal); the Rollins School of Public Health at Emory University (Atlanta, GA); the Network for Nonprofit and Social Impact at Northwestern University (Chicago, IL); and the Center for Community Research, Learning, and Action at Wilfrid Laurier University (Waterloo, ON, Canada) for hosting productive visits while I was working on this book. The following individuals generously took time to read and provide feedback on chapter drafts: Sara Ansell, Anne Brodsky, Heidi Busse, Molly Clark-Barol, Doug Perkins, Jerusha Conner, Andy Peterson, Ethen Pollard, Paul Speer, and Rod Watts. Several reviewers provided helpful insights and suggestions during the proposal process, and series editors Nicole Allen and Brad Olson helped to enhance the overall concept and organization of the book. Nicole Allen served as action editor, and I am especially grateful for her guidance and detailed comments on drafts of every chapter. Finally, collaborations and conversations with community organizers and innovative practitioners have been fundamental to inspiring the questions and challenging and refining the concepts discussed in this book.

REFERENCES

Aber, J. L., Gershoff, E. T., Ware, A., & Kotler, J. A. (2004). Estimating the effects of September 11th and other forms of violence on the mental health and social development of New York City's youth: A matter of context. *Applied Developmental Science, 8*(3), 111–129. doi:10.1207/s1532480xads0803_2

Ahmad, M. S., & Abu Talib, N. B. (2014). Analysis of community empowerment on projects sustainability: Moderating role of sense of community. *Social Indicators Research, 129*(3), 1039–1056. doi:10.1007/s11205-014-0781-9

Aiyer, S. M., Zimmerman, M. A., Morrel-Samuels, S., & Reischl, T. M. (2015). From broken windows to busy streets: A community empowerment perspective. *Health Education & Behavior, 42*(2), 137–147. doi:10.1177/1090198114558590

Akiva, T. (2005). Turning training into results: The new youth program quality assessment. *High/Scope Resource, 24*(2), 21–24.

Alexander, M. (2010). *The new Jim Crow: Mass incarceration in the age of colorblindness.* New York, NY: New Press.

Alford, R., & Friedland, R. (1985). *The powers of theory: Capitalism, the state, and democracy.* Cambridge, England: Cambridge University Press.

Alia, K. A., Freedman, D. A., Brandt, H. M., & Browne, T. (2014). Identifying emergent social networks at a federally qualified health center-based farmers' market. *American Journal of Community Psychology, 53*(3–4), 335–345. doi:10.1007/s10464-013-9616-0

Alinsky, S. D. (1971). *Rules for radicals: A pragmatic primer for realistic radicals.* New York, NY: Vintage.

Altman, I., & Rogoff, B. (1987). World views in psychology: Trait, interactional, organismic, and tranactional perspectives. In D. Stokols & I. Altman (Eds.), *Handbook of environmental psychology* (pp. 7–40). New York, NY: Wiley.

Anderson, G. L. (1998). Toward authentic participation: Deconstructing the discourses of participatory reforms in education. *American Educational Research Journal, 35*(4), 571–603.

Anderson, G. L., & Donchik, L. M. (2016). Privatizing schooling and policy making: The American Legislative Exchange Council and new political and discursive strategies of education governance. *Educational Policy, 30*(2), 322–364. doi:10.1177/0895904814528794

Anderson, M. W. (2014). The new minimal cities. *The Yale Law Journal, 123*(5), 1118–1227.

Anheier, H. K. (2009). What kind of nonprofit sector, what kind of society? *American Behavioral Scientist, 52*(7), 1082–1094. doi:10.1177/0002764208327676

Anheier, H. K. (2014). *Nonprofit organizations: Theory, management, policy* (2nd ed.). New York, NY: Routledge.

Argyris, C. (1993). *On organizational learning.* Cambridge, MA: Blackwell.

Bachrach, P., & Baratz, M. S. (1962). The two faces of power. *The American Political Science Review, 56*(4), 947–952.

Bachrach, P., & Baratz, M. S. (1970). *Power and poverty: Theory and practice.* New York, NY: Oxford University Press.

Bacigalupe, A., Esnaola, S., Martín, U., & Zuazagoitia, J. (2010). Learning lessons from past mistakes: How can health in all policies fulfill its promises? *Journal of Epidemiology and Community Health, 64*(6), 504–505. doi:10.1136/jech.2010.110437

Badland, H., Whitzman, C., Lowe, M., Davern, M., Aye, L., Butterworth, I., . . . Giles-Corti, B. (2014). Urban livability: Emerging lessons from Australia for exploring the potential for indicators to measure the social determinants of health. *Social Science & Medicine, 111,* 64–73. doi:10.1016/j.socscimed.2014.04.003

Baiocchi, G., & Ganuza, E. (2014). Participatory budgeting as if emancipation mattered. *Politics & Society, 42*(1), 29–50. doi:10.1177/0032329213512978

Bandura, A. (1982). Self-efficacy mechanism in human agency. *American Psychologist, 37*(2), 122–147. doi:10.1037/0003-066X.37.2.122

Baptist, E. E. (2014). *The half has never been told: Slavery and the making of American capitalism.* Philadelphia, PA: Basic Books.

Barker, R. G. (1968). *Ecological psychology: Concepts and methods for studying the environment of human behavior.* Stanford, CA: Stanford University Press.

Barnes, S. L. (2005). Black church culture and community action. *Social Forces, 84*(2), 967–994. doi:10.1353/sof.2006.0003

Bartle, E. E., Couchonnal, G., Canda, E. R., & Staker, M. D. (2002). Empowerment as a dynamically developing concept for practice: Lessons learned from organizational ethnography. *Social Work, 47*(1), 32–43.

Belloni, R. (2001). Civil society and peacebuilding in Bosnia and Herzegovina. *Journal of Peace Research, 38*(2), 163–180. doi:10.1177/0022343301038002003

Bentele, K. G., & O'Brien, E. E. (2013). Jim Crow 2.0? Why states consider and adopt restrictive voter access policies. *Perspectives on Politics, 11*(04), 1088–1116. doi:10.1017/s1537592713002843

Berger, P. L., & Neuhaus, R. J. (1996). *To empower people: From state to civil society* (20th anniversary edition, M. Novak, Ed.). Washington, DC: American Enterprise Institute Press. (Original work published 1977)

Bernoff, J., & Schadler, T. (2010). *Empowered: Unleash your employees, energize your customers, and transform your business.* Cambridge, MA: Harvard Business Review Press.

Bess, K. D. (2015). Reframing coalitions as systems interventions: A network study exploring the contribution of a youth violence prevention coalition to broader system capacity. *American Journal of Community Psychology, 55*(3–4), 381–395. doi:10.1007/s10464-015-9715-1

Bess, K. D., Perkins, D. D., & McCown, D. L. (2011). Testing a measure of organizational learning capacity and readiness for transformational change in human services. *Journal of Prevention & Intervention in the Community, 39*(1), 35–49. doi:10.1080/10852352.2011.530164

Bess, K. D., Speer, P. W., & Perkins, D. D. (2012). Ecological contexts in the development of coalitions for youth violence prevention: An organizational network analysis. *Health Education & Behavior, 39*(5), 526–537. doi:10.1177/1090198111419656

Bezboruah, K. C. (2013). Community organizing for health care: An analysis of the process. *Journal of Community Practice, 21*(1–2), 9–27. doi:10.1080/10705422.2013.788328

Biglan, A. (2011). Corporate externalities: A challenge to the further success of prevention science. *Prevention Science, 12*(1), 1–11. doi:10.1007/s11121-010-0190-5

Blanch, A. (2016). Social support as a mediator between job control and psychological strain. *Social Science & Medicine, 157,* 148–155. doi:10.1016/j.socscimed.2016.04.007

Bond, M. A., & Keys, C. B. (1993). Empowerment, diversity, and collaboration: Promoting synergy on community boards. *American Journal of Community Psychology, 21*(1), 37–57. doi:10.1007/BF00938206

Bonjean, C. M. (1963). Community leadership: A case study and conceptual refinement. *American Journal of Sociology, 68*(6), 672–681.

Bornstein, D. (2011, March 7). Coming together to give schools a boost. *The New York Times.* Retrieved from http://opinionator.blogs.nytimes.com/2011/03/07/coming-together-to-give-schools-a-boost/?_r=0

Bosco, F. J. (2001). Place, space, networks, and the sustainability of collective action: The Madres de Plaza de Mayo. *Global Networks, 1*(4), 307–329. doi:10.1111/1471-0374.00018

Bouie, J. (2016). White won. *Slate.* Retrieved November 13, 2016, from http://www.slate.com/articles/news_and_politics/politics/2016/11/white_won.html

Bourdieu, P. (2000). *Pascalian meditations.* Stanford, CA: Stanford University Press.

Boyd, M. J., Zaff, J. F., Phelps, E., Weiner, M. B., & Lerner, R. M. (2011). The relationship between adolescents' news media use and civic engagement: The indirect effect of interpersonal communication with parents. *Journal of Adolescence, 34*(6), 1167–1179. doi:10.1016/j.adolescence.2011.07.004

Boyd, N. M. (2011). Organization development in community contexts. *Journal of Prevention and Intervention in the Community, 39*(1), 1–4. doi:10.1080/10852352.2011.530160

Boyd, N. M. (2015). Organization theory in community contexts. *Journal of Community Psychology, 43*(6), 649–653. doi:10.1002/jcop.21767

Boyd, N. M., & Angelique, H. (2007). Resuming the dialogue on organization studies and community psychology: An introduction to the special issue. *Journal of Community Psychology, 35*(3), 281–285. doi:10.1002/jcop.20148

Boyte, H. C., & Fretz, E. (2010). Civic professionalism. *Journal of Higher Education Outreach and Engagement, 14*(2), 67–90.

Breckler, S. J. (1984). Empirical validation of affect, behavior, and cognition as distinct components of attitude. *Journal of Personality and Social Psychology, 47*(6), 1191–1205. doi:10.1037/0022-3514.47.6.1191

Brewer, R. M., & Heitzeg, N. A. (2008). The racialization of crime and punishment: Criminal justice, color-blind racism, and the political economy of the prison industrial complex. *American Behavioral Scientist, 51*(5), 625–644. doi:10.1177/0002764207307745

Brodsky, A. E., & Cattaneo, L. B. (2013). A transconceptual model of empowerment and resilience: Divergence, convergence and interactions in kindred community concepts. *American Journal of Community Psychology, 52*(3–4), 333–346. doi:10.1007/s10464-013-9599-x

Bronfenbrenner, U. (1977). Lewinian space and ecological substance. *Journal of Social Issues, 33*(4), 199–212. doi:10.1111/j.1540-4560.1977.tb02533.x

Bronfenbrenner, U. (1979). *The ecology of human development: Experiments by nature and design.* Cambridge, MA: Harvard University Press.

Broomfield, M. (2017, January 23). Women's March against Donald Trump is the largest day of protests in US history, say political scientists. *The Independent.* Retrieved January 24, 2017, from http://www.independent.co.uk/news/world/americas/womens-march-anti-donald-trump-womens-rights-largest-protest-demonstration-us-history-political-a7541081.html

Burns, R. (2013, October 23). Schoolyard syndicalists: From the Chicago public school closings, some students emerge radicalized. *In These Times.* Retrieved from http://inthesetimes.com/article/15745/schoolyard_syndicalists

Butterfoss, F. D., & Kegler, M. C. (2002). Toward a comprehensive understanding of community coalitions: Moving from practice to theory. In R. DiClemente, L. Crosby, & M. C. Kegler (Eds.), *Emerging theories in health promotion practice and research* (pp. 157–193). San Francisco, CA: Jossey-Bass.

Butterfoss, F. D., Kegler, M. C., & Francisco, V. T. (2008). Mobilizing organizations for health promotion: Theories of organizational change. In K. Glanz, B. K. Rimer, & K. Viswanath (Eds.), *Health behavior and health education: Theory, research and practice* (4th ed., pp. 335–361). San Francisco, CA: Jossey-Bass.

Calvès, A. -E. (2009). Empowerment: The history of a key concept in contemporary development discourse. *Revue Tiers Monde, 200*(4), 735–749. doi:10.3917/rtm.200.0735

Camfield, L., & Skevington, S. M. (2008). On subjective well-being and quality of life. *Journal of Health Psychology, 13*(6), 764–775. doi:10.1177/1359105308093860

Camino, L., & Zeldin, S. (2002). From periphery to center: Pathways for youth civic engagement in the day-to-day life of communities. *Applied Developmental Science, 6*(4), 213–220. doi:10.1207/S1532480XADS0604_8

Campbell, C., Cornish, F., Gibbs, A., & Scott, K. (2010). Heeding the push from below: How do social movements persuade the rich to listen to the poor? *Journal of Health Psychology, 15*(7), 962–971. doi:10.1177/1359105310372815

Cargo, M., Grams, G. D., Ottoson, J. M., Ward, P., & Green, L. W. (2003). Empowerment as fostering positive youth development and citizenship. *American Journal of Health Behavior, 27*(Suppl. 1), 66–79.

Carson, C. (1995). *In struggle: SNCC and the Black awakening of the 1960s* (2nd ed.). Cambridge, MA: Harvard University Press.

Case, R., & Caragata, L. (2009). The emergence of a new social movement: Social networks and collective action on water issues in Guelph, Ontario. *Community Development, 40*(3), 247–261. doi:10.1080/15575330903091738

Cattaneo, L. B., Calton, J. M., & Brodsky, A. E. (2014). Status quo versus status quake: Putting the power back in empowerment. *Journal of Community Psychology, 42*(4), 433–446. doi:10.1002/jcop.21619

Cattaneo, L. B., & Chapman, A. R. (2010). The process of empowerment: A model for use in research and practice. *American Psychologist, 65*(7), 646–659. doi:10.1037/a0018854

Cederbaum, J. A., Petering, R., Hutchinson, M. K., He, A. S., Wilson, J. P., Jemmott, J. B., & Jemmott, L. S. (2015). Alcohol outlet density and related use in an urban black population in Philadelphia public housing communities. *Health & Place, 31*, 31–38. doi:10.1016/j.healthplace.2014.10.007

Chambers, E. T. (2006). *Roots for radicals: Organizing for power, action, and justice.* New York, NY: Continuum.

Chaplin, A. (2010). Social movements in Bolivia: From strength to power. *Community Development Journal, 45*(3), 346–355. doi:10.1093/cdj/bsq028

Chaskin, R. J. (2001). Building community capacity: A definitional framework and case studies from a comprehensive community initiative. *Urban Affairs Review, 36*(3), 291–323. doi:10.1177/10780870122184876

Checkoway, B., & Norsman, A. (1986). Empowering citizens with disabilities. *Community Development Journal, 21*(4), 270–277.

Cheryomukhin, A., & Peterson, N. A. (2014). Measuring relational and intrapersonal empowerment: Testing instrument validity in a former Soviet country with a secular Muslim culture. *American Journal of Community Psychology, 53*(3–4), 382–393. doi:10.1007/s10464-014-9649-z

Chetkovich, C., & Kunreuther, F. (2006). *From the ground up: Grassroots organizations making social change.* Ithaca, NY: Cornell University Press.

Cho, S., Crenshaw, K. W., & McCall, L. (2013). Toward a field of intersectionality studies: Theory, applications, and praxis. *Signs, 38*(4), 785–810. doi:10.1086/669608

Chomsky, N. (2011, March 9). The Cairo-Madison connection. *Truthout.* Retrieved from: https://truthout.org/articles/the-cairomadison-connection/

Christens, B. D. (2010). Public relationship building in grassroots community organizing: Relational intervention for individual and systems change. *Journal of Community Psychology, 38*(7), 886–900. doi:10.1002/jcop.20403

Christens, B. D. (2012a). Targeting empowerment in community development: A community psychology approach to enhancing local power and well-being. *Community Development Journal, 47*(4), 538–554. doi:10.1093/cdj/bss031

Christens, B. D. (2012b). Toward relational empowerment. *American Journal of Community Psychology, 50*(1–2), 114–128. doi:10.1007/s10464-011-9483-5

Christens, B. D. (2013). In search of powerful empowerment. *Health Education Research, 28*(3), 371–374. doi:10.1093/her/cyt045

Christens, B. D., & Collura, J. J. (2012). Local community organizers and activists encountering globalization: An exploratory study of their perceptions and adaptations. *Journal of Social Issues, 68*(3), 592–611. doi:10.1111/j.1540-4560.2012.01765.x

Christens, B. D., Collura, J. C., & Tahir, F. (2013). Critical hopefulness: A person-centered analysis of the intersection of cognitive and emotional empowerment. *American Journal of Community Psychology, 52*(1–2), 170–184. doi:10.1007/s10464-013-9586-2

Christens, B. D., & Dolan, T. (2011). Interweaving youth development, community development, and social change through youth organizing. *Youth & Society, 43*(2), 528–548. doi:10.1177/0044118X10383647

Christens, B. D., & Inzeo, P. T. (2015). Widening the view: Situating collective impact among frameworks for community-led change. *Community Development, 46*(4), 420–435. doi:10.1080/15575330.2015.1061680

Christens, B. D., Inzeo, P. T., & Faust, V. (2014). Channeling power across ecological systems: Social regularities in community organizing. *American Journal of Community Psychology, 53*(3–4), 419–431. doi:10.1007/s10464-013-9620-4

Christens, B. D., Krauss, S. E., & Zeldin, S. (2016). Malaysian validation of a sociopolitical control scale for youth. *Journal of Community Psychology, 44*(4), 531–537. doi:10.1002/jcop.21777

Christens, B. D., & Lin, C. S. (2014). Influences of community and organizational participation, social support, and sense of community on psychological empowerment: Income as moderator. *Family and Consumer Sciences Research Journal, 42*(3), 211–223. doi:10.1111/fcsr.12056

Christens, B. D., & Peterson, N. A. (2012). The role of empowerment in youth development: A study of sociopolitical control as mediator of ecological systems' influence on developmental outcomes. *Journal of Youth and Adolescence, 41*(5), 623–635. doi:10.1007/s10964-011-9724-9

Christens, B. D., Peterson, C. H., & Speer, P. W. (2014). Psychological empowerment in adulthood. In T. P. Gullotta & M. Bloom (Eds.), *Encyclopedia of primary prevention and health promotion* (2nd ed., pp. 1766–1776). New York, NY: Springer.

Christens, B. D., Peterson, N. A., & Speer, P. W. (2011). Community participation and psychological empowerment: Testing reciprocal causality using a cross-lagged panel design and latent constructs. *Health Education & Behavior, 38*(4), 339–347. doi:10.1177/1090198110372880

Christens, B. D., & Speer, P. W. (2011). Contextual influences on participation in community organizing: A multilevel longitudinal study. *American Journal of Community Psychology, 47*(3–4), 253–263. doi:10.1007/s10464-010-9393-y

Christens, B. D., & Speer, P. W. (2015). Community organizing: Practice, research, and policy implications. *Social Issues and Policy Review, 9*(1), 193–222. doi:10.1111/sipr.12014

Christens, B. D., Speer, P. W., & Peterson, N. A. (2011). Social class as moderator of the relationship between (dis)empowering processes and psychological empowerment. *Journal of Community Psychology, 39*(2), 170–182. doi:10.1002/jcop.20425

Christens, B. D., Speer, P. W., & Peterson, N. A. (2016). Assessing community participation: Comparing self-reported participation data with organizational attendance records. *American Journal of Community Psychology, 57*(3–4), 415–425. doi:10.1002/ajcp.12054

Christens, B. D., Winn, L. T., & Duke, A. M. (2016). Empowerment and critical consciousness: A conceptual cross-fertilization. *Adolescent Research Review, 1*(1), 15–27. doi:10.1007/s40894-015-0019-3

Citizens United v. Federal Election Commission, 558 U.S. (2010).

Clawson, D., & Clawson, M. A. (1999). What has happened to the US labor movement? Union decline and renewal. *Annual Review of Sociology, 25*, 95–119. http://www.jstor.org/stable/223499

Clopton, A. W., & Finch, B. L. (2011). Re-conceptualizing social anchors in community development: Utilizing social anchor theory to create social capital's third dimension. *Community Development, 42*(1), 70–83. doi:10.1080/15575330.2010.505293

Cloud, D. H., Parsons, J., & Delany-Brumsey, A. (2014). Addressing mass incarceration: A clarion call for public health. *American Journal of Public Health, 104*(3), 389–391. doi:10.2105/AJPH.2013.301741

Coates, T. (2014, June). The case for reparations. *The Atlantic.* Retrieved from http://www.theatlantic.com/magazine/archive/2014/06/the-case-for-reparations/361631/

Cobb, C. E. (2015). *This nonviolent stuff'll get you killed: How guns made the civil rights movement possible* (reprint ed.). Durham, NC: Duke University Press.

Collins, J. (2012). Theorizing Wisconsin's 2011 protests: Community-based unionism confronts accumulation by dispossession. *American Ethnologist, 39*(1), 6–20. doi:10.1111/j.1548-1425.2011.01340.x

Commission on the Social Determinants of Health (CSDH). (2008). *Closing the gap in a generation: Health equity through action on the social determinants of health.* Final Report of the Commission on Social Determinants of Health. Geneva, Switzerland: World Health Organization.

Conger, J. A., & Kanungo, R. N. (1988). The empowerment process: Integrating theory and practice. *Academy of Management Review, 13*(3), 471–482.

Conner, J. (2014). Lessons that last: Former youth organizers' reflections on what and how they learned. *Journal of the Learning Sciences, 23*(3), 447–484. doi:10.1080/10508406.2014.928213

Conner, J., & Rosen, S. (2013). How students are leading us: Youth organizing and the fight for public education in philadelphia. *Penn GSE Perspectives on Urban Education, 10*(1), n1.

Conner, J., & Zaino, K. (2014). Orchestrating effective change: How youth organizing influences education policy. *American Journal of Education, 120*(2), 173–203.

Conner, J., Zaino, K., & Scarola, E. (2013). "Very powerful voices": The influence of youth organizing on educational policy in Philadelphia. *Educational Policy, 27*(3), 560–588. doi:10.1177/0895904812454001

Conner, J. O. (2011). Youth organizers as young adults: Their commitments and contributions. *Journal of Research on Adolescence, 21*(4), 923–942. doi:10.1111/j.1532-7795.2011.00766.x

Conner, J. O., & Rosen, S. M. (2015). Zombies, truants, and flash mobs: How youth organizers respond to and shape youth policy. *National Society for the Study of Education, 114*(1), 203–220.

Cooke, B., & Kothari, U. (Eds.). (2001). *Participation: The new tyranny?* New York, NY: Zed Books.

Cornish, F., Campbell, C., Shukla, A., & Banerji, R. (2012). From brothel to boardroom: Prospects for community leadership of HIV interventions in the context of global funding practices. *Health & Place, 18*(3), 468–474. doi:10.1016/j.healthplace.2011.08.018

Cornwall, A., & Anyidoho, N. A. (2010). Introduction: Women's empowerment: Contentions and contestations. *Development, 53*(2), 144–149. doi:10.1057/dev.2010.34

Craig, G., & Mayo, M. (Eds.). (1995). *Community empowerment: A reader in participation and development.* London, England: Zed Books.

Cramer Walsh, K. (2012). Putting inequality in its place: Rural consciousness and the power of perspective. *American Political Science Review, 106*(03), 517–532. doi:10.1017/S0003055412000305

Crisp, B. R., Swerissen, H., & Duckett, S. J. (2000). Four approaches to capacity building in health: Consequences for measurement and accountability. *Health Promotion International, 15*(2), 99–107. doi:10.1093/heapro/15.2.99

Crutchfield, L. R., & Grant, H. M. (2012). *Forces for good: The six practices of high-impact nonprofits* (Rev. ed.). San Francisco, CA: Jossey-Bass.

Dahl, R. A. (2005). *Who governs? Democracy and power in an American city.* (2nd ed.). New Haven, CT: Yale University Press. (Original work published 1961)

Damon, W. (2004). What is positive youth development? *The Annals of the American Academy of Political and Social Science, 591*(1), 13–24. doi:10.1177/0002716203260092

Danese, A., & McEwen, B. S. (2012). Adverse childhood experiences, allostasis, allostatic load, and age-related disease. *Physiology & Behavior, 106*(1), 29–39. doi:10.1016/j.physbeh.2011.08.019

Darnell, A. J., Barile, J. P., Weaver, S. R., Harper, C. R., Kuperminc, G. P., & Emshoff, J. G. (2013). Testing effects of community collaboration on rates of low infant birthweight at the county level. *American Journal of Community Psychology, 51*(3–4), 398–406. doi:10.1007/s10464-012-9559-x

Davis, A. Y. (2003). *Are prisons obsolete?* Toronto, ON, Canada: Publishers Group Canada.

Dean, D. G. (1961). Alienation: Its meaning and measurement. *American Sociological Review, 26,* 753–758.

De Charms, R. (1968). *Personal causation.* New York, NY: Academic Press.

de Chavez, A. C., Backett-Milburn, K., Parry, O., & Platt, S. (2005). Understanding and researching wellbeing: Its usage in different disciplines and potential for health research and health promotion. *Health Education Journal, 64*(1), 70–87.

de Sousa Santos, B. (1998). Participatory budgeting in Porto Alegre: Toward a redistributive democracy. *Politics & Society, 26*(4), 461–510. doi:10.1177/0032329298026004003

Dewey, J. (1916). *Democracy and education.* New York, NY: Macmillan.

Dewey, J. (1927). *The public and its problems.* New York, NY: Henry Holt and Company.

Dewey, J., & Bentley, A. (1949). *Knowing and the known.* Boston, MA: Beacon Press.

Diani, M. (1996). Linking mobilization frames and political opportunities: Insights from regional populism in Italy. *American Sociological Review, 61*(6), 1053–1069.

Diani, M. (2012). Interest organizations in social movements: An empirical exploration. *Interest Groups & Advocacy, 1*(1), 26–47. doi:10.1057/iga.2012.1

Diemer, M. A., & Blustein, D. L. (2006). Critical consciousness and career development among urban youth. *Journal of Vocational Behavior, 68*(2), 220–232. doi:10.1016/j.jvb.2005.07.001

Diemer, M. A., & Li, C. -H. (2011). Critical consciousness development and political participation among marginalized youth. *Child Development, 82*(6), 1815–1833. doi:10.1111/j.1467-8624.2011.01650.x

Diemer, M. A., Rapa, L. J., Park, C. J., & Perry, J. C. (2017). Development and validation of the critical consciousness scale. *Youth & Society, 49*(4), 461–483. doi:10.1177/0044118X14538289

Diener, E. (2006). Guidelines for national indicators of subjective well-being and ill-being. *Journal of Happiness Studies, 7*(4), 397–404.

Dokecki, P. R., Scanlan, P., & Strain, B. (1972). In search of a transactional model for educational intervention: Reactions to Farber and Lewis. *Peabody Journal of Education, 49*(3), 182–187. doi:10.2307/1492054

Dolan, T., Christens, B. D., & Lin, C. S. (2015). Combining youth organizing and youth participatory action research to strengthen student voice in education reform. *National Society for the Study of Education, 114*(1), 153–170.

Domhoff, G. W. (1978). *Who really rules? New Haven and community power re-examined.* New Brunswick, NJ: Transaction Books.

Domhoff, G. W. (2009). The power elite and their challengers: The role of nonprofits in American social conflict. *American Behavioral Scientist, 52*(7), 955–973. doi:10.1177/0002764208327669

Domhoff, G. W. (2013). *The myth of liberal ascendancy: Corporate dominance from the Great Depression to the Great Recession.* Boulder, CO: Paradigm.

Dowding, K. (2001). Explaining urban regimes. *International Journal of Urban and Regional Research, 25*(1), 7–19.

Dunbar-Ortiz, R. (2015). *An indigenous peoples' history of the United States.* Boston, MA: Beacon Press.

Dunn, E. C., Winning, A., Zaika, N., & Subramanian, V. (2014). Does poor health predict moving, move quality, and desire to move?: A study examining neighborhood selection in US adolescents and adults. *Health & Place, 30,* 154–164. doi:10.1016/j.healthplace.2014.08.007

Dzurinko, N., McCants, J., & Stith, J. (2011). The campaign for nonviolent schools: Students flip the script on violence in Philadelphia. *Voices in Urban Education, 2011*(Spring), 22–30.

Earls, F., & Carlson, M. (2001). The social ecology of child health and well-being. *Annual Review of Public Health, 22*(1), 143–166. doi:10.1146/annurev.publhealth.22.1.143

Economos, C. D., Hyatt, R. R., Goldberg, J. P., Must, A., Naumova, E. N., Collins, J. J., & Nelson, M. E. (2007). A community intervention reduces BMI z-score in children: Shape up Somerville first year results. *Obesity, 15*(5), 1325–1336. doi:10.1038/oby.2007.155

Edwards, M. L. (2011). "Our people are still resisting": Farmworker community organizing and the Texas agricultural system. *Organization & Environment, 24*(2), 175–191. doi:10.1177/1086026611412082

Eikenberry, A. M., & Kluver, J. D. (2004). The marketization of the nonprofit sector: Civil society at risk? *Public Administration Review, 64*(2), 132–140.

Eisman, A. B., Zimmerman, M. A., Kruger, D., Reischl, T. M., Miller, A. L., Franzen, S. P., & Morrel-Samuels, S. (2016). Psychological empowerment among urban youth: Measurement model and associations with youth outcomes. *American Journal of Community Psychology, 58*(3–4), 410–421. doi:10.1002/ajcp.12094

Ekström, M., & Östman, J. (2013). Family talk, peer talk and young people's civic orientation. *European Journal of Communication, 28*(3), 294–308. doi:10.1177/0267323113475410

Ellis, F., & Biggs, S. (2001). Evolving themes in rural development 1950s–2000s. *Development Policy Review, 19*(4), 437–448.

Eng, E., & Parker, E. (1994). Measuring community competence in the Mississippi delta: The interface between program evaluation and empowerment. *Health Education Quarterly, 21*(2), 199. doi:10.1177/109019819402100206

Escobar, A. (2006). Difference and conflict in the struggle over natural resources: A political ecology framework. *Development, 49*(3), 6–13. doi:10.1057/palgrave.development.1100267

Evans, S. D., Rosen, A. D., Kesten, S. M., & Moore, W. (2014). Miami thrives: Weaving a poverty reduction coalition. *American Journal of Community Psychology, 53*(3–4), 357–368. doi:10.1007/s10464-014-9657-z

Evans, S. M., & Boyte, H. C. (1986, 1992). *Free spaces: The sources of democratic change in America.* Chicago, IL: University of Chicago Press.

Fairclough, A. (2001). *To redeem the soul of America: The Southern Christian Leadership Conference and Martin Luther King, Jr.* Athens, GA: University of Georgia Press. (Originally published 1987)

Fawcett, S. B., Paine-Andrews, A., Francisco, V. T., Schultz, J. A., Richter, K. P., Lewis, R. K., . . . Lopez, C. M. (1995). Using empowerment theory in collaborative partnerships for community health and development. *American Journal of Community Psychology, 23*(5), 677–697.

Fedi, A., Mannarini, T., & Maton, K. I. (2009). Empowering community settings and community mobilization. *Community Development, 40*(3), 275–291. doi:10.1080/15575330903109985

Feinberg, M. E., Riggs, N. R., & Greenberg, M. T. (2005). Social networks and community prevention coalitions. *The Journal of Primary Prevention, 26*(4), 279–298. doi:10.1007/s10935-005-5390-4

Fetterman, D. M. (1994). Empowerment evaluation. *American Journal of Evaluation, 15*(1), 1–15. doi:10.1177/109821409401500101

Fetterman, D. M. (2002). Empowerment evaluation: Building communities of practice and a culture of learning. *American Journal of Community Psychology, 30*(1), 89–102.

Fine, M. (2015). Glocal provocations: Critical reflections on community based research and intervention designed at the (glocal) intersections of global dynamics and local cultures. *Community Psychology in Global Perspective, 1*(1), 5–15.

Fine, M., & Ruglis, J. (2009). Circuits and consequences of dispossession: The racialized realignment of the public sphere for US youth. *Transforming Anthropology, 17*(1), 20–33. doi:10.1111/j.1548-7466.2009.01037.x.

Fine, G. A., & Harrington, B. (2004). Tiny publics: Small groups and civil society. *Sociological Theory, 22*(3), 341–356.

Flanagan, C., & Levine, P. (2010). Civic engagement and the transition to adulthood. *The Future of Children, 20*(1), 159–179.

Flanagan, C. A., & Christens, B. D. (2011). Youth civic development: Historical context and emerging issues. *New Directions for Child and Adolescent Development, 134,* 1–9. doi:10.1002/cd.307

Flanagan, C. A., Kim, T., Collura, J., & Kopish, M. A. (2015). Community service and adolescents' social capital. *Journal of Research on Adolescence, 25*(2), 295–309. doi:10.1111/jora.12137

Flanagan, C. A., Martínez, M. L., & Cumsille, P. (2011). Civil societies as cultural and developmental contexts for civic identity formation. In L. A. Jensen (Ed.), *Bridging developmental and cultural psychology: New syntheses in theory, research, and policy* (pp. 113–137). New York, NY: Oxford University Press.

Flanagan, C. A., Martínez, M. L., Cumsille, P., & Ngomane, T. (2011). Youth civic development: Theorizing a domain with evidence from different cultural contexts. *New Directions for Child and Adolescent Development, 134,* 95–109. doi:10.1002/cd.313

Flood, J., Minkler, M., Lavery, S. H., Estrada, J., & Falbe, J. (2015). The collective impact model and its potential for health promotion: Overview and case study of a healthy retail initiative in San Francisco. *Health Education & Behavior, 42*(5), 654–668. doi:10.1177/1090198115577372

Flyvbjerg, B. (1998). *Rationality and power: Democracy in process.* Chicago, IL: University of Chicago Press.

Flyvbjerg, B. (2002). Bringing power to planning research: One researcher's praxis story. *Journal of Planning Education and Research, 21*(4), 353–366. doi:10.1177/0739456X0202100401

Forjaz, M. J., Prieto-Flores, M. -E., Ayala, A., Rodriguez-Blazquez, C., Fernandez-Mayoralas, G., Rojo-Perez, F., & Martinez-Martin, P. (2011). Measurement properties of the community wellbeing index in older adults. *Quality of Life Research, 20*(5), 733–743. doi:10.1007/s11136-010-9794-2

Foss, B., & Dyrstad, S. M. (2011). Stress in obesity: Cause or consequence? *Medical Hypotheses, 77*(1), 7–10. doi:10.1016/j.mehy.2011.03.011

Foster-Fishman, P. G., Fitzgerald, K., Brandell, C., Nowell, B., Chavis, D., & Van Egeren, L. A. (2006). Mobilizing residents for action: The role of small wins and strategic supports. *American Journal of Community Psychology, 38*(3–4), 143–152. doi:10.1007/s10464-006-9081-0

Foster-Fishman, P. G., Salem, D. A., Allen, N. A., & Fahrbach, K. (2001). Facilitating interorganizational collaboration: The contributions of interorganizational alliances. *American Journal of Community Psychology, 29*(6), 875–905. doi:10.1023/A:1012915631956

Foucault, M. (1977). *Discipline and punish: The birth of the prison.* New York, NY: Pantheon Books.

Foucault, M. (1982). The subject and power. *Critical Inquiry, 8*(4), 777–795.

Fraser, S. (2015). *The age of acquiescence: The life and death of American resistance to organized wealth and power.* New York: Little, Brown and Company.

Freire, P. (1973). *Education for critical consciousness.* New York, NY: Seabury.

Frerichs, L. M., Araz, O. M., & Huang, T. T.-K. (2013). Modeling social transmission dynamics of unhealthy behaviors for evaluating prevention and treatment interventions on childhood obesity. *PloS One, 8*(12), e82887. doi:10.1371/journal.pone.0082887

Freudenberg, N. (2002). Adverse effects of US jail and prison policies on the health and well-being of women of color. *American Journal of Public Health, 92*(12), 1895–1899.

Freudenberg, N. (2004). Community capacity for environmental health promotion: Determinants and implications for practice. *Health Education & Behavior, 31*(4), 472–490. doi:10.1177/1090198104265599

Freudenberg, N., Daniels, J., Crum, M., Perkins, T., & Richie, B. E. (2005). Coming home from jail: The social and health consequences of community reentry for women, male adolescents, and their families and communities. *American Journal of Public Health, 95*(10), 1725–1736. doi:10.2105/AJPH.2004.056325

Freudenberg, N., Fahs, M., Galea, S., & Greenberg, A. (2006). The impact of New York City's 1975 fiscal crisis on the tuberculosis, HIV, and homicide syndemic. *American Journal of Public Health, 96*(3), 424.

Friedman, T. L. (2005). *The world is flat: A brief history of the twenty-first century*. New York: Farrar, Straus and Giroux.

Frumkin, P. (2005). *On being nonprofit: A conceptual and policy primer*. Cambridge, MA: Harvard University Press.

Fuller-Rowell, T. E., Evans, G. W., & Ong, A. D. (2012). Poverty and health: The mediating role of perceived discrimination. *Psychological Science, 23*(7), 734–739. doi:10.1177/0956797612439720

Fullilove, M. T., & Wallace, R. (2011). Serial forced displacement in American cities, 1916–2010. *Journal of Urban Health, 88*(3), 381–389. doi:10.1007/s11524-011-9585-2

Galaskiewicz, J., Bielefeld, W., & Dowell, M. (2006). Networks and organizational growth: A study of community-based nonprofits. *Administrative Science Quarterly, 51*, 337–380.

Ganz, M. (2011). Public narrative, collective action, and power. In S. Odugbemi & T. Lee (Eds.), *Accountability through public opinion: From inertia to public action*. (pp. 273–289). Washington, DC: World Bank.

Gaventa, J. (1980). *Power and powerlessness: Quiescence and rebellion in an Appalachian valley*. Urbana, IL: University of Illinois Press.

Gaventa, J. (2006). Finding the spaces for change: A power analysis. *Institute for Development Studies Bulletin, 37*(6), 23–33.

Gergen, K. J. (2009). *Relational being: Beyond self and community*. New York, NY: Oxford University Press.

Gershon, D., & Straub, G. (1989). *Empowerment: The art of creating your life as you want it*. New York: High Point.

Gessen, M. (2014). *Words will break cement: The passion of Pussy Riot*. New York, NY: Riverhead Books.

Gilster, M. E. (2012). Comparing neighborhood-focused activism and volunteerism: Psychological well-being and social connectedness. *Journal of Community Psychology, 40*(7), 769–784. doi:10.1002/jcop.20528

Ginwright, S. A. (2010). Peace out to revolution! Activism among African American youth: An argument for radical healing. *Young, 18*(1), 77–96. doi:10.1177/110330880901800106

Goffman, E. (1974). *Frame analysis: An essay on the organization of experience*. Cambridge, MA: Harvard University Press.

Gone, J. P. (2013). Redressing first nations historical trauma: Theorizing mechanisms for indigenous culture as mental health treatment. *Transcultural Psychiatry, 50*(5), 683–706. doi:10.1177/1363461513487669

Goodman, R. M., Speers, M. A., Mcleroy, K., Fawcett, S. B., Kegler, M., Smith, S. R., . . . Wallerstein, N. (1998). Identifying and defining the dimensions of community capacity to provide a basis for measurement. *Health Education & Behavior, 25*(3), 258–278. doi:10.1177/109019819802500303

Gotham, K. F., & Campanella, R. (2011). Coupled vulnerability and resilience: The dynamics of cross-scale interactions in post-Katrina New Orleans. *Ecology and Society, 16*(3), art. 12. doi:10.5751/es-04292-160312

Graham, L., Brown-Jeffy, S., Aronson, R., & Stephens, C. (2011). Critical race theory as theoretical framework and analysis tool for population health research. *Critical Public Health, 21*(1), 81–93. doi:10.1080/09581596.2010.493173

Gramsci, A. (2000). *The Antonio Gramsci reader: Selected writings 1916–1935*. New York, NY: New York University Press.

Green, L. W. (2006). Public health asks of systems science: To advance our evidence-based practice, can you help us get more practice-based evidence? *American Journal of Public Health, 96*(3), 406. doi:10.2105/AJPH.2005.066035

Green, L. W., Richard, L., & Potvin, L. (1996). Ecological foundations of health promotion. *American Journal of Health Promotion, 10*(4), 270–281. doi:10.4278/0890-1171-10.4.270

Greenhouse, S. (2011). Moral support in a steady stream of pizzas. *New York Times*. Retrieved May 26, 2016, from http://www.nytimes.com/2011/02/26/us/26madison.html

Griffith, D. M., Allen, J. O., Zimmerman, M. A., Morrel-Samuels, S., Reischl, T. M., Cohen, S. E., & Campbell, K. A. (2008). Organizational empowerment in community mobilization to address youth violence. *American Journal of Preventive Medicine, 34*(3), S89–S99. doi:10.1016/j.amepre.2007.12.015

Gruber, J., & Trickett, E. J. (1987). Can we empower others? The paradox of empowerment in an alternative public high school. *American Journal of Community Psychology, 15*, 353–372. doi:10.1007/BF00922703

Gulati, R., & Gargiulo, M. (1999). Where do interorganizational networks come from? *American Journal of Sociology, 104*(5), 1439–1493.

Guo, C., & Acar, M. (2005). Understanding collaboration among nonprofit organizations: Combining resource dependency, institutional, and network perspectives. *Nonprofit and Voluntary Sector Quarterly, 34*(3), 340. doi:10.1177/0899764005275411

Gutiérrez, L. M. (1990). Working with women of color: An empowerment perspective. *Social Work, 35*(2), 149–153.

Gutiérrez, L. M., GlenMaye, L., & DeLois, K. (1995). The organizational context of empowerment practice: Implications for social work administration. *Social Work, 40*(2), 249–258.

Gutiérrez, L. M., & Lewis, E. A. (1994). Community organizing with women of color: A feminist approach. *Journal of Community Practice, 1*(2), 23–44. doi:10.1300/J125v01n02_03

Gutiérrez, L. M., & Lewis, E. A. (2012). Education, participation, and capacity building in community organizing with women of color. In M. Minkler (Ed.), *Community organizing and community building for health and welfare* (3rd ed., pp. 215–228). New Brunswick, NJ: Rutgers University Press.

Gutiérrez, L. M., Oh, H. J., & Gillmore, M. R. (2000). Toward an understanding of (em)power(ment) for HIV/AIDS prevention with adolescent women. *Sex Roles, 42*(7–8), 581–611.

Hacker, J. S., & Pierson, P. (2010). *Winner take-all politics: How Washington made the rich richer—and turned its back on the middle class.* New York, NY: Simon & Schuster.

Haiven, M., & Khasnabish, A. (2014). *The radical imagination: Social movement research in the age of austerity.* London, England: Zed Books.

Hall, P. D. (2013). Philanthropy, the nonprofit sector, and the democratic dilemma. *Daedalus,* 2013(Spring), 139–158.

Hamer, E. (2017, February 14). The Women's March happened. Now what? Experts say protests need to be a part of a "bigger strategy" to be effective. *The Badger Herald.* Retrieved February 27, 2017, from https://badgerherald.com/news/2017/02/14/the-womens-march-happened-now-what/

Hammen, C. (2005). Stress and depression. *Annual Review of Clinical Psychology, 1*(1), 293–319. doi:10.1146/annurev.clinpsy.1.102803.143938

HanleyBrown, F., Kania, J., & Kramer, M. (2012). Channeling change: Making collective impact work. *Stanford Social Innovation Review, 2012*(Winter), 1–8.

Harvey, D. (2007). Neoliberalism as creative destruction. *The Annals of the American Academy of Political and Social Science, 610*, 21–44.

Hawe, P. (2015). Lessons from complex interventions to improve health. *Annual Review of Public Health, 36*(1), 307–323. doi:10.1146/annurev-publhealth-031912-114421

Hawe, P., Shiell, A., & Riley, T. (2009). Theorising interventions as events in systems. *American Journal of Community Psychology, 43*, 267–276. doi:10.1007/s10464-009-9229-9

Hawley, A. (1963). Community power and urban renewal success. *American Journal of Sociology, 68*(4), 422–431.

Hedges, C. (2010). *The world as it is: Dispatches on the myth of human progress.* New York, NY: Nation Books.

Heller, S. B. (2014). Summer jobs reduce violence among disadvantaged youth. *Science, 346*(6214), 1219–1223. doi:10.1126/science.1257809

Helliwell, J. F., & Putnam, R. D. (2004). The social context of well-being. *Philosophical Transactions of the Royal Society B, 359*, 1435–1446. doi:10.1098/rstb.2004.1522

Heritage, Z., & Dooris, M. (2009). Community participation and empowerment in Healthy Cities. *Health Promotion International, 24*(Suppl. 1), i45–i55. doi:10.1093/heapro/dap054

Hess, D. E. (2002). Discussing controversial public issues in secondary social studies classrooms: Learning from skilled teachers. *Theory & Research in Social Education, 30*(1), 10–41. doi:10.1080/00933104.2002.10473177

Hoffman, C. (1978). Empowerment movements and mental health: Locus of control and commitment to the united farm workers. *Journal of Community Psychology, 6*(3), 216–221.

Hope, E. C., & Jagers, R. J. (2014). The role of sociopolitical attitudes and civic education in the civic engagement of black youth. *Journal of Research on Adolescence, 24*(3), 460–470. doi:10.1111/jora.12117

Hughey, J., Speer, P. W., & Peterson, N. A. (1999). Sense of community in community organizations: Structure and evidence of validity. *Journal of Community Psychology, 27*(1), 97–113. doi:10.1002/(SICI)1520-6629(199901)27:1<97::AID-JCOP7>3.0.CO;2-K

Hunter, F. (1953). *Community power structure: A study of decision makers.* Chapel Hill, NC: University of North Carolina Press.

Hunter, F., Schaffer, R. C., & Sheps, C. G. (1956). *Community organization: Action and inaction.* Chapel Hill, NC: University of North Carolina Press.

Hurd, N. M., Stoddard, S. A., & Zimmerman, M. A. (2013). Neighborhoods, social support, and African American adolescents' mental health outcomes: A multilevel path analysis. *Child Development, 84*(3), 858–874. doi:10.1111/cdev.12018

Imbroscio, D. (2013). From redistribution to ownership: Toward an alternative urban policy for America's cities. *Urban Affairs Review, 49*(6), 787–820. doi:10.1177/1078087413495362

INCITE! Women of Color Against Violence (Ed.). (2009). *The revolution will not be funded: Beyond the non-profit industrial complex.* Brooklyn, NY: South End Press.

Israel, B. A., Checkoway, B., Schulz, A., & Zimmerman, M. (1994). Health education and community empowerment: Conceptualizing and measuring perceptions of individual, organizational, and community control. *Health Education Quarterly, 21*(2), 149–170. doi:10.1177/109019819402100203

Itzhaky, H., & York, A. S. (2000). Sociopolitical control and empowerment: An extended replication. *Journal of Community Psychology, 28*(4), 407–415. doi:10.1002/1520-6629(200007)28:4<407::AID-JCOP3>3.0.CO;2-R

Itzhaky, H., & York, A. S. (2002). Showing results in community organization. *Social Work, 47*(2), 125–131.

Jacobs, J. (1961). *The death and life of great American cities.* New York, NY: Random House.

Jason, L. A., Stevens, E., Ram, D., Miller, S. A., Beasley, C. R., & Gleason, K. (2016). Theories in the field of community psychology. *Global Journal of Community Psychology Practice, 7*(2), 1–27. Retrieved from https://www.gjcpp.org/en/article.php?issue=22&article=125

Jonas, E. G., & Wilson, D. (Eds.). (1999). *The urban growth machine: Critical perspectives, two decades later.* Albany, NY: State University of New York Press.

Jones, C. P. (2000). Levels of racism: A theoretic framework and a gardener's tale. *American Journal of Public Health, 90*(8), 1212–1215.

Jones, B. D., & Baumgartner, F. R. (2012). From there to here: Punctuated equilibrium to the general punctuation thesis to a theory of government information processing. *The Policy Studies Journal, 40*(1), 1–19.

Jost, J. T., Banaji, M. R., & Nosek, B. A. (2004). A decade of system justification theory: Accumulated evidence of conscious and unconscious bolstering of the status quo. *Political Psychology, 25*(6), 881–919. doi:10.1111/j.1467-9221.2004.00402.x

Jost, J. T., Ledgerwood, A., & Hardin, C. D. (2008). Shared reality, system justification, and the relational basis of ideological beliefs. *Social and Personality Psychology Compass, 2*(1), 171–186. doi:10.1111/j.1751-9004.2007.00056.x

Kahne, J., & Middaugh, E. (2008). *Democracy for some: The civic opportunity gap in high school.* Medford, MA: Center for Information & Research on Civic Learning & Engagement (CIRCLE).

Kaiser, A. A., & Rusch, L. (2015). Trade-offs in empowerment through social action: Voices from Detroit. *Community Development, 46*(4), 361–379. doi:10.1080/15575330.2015.1063527

Kane, L. (2010). Community development: Learning from popular education in Latin America. *Community Development Journal, 45*(3), 276–286. doi:10.1093/cdj/bsq021

Kania, J., & Kramer, M. (2011). Collective impact. *Stanford Social Innovation Review, 2011*, 36–41.

Kasmel, A., & Tanggaard, P. (2011). Evaluation of changes in individual community-related empowerment in community health promotion interventions in Estonia. *International Journal of Environmental Research and Public Health, 8*(6), 1772–1791. doi:10.3390/ijerph8061772

Kawachi, I., & Berkman, L. (2001). Social ties and mental health. *Journal of Urban Health, 78*(3), 458–467. doi:10.1093/jurban/78.3.458

Kay, A. C., & Jost, J. T. (2003). Complementary justice: Effects of "poor but happy" and "poor but honest" stereotype exemplars on system justification and implicit activation of the justice motive. *Journal of Personality and Social Psychology, 85*(5), 823–837. doi:10.1037/0022-3514.85.5.823

Kegler, M. C., Rigler, J., & Honeycutt, S. (2010). How does community context influence coalitions in the formation stage? A multiple case study based on the community coalition action theory. *BMC Public Health, 10*, 90. doi:10.1186/1471-2458-10-90

Kegler, M. C., Rigler, J., & Ravani, M. K. (2010). Using network analysis to assess the evolution of organizational collaboration in response to a major environmental health threat. *Health Education Research, 25*(3), 413–424. doi:10.1093/her/cyq022

Kegler, M. C., & Swan, D. W. (2011). An initial attempt at operationalizing and testing the community coalition action theory. *Health Education & Behavior, 38*(3), 261–270. doi:10.1177/1090198110372875

Kegler, M. C., & Swan, D. W. (2012). Advancing coalition theory: The effect of coalition factors on community capacity mediated by member engagement. *Health Education Research, 27*(4), 572–584. doi:10.1093/her/cyr083

Kelley, R. D. G. (2003). *Freedom dreams: The black radical imagination.* Boston, MA: Beacon Press.

Kellogg Foundation. (2004). *Logic model development guide: Using logic models to bring together planning, evaluation, and action.* Battle Creek, MI: Author.

Kelly, J. G., & Hess, R. (Eds.). (1986). *The ecology of prevention: Illustrating mental health consultation.* New York, NY: Haworth.

Kelly, S. (2014). Towards a negative ontology of leadership. *Human Relations, 67*(8), 905–922. doi:10.1177/0018726713503177

Kemble, R. (2013, March 12). Madison's solidarity sing along, two years in. *The Progressive.* Retrieved from http://www.progressive.org/news/2013/03/181227/madison's-solidarity-sing-along-two-years

Kerrissey, J. (2015). Collective labor rights and income inequality. *American Sociological Review, 80*(3), 626–653. doi:10.1177/0003122415583649

Kieffer, C. H. (1984). Citizen empowerment: A developmental perspective. In J. Rappaport & R. Hess (Eds.), *Studies in empowerment: Steps toward understanding and action* (pp. 9–36). New York, NY: Haworth Press.

King, P. (2006). Ida B. Wells and the management of nonviolence. *Critical Review of International Social and Political Philosophy, 7*(4), 111–146. doi:10.1080/1369823042000330060

Kirshner, B. (2009). Power in numbers: Youth organizing as a context for exploring civic identity. *Journal of Research on Adolescence, 19*(3), 414–440. doi:10.1111/j.1532-7795.2009.00601.x

Kirshner, B., Hipolito-Delgado, C., & Zion, S. (2015). Sociopolitical development in educational systems: From margins to center. *The Urban Review, 47*(5), 803–808. doi:10.1007/s11256-015-0335-8

Kivimäki, M., Ferrie, J. E., Head, J., Shipley, M. J., Vahtera, J., & Marmot, M. G. (2004). Organisational justice and change in justice as predictors of employee health: The Whitehall II study. *Journal of Epidemiology and Community Health, 58*(11), 931–937. doi:10.1136/jech.2003.019026

Klandermans, B. (1984). Mobilization and participation: Social-psychological expansions of resource mobilization theory. *American Sociological Review, 49*(5), 583–600.

Klar, M., & Kasser, T. (2009). Some benefits of being an activist: Measuring activism and its role in psychological well-being. *Political Psychology, 30*(5), 755–777. doi:10.1111/j.1467-9221.2009.00724.x

Klein, D. (1968). *Community dynamic and mental health.* New York, NY: Wiley.

Klein, E. (2016, December 23). Partisanship is a helluva drug. *Vox.* Retrieved January 4, 2017, from https://www.vox.com/policy-and-politics/2016/12/23/14062616/republicans-trump-ideology-conservatives

Knight, L. W. (2010). *Jane Addams: Spirit in action.* New York, NY: Norton.

Kocieniewski, D. (2012). But nobody pays that [series]. *The New York Times.* Retrieved from http://topics.nytimes.com/top/features/timestopics/series/but_nobody_pays_that/index.html

Krauss, S. E., Collura, J., Zeldin, S., Ortega, A., Abdullah, H., & Sulaiman, A. H. (2014). Youth-adult partnership: Exploring contributions to empowerment, agency and community connections in malaysian youth programs. *Journal of Youth and Adolescence, 43*(9), 1–13. doi:10.1007/s10964-013-0027-1

Krieger, N. (2008). Proximal, distal, and the politics of causation: What's level got to do with it? *American Journal of Public Health, 98*(2), 221–230. doi:10.2105/AJPH.2007.111278

Krieger, N. (2014). Discrimination and health inequities. *International Journal of Health Services, 44*(4), 643–710. doi:10.2190/HS.44.4.b

Kroll, A. (2011, February 28). The spirit of Egypt in Madison: Eating Egyptian pizza in downtown Madison. *Mother Jones.* Retrieved from https://www.motherjones.com/politics/2011/02/egypt-madison-ians-pizza/

Kronenberg, C., & Kalter, F. (2012). Rational choice theory and empirical research: Methodological and theoretical contributions. *Annual Review of Sociology, 38*, 73–92. doi:10.1146/annurev-soc-071811-145441

Labonte, R. (1994). Health promotion and empowerment: Reflections on professional practice. *Health Education Quarterly, 21*(2), 253. doi:10.1177/109019819402100209

Lamore, R. L., Link, T., & Blackmond, T. (2006). Renewing people and places: Institutional investment policies that enhance social capital and improve the built environment of distressed communities. *Journal of Urban Affairs, 28*(5), 429–442. doi:10.1111/j.1467-9906.2006.00308.x

Langhout, R. D., Collins, C., & Ellison, E. R. (2014). Examining relational empowerment for elementary school students in a yPAR program. *American Journal of Community Psychology, 53*(3–4), 369–381. doi:10.1007/s10464-013-9617-z

Lasch-Quinn, E. (1993). *Black neighbors: Race and the limits of reform in the American settlement house movement, 1890–1945.* Chapel Hill, NC: University of North Carolina Press.

Lasker, R. D., Weiss, E. S., & Miller, R. (2001). Partnership synergy: A practical framework for studying and strengthening the collaborative advantage. *Milbank Quarterly, 79*(2), 179–205. doi:10.1111/1468-0009.00203

Laverack, G. (2001). An identification and interpretation of the organizational aspects of community empowerment. *Community Development Journal, 36*(2), 134–145. doi:10.1093/cdj/36.2.134

Laverack, G. (2006). Using a "domains" approach to build community empowerment. *Community Development Journal, 41*(1), 4–12. doi:10.1093/cdj/bsi038

Laverack, G., & Wallerstein, N. (2001). Measuring community empowerment: A fresh look at organizational domains. *Health Promotion International, 16*(2), 179–185. doi:10.1093/heapro/16.2.179

Laverack, G., & Whipple, A. (2010). The sirens' song of empowerment: A case study of health promotion and the New Zealand Prostitutes Collective. *Global Health Promotion, 17*(1), 33–38. doi:10.1177/1757975909356630

Le, V. (2015). Why communities of color are getting frustrated with collective impact. Retrieved March 2, 2016, from http://nonprofitwithballs.com/2015/11/why-communities-of-color-are-getting-frustrated-with-collective-impact/

Lecy, J. D., & Van Slyke, D. M. (2013). Nonprofit sector growth and density: Testing theories of government support. *Journal of Public Administration Research and Theory, 23*(1), 189–214. doi:10.1093/jopart/mus010

Ledwith, M. (2011). *Community development: A critical approach* (2nd ed.). Bristol, UK: The Policy Press.

Lee, N.-J., Shah, D. V., & McLeod, J. M. (2013). Processes of political socialization: A communication mediation approach to youth civic engagement. *Communication Research, 40*(5), 669–697. doi:10.1177/0093650212436712

Leischow, S. J., Best, A., Trochim, W. M., Clark, P. I., Gallagher, R. S., Marcus, S. E., & Matthews, E. (2008). Systems thinking to improve the public's health. *American Journal of Preventive Medicine, 35*(2, Suppl.), S196–S203. doi:10.1016/j.amepre.2008.05.014

Lerner, M. (1999). *Surplus powerlessness: The psychodynamics of everyday life—and the psychology of individual and social transformation.* Amherst, NY: Humanity Books.

Levin, J. (2013, December 19). The welfare queen. *Slate.* Retrieved from http://www.slate.com/articles/news_and_politics/history/2013/12/linda_taylor_welfare_queen_ronald_reagan_made_her_a_notorious_american_villain.html

Levine, M., & Levine, A. (1970). *A social history of the helping professions.* New York, NY: Appleton-Century-Crofts.

Levine, M., & Levine, A. (2012). Education deformed: No child left behind and the race to the top. "This almost reads like our business plans." *The American Journal of Orthopsychiatry, 82*(1), 104–113. doi:10.1111/j.1939-0025.2011.01142.x

Levine, O. H., Britton, P. J., James, T. C., Jackson, A. P., Hobfoll, S. E., & Lavin, J. P. (1993). The empowerment of women: A key to HIV prevention. *Journal of Community Psychology, 21,* 320–334.

Levinson, M. (2012). *No citizen left behind.* Cambridge, MA: Harvard University Press.

Lewin, K. (1951). *Field theory in social science.* New York, NY: Harper & Row.

Lin, C. S., Pykett, A. A., Flanagan, C., & Chávez, K. R. (2016). Engendering the prefigurative: Feminist praxes that bridge a politics of prefigurement and survival. *Journal of Social and Political Psychology, 4*(1), 302–317. doi:10.5964/jspp.v4i1.537

Lindqvist, A. K., Mikaelsson, K., Westerberg, M., Gard, G., & Kostenius, C. (2014). Moving from idea to action: Promoting physical activity by empowering adolescents. *Health Promotion Practice, 15*(6), 812–818. doi:10.1177/1524839914535777

Lippman, S. A., Maman, S., MacPhail, C., Twine, R., Peacock, D., Kahn, K., & Pettifor, A. (2013). Conceptualizing community mobilization for HIV prevention: Implications for HIV prevention programming in the African context. *PloS One, 8*(10), e78208. doi:10.1371/journal.pone.0078208

Lippman, S. A., Neilands, T. B., Leslie, H. H., Maman, S., MacPhail, C., Twine, R., . . . Pettifor, A. (2016). Development, validation, and performance of a scale to measure community mobilization. *Social Science & Medicine, 157,* 127–137. doi:10.1016/j.socscimed.2016.04.002

Lissak, R. S. (1989). *Pluralism and progressives: Hull House and the new immigrants, 1890–1917.* Chicago, IL: University of Chicago Press.

Livingood, W. C., Brady, C., Pierce, K., Atrash, H., Hou, T., & Bryant, T. (2010). Impact of preconception health care: Evaluation of a social determinants focused intervention. *Maternal and Child Health Journal, 14*(3), 382–391. doi:10.1007/s10995-009-0471-4

Long, N. E. (1958). The local community as an ecology of games. *The American Journal of Sociology, 64*(3), 251–261. doi:10.1086/222468

Lu, M. C., & Halfon, N. (2003). Racial and ethnic disparities in birth outcomes: A life-course perspective. *Maternal and Child Health Journal, 7*(1), 13–30. doi:10.1023/A:1022537516969

Luke, D. A., & Stamatakis, K. A. (2012). Systems science methods in public health: Dynamics, networks, and agents. *Annual Review of Public Health, 33,* 357–376. doi:10.1146/annurev-publhealth-031210-101222

Lukes, S. (1974). *Power: A radical view.* New York, NY: Humanities Press.

Lukes, S. (2005). *Power: A radical view* (2nd ed.). New York, NY: Palgrave Macmillan.

Madigan, S., Wade, M., Plamondon, A., & Jenkins, J. M. (2016). Neighborhood collective efficacy moderates the association between maternal adverse childhood experiences and marital conflict. *American Journal of Community Psychology, 57*(3–4), 437–447. doi:10.1002/ajcp.12053

Mahatmya, D., & Lohman, B. J. (2012). Predictors and pathways to civic involvement in emerging adulthood: Neighborhood, family, and school influences. *Journal of Youth and Adolescence, 41*(9), 1168–1183. doi:10.1007/s10964-012-9777-4

Mair, C., Diez Roux, A. V., Golden, S. H., Rapp, S., Seeman, T., & Shea, S. (2015). Change in neighborhood environments and depressive symptoms in New York City: The multi-ethnic study of atherosclerosis. *Health & Place, 32*, 93–98. doi:10.1016/j.healthplace.2015.01.003

Maraniss, D. (2003). *They marched into sunlight: War and peace in Vietnam and America, October 1967.* New York, NY: Simon & Schuster.

Marayuma, M. (1983). Cross-cultural perspectives on social and community change. In E. Seidman (Ed.), *Handbook of social intervention.* Beverly Hills, CA: Sage.

Marmot, M., & Allen, J. J. (2014). Social determinants of health equity. *American Journal of Public Health, 104*(S4), S517–S519. doi:10.2105/AJPH.2014.302200

Marmot, M., Friel, S., Bell, R., Houweling, T. A., & Taylor, S. (2008). Closing the gap in a generation: Health equity through action on the social determinants of health. *The Lancet, 372*(9650), 1661–1669.

Marsick, V. J., & Watkins, K. E. (2003). Demonstrating the value of an organization's learning culture: The dimensions of the learning organization questionnaire. *Advances in Developing Human Resources, 5*(2), 132–151. doi:10.1177/1523422303251341

Martínez, M. L., Peñaloza, P., & Valenzuela, C. (2012). Civic commitment in young activists: Emergent processes in the development of personal and collective identity. *Journal of Adolescence, 35*(3), 474–484. doi:10.1016/j.adolescence.2011.11.006

Maton, K. I. (1988). Social support, organizational characteristics, psychological well-being, and group appraisal in three self-help group populations. *American Journal of Community Psychology, 16*(1), 53–77. doi:10.1007/BF00906072

Maton, K. I. (1990). Meaningful involvement in instrumental activity and well-being: Studies of older adolescents and at risk urban teen-agers. *American Journal of Community Psychology, 18*(2), 297–320.

Maton, K. I. (2008). Empowering community settings: Agents of individual development, community betterment, and positive social change. *American Journal of Community Psychology, 41*, 4–21. doi:10.1007/s10464-007-9148-6

Maton, K. I., & Brodsky, A. (2011). Empowering community settings: Theory, research and action. In M. S. Aber, K. I. Maton, & E. Seidman (Eds.), *Empowering settings and voices for social change* (pp. 38–64). New York, NY: Oxford University Press.

Maton, K. I., & Salem, D. A. (1995). Organizational characteristics of empowering community settings: A multiple case study approach. *American Journal of Community Psychology, 23*(5), 631–656. doi:10.1007/BF02506985

Maton, K. I., Seidman, E., & Aber, M. S. (2011). Empowering settings and voices for social change: An introduction. In M. S. Aber, K. I. Maton, & E. Seidman (Eds.), *Empowering settings and voices for social change* (pp. 1–11). New York, NY: Oxford University Press.

Maurizi, L. K., Ceballo, R., Epstein-Ngo, Q., & Cortina, K. S. (2013). Does neighborhood belonging matter? Examining school and neighborhood belonging as protective factors for Latino adolescents. *The American Journal of Orthopsychiatry, 83*(2, Pt. 3), 323–334. doi:10.1111/ajop.12017

Mayne, S. L., Auchincloss, A. H., & Michael, Y. L. (2015). Impact of policy and built environment changes on obesity-related outcomes: A systematic review of naturally occurring experiments. *Obesity Reviews, 16*(5), 362–375. doi:10.1111/obr.12269

McAdam, D. (1999). *Political process and the development of black insurgency, 1930–1970* (2nd Ed.). Chicago: University of Chicago Press.

McAdam, D., McCarthy, J. D., & Zald, M. N. (1996). *Comparative perspectives on social movements: Political opportunities, mobilizing structures, and cultural framings.* Cambridge, England: Cambridge University Press.

McAdam, D., Tarrow, S., & Tilly, C. (2008). Methods for measuring mechanisms of contention. *Qualitative Sociology, 31*(4), 307–331. doi:10.1007/s11133-008-9100-6

McAlevey, J. F. (2016). *No shortcuts: Organizing for power in the new gilded age.* New York, NY: Oxford University Press.

McAvoy, P., & Hess, D. (2013). Classroom deliberation in an era of political polarization. *Curriculum Inquiry, 43*(1), 14–47. doi:10.1111/curi.12000

McCarthy, J. (2003). Regeneration and community involvement. *City, 7*(1), 95–105. doi:10.1080/13604810302219

McCarthy, J. D., & Walker, E. T. (2004). Alternative organizational repertoires of poor people's social movement organizations. *Nonprofit and Voluntary Sector Quarterly, 33*(3), 97s–119s. doi:10.1177/0899764004266200

McCarthy, J. D., & Zald, M. N. (1977). Resource mobilization and social movements: A partial theory. *The American Journal of Sociology, 82*(6), 1212–1241.

McKeever, B. S., & Pettijohn, S. L. (2014). *The nonprofit sector in brief 2014: Public charities, giving, and volunteering.* Washington, DC: Urban Institute, Center on Nonprofits and Philanthropy.

McKenzie, B. D. (2014). Political perceptions in the Obama era: Diverse opinions of the great recession and its aftermath among whites, Latinos, and blacks. *Political Research Quarterly, 67*(4), 823–836. doi:10.1177/1065912914541702

McNulty, J. K., & Fincham, F. D. (2012). Beyond positive psychology? Toward a contextual view of psychological processes and well-being. *The American Psychologist, 67*(2), 101–110. doi:10.1037/a0024572

Menand, L. (2001). *The metaphysical club: A story of ideas in America.* New York, NY: Farrar, Straus and Giroux.

Mesch, S. M. (2017). Estimated 75,000 to 100,000 protesters rally for Women's March on Madison. *Wisconsin State Journal.* Retrieved January 24, 2017, from http://host.madison.com/wsj/news/local/govt-and-politics/estimated-to-protesters-rally-for-women-s-march-on-madison/article_2bdcbf0e-8e4d-528e-b0d3-566c8c1ec991.html

Metzger, A., & Smetana, J. G. (2009). Adolescent civic and political engagement: Associations between domain-specific judgments and behavior. *Child Development, 80*(2), 433–441. doi:10.1111/j.1467-8624.2009.01270.x

Mialon, M., Swinburn, B., & Sacks, G. (2015). A proposed approach to systematically identify and monitor the corporate political activity of the food industry with respect to public health using publicly available information. *Obesity Reviews, 16*(7), 519–530. doi:10.1111/obr.12289

Miller, P. M., Brown, T., & Hopson, R. (2011). Centering love, hope, and trust in the community: Transformative urban leadership informed by Paulo Freire. *Urban Education, 46*(5), 1078–1099. doi:10.1177/0042085910395951

Miller, R. L., & Campbell, R. (2006). Taking stock of empowerment evaluation: An empirical review. *American Journal of Evaluation, 27*(3), 296–319. doi:10.1177/1098214006027003303

Miller, R. L., & Campbell, R. (2007). Taking stock again results in the same conclusions. *American Journal of Evaluation, 28*(4), 579–581. doi:10.1177/1098214007308901

Mills, C. W. (2000). *The power elite.* New York, NY: Oxford University Press. (Original work published 1956)

Milward, H. B. B., & Provan, K. G. G. (2000). Governing the Hollow State. *Journal of Public Administration Research and Theory, 10*(2), 359–379.

Minkler, M., & Wallerstein, N. (Eds.). (2008). *Community-based participatory research for health: From process to outcomes* (2nd ed.). San Francisco, CA: Jossey-Bass.

Molix, L., & Bettencourt, B. (2010). Predicting well-being among ethnic minorities: Psychological empowerment and group identity. *Journal of Applied Social Psychology, 40*(3), 513–533. doi:10.1111/j.1559-1816.2010.00585.x

Molotch, H. (1976). The city as a growth machine: Toward a political economy of place. *The American Journal of Sociology, 82*(2), 309–332.

Mondros, J. B., & Wilson, S. M. (1994). *Organizing for power and empowerment.* New York, NY: Columbia University Press.

Mooney, G. (2012). Neoliberalism is bad for our health. *International Journal of Health Services, 42*(3), 383–401.

Morenoff, J. D., Sampson, R. J., & Raudenbush, S. W. (2001). Neighborhood inequality, collective efficacy, and the spatial dynamics of urban violence. *Criminology, 39*(3), 517–560.

Morris, A. D. (1986). *The origins of the civil rights movement: Black communities organizing for change.*

National Association of County & City Health Officials (NACCHO). (2011). *Healthy communities, healthy behaviors: Using policy, systems, and environmental change to combat chronic disease.* Washington, DC: NACCHO. Retrieved from http://archived.naccho.org/topics/HPDP/ mcah/upload/issuebrief_pse_webfinal.pdf

Neal, J. W. (2014). Exploring empowerment in settings: Mapping distributions of network power. *American Journal of Community Psychology, 53*(3–4), 394–406. doi:10.1007/ s10464-013-9609-z

Neal, J. W., & Christens, B. D. (2014). Linking the levels: Network and relational perspectives for community psychology. *American Journal of Community Psychology, 53*(3–4), 314–323. doi:10.1007/s10464-014-9654-2

Neal, J. W., & Neal, Z. P. (2013). Nested or networked? Future directions for ecological systems theory. *Social Development, 22*(4), 722–737. doi:10.1111/sode.12018

Neal, Z. P. (2014). A network perspective on the processes of empowered organizations. *American Journal of Community Psychology, 53*(3–4), 407–418. doi:10.1007/s10464-013-9623-1

Nelson, G. (2013). Community psychology and transformative policy change in the neoliberal era. *American Journal of Community Psychology, 52*(3–4), 211–223. doi:10.1007/ s10464-013-9591-5

Nelson, G., Hall, G. B., & Walsh-Bowers, R. (1998). The relationship between housing characteristics, emotional well-being and the personal empowerment of psychiatric consumer/survivors. *Community Mental Health Journal, 34*(1), 57–69.

Nelson, J. B. (2014, September 18). Economists say time has run out on top campaign promise. *PolitiFact Wisconsin.* Retrieved May 24, 2016, from http://www.politifact.com/wisconsin/ promises/walk-o-meter/promise/526/create-250000-new-jobs/

Newbrough, J. R. (1973). Community psychology: A new holism. *American Journal of Community Psychology, 1*(3), 201–211. doi:10.1007/BF00881567

Newbrough, J. R. (1980). Community psychology and the public interest. *American Journal of Community Psychology, 8*(1), 1–17. doi:10.1007/BF00892277

Nicholls, W., Miller, B., & Beaumont, J. (Eds.). (2016). *Spaces of contention: Spatialities and social movements.* New York, NY: Routledge.

Nichols, J. (2012). *Uprising: How Wisconsin renewed the politics of protest, from Madison to Wall Street.* New York, NY: Nation Books.

Nickel, P. M., & Eikenberry, A. M. (2009). A critique of the discourse of marketized philanthropy. *American Behavioral Scientist, 52*(7), 974–989. doi:10.1177/0002764208327670

Niebuhr, R. (1932). *Moral man and immoral society.* New York: Charles Scribner's Sons.

Nkansah-Amankra, S., Agbanu, S. K., & Miller, R. J. (2013). Disparities in health, poverty, incarceration, and social justice among racial groups in the United States: A critical review of evidence of close links with neoliberalism. *International Journal of Health Services, 43*(2), 217–240.

Nowell, B. (2009). Profiling capacity for coordination and systems change: The relative contribution of stakeholder relationships in interorganizational collaboratives. *American Journal of Community Psychology, 44,* 196–212. doi:10.1007/s10464-009-9276-2

Nowell, B., & Foster-Fishman, P. (2011). Examining multi-sector community collaboratives as vehicles for building organizational capacity. *American Journal of Community Psychology, 48*(3–4), 193–207. doi:10.1007/s10464-010-9364-3

Nowell, B., & Harrison, L. M. (2011). Leading change through collaborative partnerships: A profile of leadership and capacity among local public health leaders. *Journal of Prevention & Intervention in the Community, 39*(1), 19–34. doi:10.1080/10852352.2011.530162

Noy, D. (2008). Power mapping: Enhancing sociological knowledge by developing generalizable analytical public tools. *The American Sociologist, 39*(1), 3–18. doi:10.1007/s12108-008-9030-5

Oakley, D., & Tsao, H. (2006). A new way of revitalizing distressed urban communities? Assessing the impact of the federal empowerment zone program. *Journal of Urban Affairs, 28*(5), 443–471.

O'Brien, M. S. (2013). This is what democracy sounds like: Live and mediated soundscapes of the Wisconsin uprising. *Music and Politics, 7*(2), 1–19. doi:10.3998/mp.9460447.0007.204

O'Campo, P. (2012). Are we producing the right kind of actionable evidence for the social determinants of health? *Journal of Urban Health, 89*(6), 881–893.

Odgers, C. L., Moffitt, T. E., Tach, L. M., Sampson, R. J., Taylor, A., Matthews, C. L., & Caspi, A. (2009). The protective effects of neighborhood collective efficacy on British children growing up in deprivation: A developmental analysis. *Developmental Psychology, 45*(4), 942–957. doi:10.1037/a0016162

Oliver, P. E. (2015). Rational action. In D. Della Porta & M. Diani (Eds.), *The Oxford handbook of social movements* (pp. 246–263). New York, NY: Oxford University Press.

Ollstein, A. (2015). Scott Walker's baffling war on bikes. *ThinkProgress.* Retrieved April 12, 2016, from http://thinkprogress.org/politics/2015/06/03/3664754/scott-walkers-war-bikes/

The Onion. (1999, September 15). Small, dedicated group of concerned citizens fails to change world. Retrieved from http://www.theonion.com/article/small-dedicated-group-of-concerned-citizens-fails--657

Oser, J., Hooghe, M., & Marien, S. (2013). Is online participation distinct from offline participation? A latent class analysis of participation types and their stratification. *Political Research Quarterly, 66*(1), 91–101. doi:10.1177/1065912912436695

Ostrander, S. A. (2007). The growth of donor control: Revisiting the social relations of philanthropy. *Nonprofit and Voluntary Sector Quarterly, 36*(2), 356–372. doi:10.1177/0899764007300386

Ottersen, O. P., Dasgupta, J., Blouin, C., Buss, P., Chongsuvivatwong, V., Frenk, J., . . . Scheel, I. B. (2014). The political origins of health inequity: Prospects for change. *The Lancet, 383*(9917), 630–667. doi:10.1016/S0140-6736(13)62407-1

Park, R. E. (1936). Human ecology. *The American Journal of Sociology, 42*(1), 1–15.

Patton, M. Q. (2005). Book review: Empowerment evaluation principles in practice. *American Journal of Evaluation, 26*(3), 408–414. doi:10.1177/1098214005277353

Patton, M. Q. (2015). Book review: Empowerment evaluation: Knowledge and truth for self-assessment, evaluation capacity building, and accountability. *Evaluation and Program Planning, 52,* 15–18. doi:10.1016/j.evalprogplan.2015.03.003

Peirson, L. J., Boydell, K. M., Ferguson, H. B., & Ferris, L. E. (2011). An ecological process model of systems change. *American Journal of Community Psychology, 47*(3–4), 307–321. doi:10.1007/s10464-010-9405-y

Perkins, D. D. (1995). Speaking truth to power: Empowerment ideology as social intervention and policy. *American Journal of Community Psychology, 23*(5), 765–794.

Perkins, D. D., Bess, K. D., Cooper, D. G., Jones, D. L., Armstead, T., & Speer, P. W. (2007). Community organizational learning: Case studies illustrating a three-dimensional model of levels and orders of change. *Journal of Community Psychology, 35*(3), 303–328.

Perkins, D. D., Brown, B. B., & Taylor, R. B. (1996). The ecology of empowerment: Predicting participation in community organizations. *Journal of Social Issues, 52*(1), 85–110. doi:10.1111/j.1540-4560.1996.tb01363.x

Perkins, D. D., & Taylor, R. B. (1996). Ecological assessments of community disorder: Their relationship to fear of crime and theoretical implications. *American Journal of Community Psychology, 24*(1), 63–107.

Perkins, K. L., & Sampson, R. J. (2015). Compounded deprivation in the transition to adulthood: The intersection of racial and economic inequality among Chicagoans, 1995–2013. *RSF: The Russell Sage Foundation Journal of the Social Sciences, 1*(1), 35–54.

Perreault, T. (2003). Changing places: Transnational networks, ethnic politics, and community development in the Ecuadorian Amazon. *Political Geography, 22*(1), 61–88. doi:10.1016/S0962-6298(02)00058-6

Peters, D. H. (2014). The application of systems thinking in health: Why use systems thinking? *Health Research Policy and Systems, 12*(1), 1.

Peterson, N. A. (2014). Empowerment theory: Clarifying the nature of higher-order multidimensional constructs. *American Journal of Community Psychology, 53*, 96–108. doi:10.1007/s10464-013-9624-0

Peterson, N. A., Hamme, C. L., & Speer, P. W. (2002). Cognitive empowerment of African Americans and Caucasians: Differences in understandings of power, political functioning, and shaping ideology. *Journal of Black Studies, 32*(3), 336–351. doi:10.1177/0021934702032003304

Peterson, N. A., & Hughey, J. (2002). Tailoring organizational characteristics for empowerment: Accommodating individual economic resources. *Journal of Community Practice, 10*(3), 41–59. doi:10.1300/J125v10n03_03

Peterson, N. A., Lowe, J. B., Aquilino, M. L., & Schneider, J. E. (2005). Linking social cohesion and gender to intrapersonal and interactional empowerment: Support and new implications for theory. *Journal of Community Psychology, 33*(2), 233–244. doi:10.1002/jcop.20047

Peterson, N. A., Lowe, J. B., Hughey, J., Reid, R. J., Zimmerman, M. A., & Speer, P. W. (2006). Measuring the intrapersonal component of psychological empowerment: Confirmatory factor analysis of the sociopolitical control scale. *American Journal of Community Psychology, 38*(3–4), 287–297. doi:10.1007/s10464-006-9070-3

Peterson, N. A., Peterson, C. H., Agre, L., Christens, B. D., & Morton, C. M. (2011). Measuring youth empowerment: Validation of a sociopolitical control scale for youth in an urban community context. *Journal of Community Psychology, 39*(5), 592–605. doi:10.1002/jcop.20456

Peterson, N. A., Gilmore Powell, K., Hamme Peterson, C., & Reid, R. J. (2017). Testing the phrase completion response option format in a sociopolitical control scale for youth. *Community Psychology in Global Perspective, 3*(1), 57–71.

Peterson, N. A., & Reid, R. J. (2003). Paths to psychological empowerment in an urban community: Sense of community and citizen participation in substance abuse prevention activities. *Journal of Community Psychology, 31*(1), 25–38. doi:10.1002/jcop.10034

Peterson, N. A., & Speer, P. W. (2000). Linking organizational characteristics to psychological empowerment: Contextual issues in empowerment theory. *Administration in Social Work, 24*(4), 39–58. doi:10.1300/J147v24n04_03

Peterson, N. A., Speer, P. W., Hughey, J., Armstead, T., Schneider, J. E., & Sheffer, M. A. (2008). Community organizations and sense of community: Further development in theory and measurement. *Journal of Community Psychology, 36*(6), 798–813. doi:10.1002/jcop.20260

Peterson, N. A., & Zimmerman, M. A. (2004). Beyond the individual: Toward a nomological network of organizational empowerment. *American Journal of Community Psychology, 34*(1/2), 129–145. doi:10.1023/B:AJCP.0000040151.77047.58

Philadelphia Student Union. (2017). Mission. Retrieved March 17, 2017, from http://phillystudentunion.org/mission/

Piketty, T. (2014). *Capital in the 21st century*. Cambridge, MA: Harvard University Press.

Piketty, T., & Saez, E. (2007). How progressive is the US federal tax system? A historical and international perspective. *Journal of Economic Perspectives, 21*(1), 3–24.

Polletta, F. (1999). "Free spaces" in collective action. *Theory and Society, 28*(1), 1–38. doi:10.1023/A:1006941408302

Polsby, N. W. (1960). How to study community power: The pluralist alternative. *The Journal of Politics, 22*(3), 474–484.

Preskill, S., & Brookfield, S. D. (2009). *Learning as a way of leading: Lessons from the struggle for social justice.* San Francisco, CA: Jossey-Bass.

Prestby, J. E., Wandersman, A., Florin, P., Rich, R., & Chavis, D. (1990). Benefits, costs, incentive management and participation in voluntary organizations: A means to understanding and promoting empowerment. *American Journal of Community Psychology, 18*(1), 117–149. doi:10.1007/BF00922691

Price, J. R. (1992). *Empowerment: You can do, be, and have all things!* Carlsbad, CA: Hay House, Inc.

Prilleltensky, I. (1994). *The morals and politics of psychology: Psychological discourse and the status quo.* Albany, NY: State University of New York Press.

Prilleltensky, I. (1997). Values, assumptions, and practices: Assessing the moral implications of psychological discourse and action. *American Psychologist, 52*(5), 517–535. doi:10.1037/0003-066X.52.5.517

Prilleltensky, I. (2008). The role of power in wellness, oppression, and liberation: The promise of psychopolitical validity. *Journal of Community Psychology, 36*(2), 116–136. doi:10.1002/jcop.20225

Prilleltensky, I., Dietz, S., Prilleltensky, O., Myers, N. D., Rubenstein, C. L., Jin, Y., & McMahon, A. (2015). Assessing multidimensional well-being: Development and validation of the I COPPE scale. *Journal of Community Psychology, 43*(2), 199–226. doi:10.1002/jcop.21674

Provan, K. G., Nakama, L., Veazie, M. A., Teufel-Shone, N. I., & Huddleston, C. (2003). Building community capacity around chronic disease services through a collaborative interorganizational network. *Health Education & Behavior, 30*(6), 646–662. doi:10.1177/1090198103255366

Putnam, R. D. (2001). *Bowling alone: The collapse and revival of American community.* New York, NY: Simon and Schuster.

Qouta, S., Punamäki, R. L., & El Sarraj, E. (2008). Child development and family mental health in war and military violence: The Palestinian experience. *International Journal of Behavioral Development, 32*(4), 310–321. doi:10.1177/0165025408090973

Quinn, R. E., & Spreitzer, G. M. (1991). The psychometrics of the competing values culture instrument and an analysis of the impact of organizational culture on quality of life. In R. W. Pasmore & W. A. Pasmore (Eds.), *Research in organizational change and development* (pp. 115–142). Greenwich, CT: Jai Press.

Raelin, J. (2011). From leadership-as-practice to leaderful practice. *Leadership, 7*(2), 195–211. doi:10.1177/1742715010394808

Raison, C. L., & Miller, A. H. (2013). Malaise, melancholia and madness: The evolutionary legacy of an inflammatory bias. *Brain, Behavior, and Immunity, 31*, 1–8. doi:10.1016/j.bbi.2013.04.009

Ramos-Vidal, I., & Maya-Jariego, I. (2014). Sentido de comunidad, empoderamiento psicológico y participación ciudadana en trabajadores de organizaciones culturales. *Psychosocial Intervention, 23*(3), 169–176. doi:10.1016/j.psi.2014.04.001

Ramraj, C., Shahidi, F. V., Darity, W., Kawachi, I., Zuberi, D., & Siddiqi, A. (2016). Equally inequitable? A cross-national comparative study of racial health inequalities in the United States and Canada. *Social Science & Medicine, 161*, 19–26. doi:10.1016/j.socscimed.2016.05.028

Ransby, B. (2003). *Ella Baker and the black freedom movement: A radical democratic vision.* Chapel Hill, NC: University of North Carolina Press.

Rappaport, J. (1981). In praise of paradox: A social policy of empowerment over prevention. *American Journal of Community Psychology, 9*(1), 1–25. doi:10.1007/BF00919275

Rappaport, J. (1987). Terms of empowerment/ exemplars of prevention: Toward a theory for community psychology. *American Journal of Community Psychology, 15*(2), 121–148. doi:10.1007/BF00919275

Rappaport, J. (2011). Empowerment, crossing boundaries, and telling our story. In M. Aber, K. Maton, & E. Seidman (Eds.), *Empowering settings and voices for social change* (pp. 232–237). New York, NY: Oxford University Press.

Reiche, E. M. V., Nunes, S. O. V., & Morimoto, H. K. (2004). Stress, depression, the immune system, and cancer. *The Lancet Oncology, 5*(10), 617–625.

Remington, P. L., Catlin, B. B., & Gennuso, K. P. (2015). The county health rankings: Rationale and methods. *Population Health Metrics, 13*(1), 11. doi:10.1186/s12963-015-0044-2

Rifkin, S. B., Muller, F., & Bichmann, W. (1988). Primary health care: on measuring participation. *Social Science & Medicine, 26*(9), 931–940.

Riger, S. (1993). What's wrong with empowerment. *American Journal of Community Psychology, 21*(3), 279–292. doi:10.1007/BF00941504

Riger, S. (1994). Challenges of success: Stages of growth in feminist organizations. *Feminist Studies, 20*(2), 275–300.

Rissel, C. (1994). Empowerment: The holy grail of health promotion? *Health Promotion International, 9*(1), 39.

Rogell, A., & Olsson, G. (2011). *The Black Power mixtape 1967–1975* [motion picture]. Stockholm, Sweden: Story AB.

Rogers, J., Mediratta, K., & Shah, S. (2012). Building power, learning democracy: Youth organizing as a site of civic development. *Review of Research in Education, 36*(1), 43–66. doi:10.3102/0091732X11422328

Rogers, J., & Oakes, J. (2005). John Dewey speaks to Brown: Research, democratic social movement strategies, and the struggle for education on equal terms. *Teachers College Record, 107*(9), 2178–2203.

Rosen, S. M. (2012). Making space for youth: Individual and organizational identities in the Philadelphia Student Union. PhD dissertation. University of Pennsylvania, Philadelphia.

Rosen, S. M. (2016). Identity performance and collectivist leadership in the Philadelphia Student Union. *International Journal of Leadership in Education, 19*(2), 224–240. doi: 10.1080/13603124.2014.954628

Rothman, J., & Mizrahi, T. (2014). Balancing micro and macro practice: A challenge for social work. *Social Work, 59*(1), 91–93. doi:10.1093/sw/swt067

Rothschild, M. (2012, June 7). How the Wisconsin solidarity movement failed in imagination and nerve. *The Isthmus.* Retrieved from http://isthmus.com/opinion/opinion/how-the-wisconsin-solidarity-movement-failed-in-imagination-and-nerve/

Rusch, L., & Swarts, H. (2015). Practices of engagement: Comparing and integrating deliberation and organizing. *Journal of Community Practice, 23*(1), 5–26. doi:10.1080/10705422.2014.985411

Russell, S. T., Muraco, A., Subramaniam, A., & Laub, C. (2009). Youth empowerment and high school gay-straight alliances. *Journal of Youth and Adolescence, 38*(7), 891–903. doi:10.1007/s10964-008-9382-8

Salamon, L. M. (1994). The rise of the nonprofit sector. *Foreign Affairs, 73*(4), 109–122.

Salamon, L. M. (2010). Putting the civil society sector on the economic map of the world. *Annals of Public and Cooperative Economics, 81*(2), 167–210. doi:10.1111/j.1467-8292.2010.00409.x

Salamon, L. M., & Van Evera, S. (1973). Fear, apathy, and discrimination: A test of three explanations of political participation. *American Political Science Review, 67*(4), 1288–1306. doi:10.2307/1956549

Sampson, R. J. (2003). The neighborhood context of well-being. *Perspectives in Biology and Medicine, 46*(3), S53–S64.

Sampson, R. J. (2004). Neighbourhood and community: Collective efficacy and community safety. *New Economy, 11*, 106–113.

Sampson, R. J. (2012). *Great American city: Chicago and the enduring neighborhood effect.* Chicago, IL: University of Chicago Press.

Sampson, R. J. (2013). The place of context: A theory and strategy for criminology's hard problems. *Criminology, 51*(1), 1–31. doi:10.1111/1745-9125.12002

Sampson, R. J., McAdam, D., MacIndoe, H., & Weffer-Elizondo, S. (2005). Civil society reconsidered: The durable nature and community structure of collective civic action. *The American Journal of Sociology, 111*(3), 673–714.

Sampson, R. J., Raudenbush, S. W., & Earls, F. (1997). Neighborhoods and violent crime: A multilevel study of collective efficacy. *Science, 277*(5328), 918–924.

Santiago, C. D. C., Wadsworth, M. E., & Stump, J. (2011). Socioeconomic status, neighborhood disadvantage, and poverty-related stress: Prospective effects on psychological syndromes among diverse low-income families. *Journal of Economic Psychology, 32*(2), 218–230. doi:10.1016/j.joep.2009.10.008

Sarason, S. B. (1984). *The psychological sense of community: Prospects for a community psychology.* San Francisco, CA: Jossey-Bass.

Sardenberg, C. (2008). Liberal vs. liberating empowerment: A Latin American feminist perspective on conceptualising women's empowerment. *IDS Bulletin, 39*(6), 18–27.

Sarmiento, C. S., & Beard, V. A. (2013). Traversing the border: Community-based planning and transnational migrants. *Journal of Planning Education and Research, 33*(3), 336–347. doi:10.1177/0739456X13499934

Sarmiento, C. S., & Sims, J. R. (2015). Facades of equitable development: Santa Ana and the affordable housing complex. *Journal of Planning Education and Research, 35*(3), 323–336. doi:10.1177/0739456X15586629

Sassen, S. (1996). *Losing control? Sovereignty in an age of globalization.* New York, NY: Columbia University Press.

Sassen, S. (2014). *Expulsions: Brutality and complexity in the global economy.* Cambridge, MA: Harvard University Press.

Schnittker, J. (2014). The psychological dimensions and the social consequences of incarceration. *The Annals of the American Academy of Political and Social Science, 651*(1), 122–138. doi:10.1177/0002716213502922

Schulz, A., & Northridge, M. E. (2004). Social determinants of health: Implications for environmental health promotion. *Health Education & Behavior, 31*(4), 455–471. doi:10.1177/1090198104265598

Seidman, E. (1988). Back to the future, community psychology: Unfolding a theory of social intervention. *American Journal of Community Psychology, 16*(1), 4–24. doi:10.1007/BF00906069

Seidman, E. (2012). An emerging action science of social settings. *American Journal of Community Psychology, 50*(1–2), 1–16. doi:10.1007/s10464-011-9469-3

Seif, H. (2011). "Unapologetic and unafraid": Immigrant youth come out from the shadows. *New Directions for Child and Adolescent Development, 134,* 59–75. doi:10.1002/cd.311

Seligman, M. E. P. (1975). *Helplessness.* San Francisco, CA: Freeman.

Sen, G., & Grown, C. (1987). *Development, crises and alternative visions: Third world women's perspectives.* New York, NY: Monthly Review Press.

Senge, P. (1990). *The fifth discipline: The art and practice of the learning organization.* Chatham, MA: Doubleday.

Shah, S., & Mediratta, K. (2008) Negotiating reform: Young people's leadership in the educational arena. *New Directions for Youth Development, 2000*(117), 43–59. doi:10.1002/yd.246

Shapiro, V. B., Oesterle, S., Abbott, R. D., Arthur, M. W., & Hawkins, J. D. (2013). Measuring dimensions of coalition functioning for effective and participatory community practice. *Social Work Research, 37*(4), 349–359. doi:10.1093/swr/svt028

Shinn, M., & Rapkin, B. D. (2000). Cross-level research without cross-ups in community psychology. In J. Rappaport & E. Seidman (Eds.), *Handbook of community psychology* (pp. 669–695). New York, NY: Kluwer Academic/Plenum.

Shonkoff, J. P., Boyce, W. T., & McEwen, B. S. (2009). Neuroscience, molecular biology, and the childhood roots of health disparities. *JAMA: The Journal of the American Medical Association, 301*(21), 2252–2259.

Sibal, B. (2006). People's power in people's hands: The lesson we need to learn. *Journal of Epidemiology and Community Health, 60*(6), 521.

Siegrist, J., & Marmot, M. (2004). Health inequalities and the psychosocial environment—two scientific challenges. *Social Science & Medicine, 58*(8), 1463–1473. doi:10.1016/S0277-9536(03)00349-6

Silverman, R. M. (2012). The nonprofitization of public education: Implications of requiring charter schools to be nonprofits in New York. *Nonprofit Policy Forum, 3*(1), Article 6. doi:10.1515/2154-3348.1046

Silverman, R. M. (2014). Urban, suburban, and rural contexts of school districts and neighborhood revitalization strategies: Rediscovering equity in education policy and urban planning. *Leadership and Policy in Schools, 13*(1), 3–27. doi:10.1080/15700763.2013.876051

Simon, B. L. (1994). *The empowerment tradition in American social work*. New York, NY: Columbia University Press.

Sirianni, C., & Friedland, L. (2001). *Civic innovation in America: Community empowerment, public policy, and the movement for civic renewal*. Berkeley, CA: University of California Press.

Sirota, D. (2014, February 13). How PBS is becoming the Plutocratic Broadcasting Service. Retrieved April 14, 2016 from https://pando.com/2014/02/13/how-pbs-is-becoming-the-plutocratic-broadcasting-service/

Sites, W. (2007). Beyond trenches and grassroots? Reflections on urban mobilization, fragmentation, and the anti-Wal-Mart campaign in Chicago. *Environment and Planning A, 39*(11), 2632–2651. doi:10.1068/a38339

Skocpol, T. (2004). *Diminished democracy: From membership to management in American civic life*. Norman, OK: University of Oklahoma Press.

Skocpol, T., & Fiorina, M. P. (Eds.). (1999). *Civic engagement in American democracy*. Washington, DC: Brookings Institution Press.

Sloop, J. M. (1996). *The cultural prison: Discourse, prisoners, and punishment*. Tuscaloosa, AL: University of Alabama Press.

Smith, N. (1992). New city, new frontier: The lower east side as wild, wild west. In M. Sorkin (Ed.), *Variations on a theme park: The new American city and the end of public space* (pp. 61–93). New York, NY: Hill and Wang.

Smith, N. (1996). *The new urban frontier: Gentrification and the revanchist city*. New York, NY: Routledge.

Snow, D. A. (2013). Framing and social movements. In *The Wiley-Blackwell encyclopedia of social and political movements*. Oxford, UK: Blackwell. doi:10.1002/9780470674871.wbespm434

Snow, D. A., Zurcher, L. A., & Ekland-Olson, S. (1980). Social networks and social movements: A microstructural approach to differential recruitment. *American Sociological Review, 45*(5), 787–801.

Snyder, M. (2009). In the footsteps of Kurt Lewin: Practical theorizing, action research, and the psychology of social action. *Journal of Social Issues, 65*(1), 225–245. doi:10.1111/j.1540-4560.2008.01597.x

Soja, E. (2000). *Postmetropolis: Critical studies of cities and regions*. Malden, MA: Blackwell.

Solomon, B. B. (1976). *Black empowerment: Social work in oppressed communities*. New York, NY: Columbia University Press.

Speer, P. W. (2000). Intrapersonal and interactional empowerment: Implications for theory. *Journal of Community Psychology, 28*(1), 51–61. doi:10.1002/(SICI)1520-6629(200001)28:1<51::AID-JCOP6>3.0.CO;2-6

Speer, P. W. (2008). Social power and forms of change: Implications for psychopolitical validity. *Journal of Community Psychology, 36*(2), 199–213. doi:10.1002/jcop.20231

Speer, P. W., & Christens, B. D. (2012). Local community organizing and change: Altering policy in the housing and community development system in Kansas City. *Journal of Community & Applied Social Psychology, 22*(5), 414–427. doi:10.1002/casp.1132

Speer, P. W., & Christens, B. D. (2013). An approach to scholarly impact through strategic engagement in community-based research. *Journal of Social Issues, 69*(4), 734–753. doi:10.1111/josi.12039

Speer, P. W., & Hughey, J. (1995). Community organizing: An ecological route to empowerment and power. *American Journal of Community Psychology, 23*(5), 729–748. doi:10.1007/BF02506989

Speer, P. W., Hughey, J., Gensheimer, L. K., & Adams-Leavitt, W. (1995). Organizing for power: A comparative case study. *Journal of Community Psychology, 23*(1), 57–73. doi:10.1002/1520-6629(199501)23:1<57::AID-JCOP2290230106>3.0.CO;2-9

Speer, P. W., Jackson, C. B., & Peterson, N. A. (2001). The relationship between social cohesion and empowerment: Support and new implications for theory. *Health Education & Behavior, 28*(6), 716–732. doi:10.1177/109019810102800605

Speer, P. W., Ontkush, M., Schmitt, B., Raman, P., Jackson, C., Rengert, K. M., & Peterson, N. A. (2003). The intentional exercise of power: Community organizing in Camden, New Jersey. *Journal of Community & Applied Social Psychology, 13*(5), 399–408. doi:10.1002/casp.745

Speer, P. W., & Peterson, N. A. (2000). Psychometric properties of an empowerment scale: Testing cognitive, emotional, and behavioral domains. *Social Work Research, 24*(2), 109–118.

Speer, P. W., Peterson, N. A., Armstead, T. L., & Allen, C. T. (2013). The influence of participation, gender and organizational sense of community on psychological empowerment: The moderating effects of income. *American Journal of Community Psychology, 51*(1–2), 103–113. doi:10.1007/s10464-012-9547-1

Speer, P. W., Tesdahl, E. A., & Ayers, J. F. (2014). Community organizing practices in a globalizing era: Building power for health equity at the community level. *Journal of Health Psychology, 19*(1), 159–169. doi:10.1177/1359105313500255

Stanley, J. (2016, November 4). Beyond lying: Donald Trump's authoritarian reality. *The New York Times*. Retrieved January 4, 2017, from http://www.nytimes.com/2016/11/05/opinion/beyond-lying-donald-trumps-authoritarian-reality.html

Steiner, B. D. (2001). The consciousness of crime and punishment: Reflections on identity politics and lawmaking in the war on drugs. *Studies in Law Politics and Society, 23*, 185–212.

Steptoe, A., & Kivimäki, M. (2013). Stress and cardiovascular disease: An update on current knowledge. *Annual Review of Public Health, 34*, 337–354. doi:10.1146/annurev-publhealth-031912-114452

Stiglitz, J. (2006). *Making globalization work*. New York, NY: Norton.

Stoecker, R. (1995). Community organizing and community-based redevelopment in Cedar-Riverside and East Toledo: A comparative study. *Journal of Community Practice, 2*(3), 1–23. doi:10.1300/J125v02n03_01

Stokols, D. (1992). Establishing and maintaining healthy environments: Toward a social ecology of health promotion. *American Psychologist, 47*(1), 6–22. doi:10.1037/0003-066X.47.1.6

Stolle, D., Hooghe, M., & Micheletti, M. (2005). Politics in the supermarket: Political consumerism as a form of political participation. *International Political Science Review, 26*(3), 245–269.

Stone, C. N. (2006). Power, reform, and urban regime analysis. *City & Community, 5*(1), 23–38. doi:10.1111/j.1540-6040.2006.00151.x

Sudhipongpracha, T. (2013). Measuring community empowerment as a process and an outcome: Preliminary evaluation of the decentralized primary health care programs in northeast Thailand. *Community Development, 44*(5), 551–566. doi:10.1080/15575330.2013.849748

Suess, G. E. L., & Lewis, K. S. (2007). The time is now: Youth organize to transform Philadelphia high schools. *Children, Youth and Environments, 17*(2), 364–379.

Swarts, H. (2011). Drawing new symbolic boundaries over old social boundaries: Forging social movement unity in congregation-based community organizing. *Sociological Perspectives, 54*(3), 453–477. doi:10.1525/sop.2011.54.3.453

Swartz, D. L. (2007). Recasting power in its third dimension. *Theory and Society, 36*(1), 103–109. doi:10.1007/s11186-006-9018-5

Swift, C., & Levin, G. (1987). Empowerment: An emerging mental health technology. *The Journal of Primary Prevention, 8*(1), 71–94. doi:10.1007/BF01695019

Taylor, K.-Y. (2016). *From #blacklivesmatter to black liberation*. Chicago, IL: Haymarket Books.

Terriquez, V. (2011). Schools for democracy: Labor union participation and Latino immigrant parents' school-based civic engagement. *American Sociological Review, 76*(4), 581–601. doi:10.1177/0003122411414815

Terriquez, V. (2015). Training young activists: Grassroots organizing and youths' civic and political trajectories. *Sociological Perspectives, 58*(2), 223–242. doi:10.1177/0731121414556473

Thoits, P. A. (2010). Stress and health: Major findings and policy implications. *Journal of Health and Social Behavior,)51*(Suppl.), S41–S53. doi:10.1177/0022146510383499

Thoits, P. A. (2011). Mechanisms linking social ties and support to physical and mental health. *Journal of Health and Social Behavior, 52*(2), 145–161. doi:10.1177/0022146510395592

Thompson, R., Proctor, L. J., English, D. J., Dubowitz, H., Narasimhan, S., & Everson, M. D. (2012). Suicidal ideation in adolescence: Examining the role of recent adverse experiences. *Journal of Adolescence, 35*(1), 175–186. doi:10.1016/j.adolescence.2011.03.003

Tilly, C., & Tarrow, S. (2015). *Contentious politics* (2nd ed.). New York, NY: Oxford University Press.

Timmermans, S., Orrico, L. A., & Smith, J. (2014). Spillover effects of an uninsured population. *Journal of Health and Social Behavior, 55*(3), 360–374. doi:10.1177/0022146514543523

Tocqueville, A. (1945). *Democracy in America* (Vol. 2). New York, NY: Vintage Books. (Originally published 1840)

Todd, N. R., Houston, J. D., & Suffrin, R. L. (2015). Applying affiliation social network analysis to understand interfaith groups. *Psychosocial Intervention, 24*(3), 147–154.

Toomey, A. H. (2011). Empowerment and disempowerment in community development practice: Eight roles practitioners play. *Community Development Journal, 46*(2), 181–195. doi:10.1093/cdj/bsp060

Torney-Purta, J. (2002). The school's role in developing civic engagement: A study of adolescents in twenty-eight countries. *Applied Developmental Science, 6*(4), 203–212.r4ire

Tough, P. (2008). *Whatever it takes: Geoffrey Canada's quest to change Harlem and America.* New York, NY: Houghton Mifflin.

Trickett, E. J. (1984). Toward a distinctive community psychology: An ecological metaphor for the conduct of community research and the nature of training. *American Journal of Community Psychology, 12*(3), 261–279. doi:10.1007/BF00896748

Trickett, E. J. (2011). Settings and empowerment. In M. S. Aber, K. I. Maton, & E. Seidman (Eds.), *Empowering settings and voices for social change* (pp. 94–106). New York, NY: Oxford University Press.

Tsouros, A. (2009). City leadership for health and sustainable development: The World Health Organization European Healthy Cities Network. *Health Promotion International, 24*(Suppl. 1), i4–i10. doi:10.1093/heapro/dap050

Turney, K. (2014). Stress proliferation across generations? Examining the relationship between parental incarceration and childhood health. *Journal of Health and Social Behavior, 55*(3), 302–319. doi:10.1177/0022146514544173

Umberson, D., Williams, K., Thomas, P. A., Liu, H., & Thomeer, M. B. (2014). Race, gender, and chains of disadvantage: Childhood adversity, social relationships, and health. *Journal of Health and Social Behavior, 55*(1), 20–38. doi:10.1177/0022146514521426

Underlid, K. (2007). Poverty and experiences of insecurity. A qualitative interview study of 25 long-standing recipients of social security. *International Journal of Social Welfare, 16*(1), 65–74.

Valente, T. W., Chou, C. P., & Pentz, M. A. (2007). Community coalition networks as systems: Effects of network change on adoption of evidence-based prevention. *American Journal of Public Health, 97*(3), 1–7. doi:10.2105/AJPH.2005.063644

van der Toorn, J., Feinberg, M., Jost, J. T., Kay, A. C., Tyler, T. R., Willer, R., & Wilmuth, C. (2015). A sense of powerlessness fosters system justification: Implications for the legitimation of authority, hierarchy, and government. *Political Psychology, 36*(1), 93–110. doi:10.1111/pops.12183

Vieno, A., Lenzi, M., Canale, N., & Santinello, M. (2014). Italian validation of the Sociopolitical Control Scale for Youth (SPCS-Y). *Journal of Community Psychology, 42*(4), 463–468. doi:10.1002/jcop.21621

Walker, E. T., & McCarthy, J. D. (2007). The influence of organizational structure, membership composition and resources on the survival of poor people's social movement organizations. In

M. Chen, R. Jhabvala, R. Kanbur, & C. Richards (Eds.), *Membership based organizations of the poor* (pp. 43–62). New York, NY: Routledge.

Wallace, D., & Wallace, R. (1998a). *A plague on your houses: How New York was burned down and national public health crumbled.* New York, NY: Verso.

Wallace, D., & Wallace, R. (1998b). Scales of geography, time, and population: The study of violence as a public health problem. *American Journal of Public Health, 88*(12), 1853–1858.

Wallace, D., & Wallace, R. (2000). Life and death in Upper Manhattan and the Bronx: Toward an evolutionary perspective on catastrophic social change. *Environment and Planning A, 32,* 1245–1266. doi:10.1068/a32208

Wallace, D., & Wallace, R. (2008). Urban systems during disasters: Factors for resilience. *Ecology and Society, 13*(1), 18.

Wallace, R., & Wallace, D. (1990). Origins of public health collapse in New York City: The dynamics of planned shrinkage, contagious urban decay and social disintegration. *Bulletin of the New York Academy of Medicine, 66*(5), 391–434.

Wallerstein, N. (1992). Powerlessness, empowerment, and health: Implications for health promotion programs. *American Journal of Health Promotion, 6*(3), 197.

Wallerstein, N. (1993). Empowerment and health: The theory and practice of community change. *Community Development Journal, 28*(3), 218–227. doi:10.1093/cdj/28.3.218

Wallerstein, N. (2002). Empowerment to reduce health disparities. *Scandinavian Journal of Public Health, 30*(59, Suppl.), 72–77. doi:10.1177/14034948020300031201

Wallerstein, N., & Bernstein, E. (1988). Empowerment education: Freire's ideas adapted to health education. *Health Education Quarterly, 15*(4), 379–394. doi:10.1177/109019818801500402

Walzer, N., Weaver, L., & McGuire, C. (2016). Collective impact approaches and community development issues. *Community Development, 47*(2), 156–166. doi:10.1080/15575330.2015.1133686

Wang, Q., Chen, X., & Chen, Y. (2011). Development of a scale to measure residents' psychological empowerment in Chinese urban community. *Journal of Community Psychology, 39*(2), 202–211. doi:10.1002/jcop.20427

Watts, R. J., Diemer, M. A., & Voight, A. M. (2011). Critical consciousness: Current status and future directions. *New Directions for Child and Adolescent Development, 134,* 43–57. doi:10.1002/cd.310

Watts, R. J., & Flanagan, C. (2007). Pushing the envelope on youth civic engagement: A developmental and liberation psychology perspective. *Journal of Community Psychology, 35*(6), 779–792. doi:10.1002/jcop.20178

Watts, R. J., & Hipolito-Delgado, C. P. (2015). Thinking ourselves to liberation?: Advancing sociopolitical action in critical consciousness. *The Urban Review, 47*(5), 847–867. doi:10.1007/s11256-015-0341-x

Watts, R. J., Williams, N. C., & Jagers, R. J. (2003). Sociopolitical development. *American Journal of Community Psychology, 31*(1/2), 185–194. doi:10.1023/A:1023091024140

Weaver, L. (2014). The promise and peril of collective impact. *The Philanthropist, 26*(1), 11–19.

Weick, K. E. (1984). Small wins. *American Psychologist, 39*(1), 40–49.

Wells, R., Ford, E. W., McClure, J. A., Holt, M. L., & Ward, A. (2007). Community-based coalitions' capacity for sustainable action: The role of relationships. *Health Education & Behavior, 34*(1), 124. doi:10.1177/1090198105277851

Wells, R., Ward, A. J., Feinberg, M., & Alexander, J. A. (2008). What motivates people to participate more in community-based coalitions? *American Journal of Community Psychology, 42*(1/2), 94–104. doi:10.1007/s10464-008-9182-z

Wernick, L. J. (2016). Critical consciousness development impact on social justice movement giving among wealthy activists. *Social Work Research.* doi:10.1093/swr/svw012

West, C. (2001). *Race matters.* New York, NY: Vintage.

West, C. (2014). *Black prophetic fire: Cornel West on Ella Baker (Part One).* Oakland, CA: Ella Baker Center. Retrieved from http://ellabakercenter.org/blog/2014/11/black-prophetic-fire-cornel-west-on-ella-baker-part-one

Western, B. (2014). Incarceration, inequality, and imagining alternatives. *The Annals of the American Academy of Political and Social Science, 651*(1), 302–306. doi:10.1177/0002716213503107

Western, B., & Rosenfeld, J. (2011). Unions, norms, and the rise in US wage inequality. *American Sociological Review, 76*(4), 513–537. doi:10.1177/0003122411414817

Westoby, P., & Owen, J. (2010). The sociality and geometry of community development practice. *Community Development Journal, 45*(1), 58–74. doi:10.1093/cdj/bsp005

White, M. (2017, January 19). Without a path from protest to power, the Women's March will end up like Occupy. *The Guardian.* Retrieved January 22, 2017, from https://www.theguardian.com/world/2017/jan/19/womens-march-washington-occupy-protest

Wildeman, C. (2014). Parental incarceration, child homelessness, and the invisible consequences of mass imprisonment. *The ANNALS of the American Academy of Political and Social Science, 651*(1), 74–96. doi:10.1177/0002716213502921

Wilke, L. A., & Speer, P. W. (2011). The mediating influence of organizational characteristics in the relationship between organizational type and relational power: An extension of psychological empowerment research. *Journal of Community Psychology, 39*(8), 972–986. doi:10.1002/jcop.20484

Wilkinson, R., & Pickett, K. (2010). *The spirit level: Why greater equality makes societies stronger.* New York, NY: Bloomsbury Press.

Wirth, L. (1945). Human ecology. *The American Journal of Sociology, 50*(6), 483–488.

Wisconsin State Journal. (2011). Transcript of prank Koch-Walker conversation. Retrieved March 31, 2016, from http://host.madison.com/wsj/transcript-of-prank-koch-walker-conversation/article_531276b6-3f6a-11e0-b288-001cc4c002e0.html

Wiseman, J., & Brasher, K. (2008). Community wellbeing in an unwell world: Trends, challenges, and possibilities. *Journal of Public Health Policy, 29*(3), 353–366. doi:10.1057/jphp.2008.16

Wolff, T. (2001). A practitioner's guide to successful coalitions. *American Journal of Community Psychology, 29*(2), 173–191. doi:10.1023/A:1010366310857

Wolff, T. (2010). *The power of collaborative solutions: Six principles and effective tools for building healthy communities.* San Francisco, CA: Jossey-Bass.

Wolff, T. (2016). Voices from the field: 10 places where collective impact gets it wrong. *The Nonprofit Quarterly,* April 28. Retrieved from https://nonprofitquarterly.org/2016/04/28/voices-from-the-field-10-places-where-collective-impact-gets-it-wrong/

Wolff, T., Minkler, M., Wolfe, S. M., Berkowitz, B., Bowen, L., Butterfoss, F. D., . . . Lee, K. S. (2016). Collaborating for equity and justice: Moving beyond collective impact. *The Nonprofit Quarterly, 23*(4), 42–53.

Wolfinger, R. E. (1960). Reputation and reality in the study of "community power." *American Sociological Review, 25*(5), 636–644.

Wong, N. T., Zimmerman, M. A., & Parker, E. A. (2010). A typology of youth participation and empowerment for child and adolescent health promotion. *American Journal of Community Psychology, 46*, 100–114. doi:10.1007/s10464-010-9330-0

Wood, R. L., Partridge, K., & Fulton, B. (2013). *Building bridges, building power: Developments in institution-based community organizing.* Longmont, CO: Interfaith Funders.

Woodall, J. R., Warwick-Booth, L., & Cross, R. (2012). Has empowerment lost its power? *Health Education Research, 27*(4), 742–745. doi:10.1093/her/cys064

World Bank. (2001). *World development report 2000/2001: Attacking poverty.* New York, NY: Oxford University Press.

World Health Organization (WHO). (1986). *Ottawa charter for health promotion.* Geneva, Switzerland: World Health Organization.

Wray-Lake, L., & Flanagan, C. A. (2012). Parenting practices and the development of adolescents' social trust. *Journal of Adolescence, 35*(3), 549–560. doi:10.1016/j.adolescence.2011.09.006

Wright, E. O. (1994). *Interrogating inequality: Essays on class analysis, socialism and Marxism.* New York, NY: Verso.

Wright, E. O. (2010). *Envisioning real utopias*. New York, NY: Verso.

Wright, E. O. (2013). Transforming capitalism through real utopias. *American Sociological Review,* *78*(1), 1–25. doi:10.1177/0003122412468882

Yan, M. C., & Sin, R. (2011). The resilience of the settlement-house tradition in community development: A study of neighborhood centers in San Francisco. *Community Development, 42*(1), 106–124. doi:10.1080/15575330.2010.488740

Yan, R., Bastian, N. D., & Griffin, P. M. (2015). Association of food environment and food retailers with obesity in US adults. *Health & Place, 33,* 19–24. doi:10.1016/j.healthplace.2015.02.004

Yates, M. D. (Ed.). (2010). *Wisconsin uprising: Labor fights back.* New York, NY: Monthly Review Press.

Youniss, J. (2011). Civic education: What schools can do to encourage civic identity and action. *Applied Developmental Science, 15*(2), 98–103. doi:10.1080/10888691.2011.560814

Yoshikawa, H., & Ramos Olazagasti, M. A. (2011). The neglected role of community narratives in culturally anchored prevention and public policy. In M. S. Aber, K. I. Maton, & E. Seidman (Eds.), *Empowering settings and voices for social change* (pp. 173–192). New York, NY: Oxford University Press.

Zaff, J. F., Kawashima-Ginsberg, K., Lin, E. S., Lamb, M., Balsano, A., & Lerner, R. M. (2011). Developmental trajectories of civic engagement across adolescence: Disaggregation of an integrated construct. *Journal of Adolescence, 34*(6), 1207–1220. doi:10.1016/j.adolescence.2011.07.005

Zakocs, R. C., & Edwards, E. M. (2006). What explains community coalition effectiveness? A review of the literature. *American Journal of Preventive Medicine, 30*(4), 351–361. doi:10.1016/j.amepre.2005.12.004

Zeldin, S. (2004). Youth as agents of adult and community development: Mapping the processes and outcomes of youth engaged in organizational governance. *Applied Developmental Science, 8*(2), 75–90. doi:10.1207/s1532480xads0802_2

Zeldin, S., Christens, B. D., & Powers, J. (2013). The psychology and practice of youth-adult partnership: Bridging generations for youth development and community change. *American Journal of Community Psychology, 51*(3–4), 385–397. doi:10.1007/s10464-012-9558-y

Zeldin, S., Krauss, S. E., Collura, J., Lucchesi, M., & Sulaiman, A. H. (2014). Conceptualizing and measuring youth-adult partnership in community programs: A cross national study. *American Journal of Community Psychology, 54*(3–4), 337–347. doi:10.1007/s10464-014-9676-9

Zhao, X., Haste, H., Selman, R. L., & Luan, Z. (2014). Compliant, cynical, or critical: Chinese youth's explanations of social problems and individual civic responsibility. *Youth & Society, 49*(8), 1123–1140. doi:10.1177/0044118x14559504

Zimmerman, M. A. (1990a). Taking aim on empowerment research: On the distinction between individual and psychological conceptions. *American Journal of Community Psychology, 18*(1), 169–177. doi:10.1007/BF00922695

Zimmerman, M. A. (1990b). Toward a theory of learned hopefulness: A structural model analysis of participation and empowerment. *Journal of Research in Personality, 24*(1), 71–86. doi:10.1016/0092-6566(90)90007-S

Zimmerman, M. A. (1995). Psychological empowerment: Issues and illustrations. *American Journal of Community Psychology, 23*(5), 581–599. doi:10.1007/BF02506983

Zimmerman, M. A. (2000). Empowerment theory: Psychological, organizational and community levels of analysis. In J. Rappaport & E. Seidman (Eds.), *Handbook of community psychology* (pp. 43–63). New York, NY: Kluwer Academic/Plenum.

Zimmerman, M. A., Ramírez-Valles, J., & Maton, K. I. (1999). Resilience among urban African American male adolescents: A study of the protective effects of sociopolitical control on their mental health. *American Journal of Community Psychology, 27*(6), 733–751. doi:10.1023/A:1022205008237

Zimmerman, M. A., Ramírez-Valles, J., Zapert, K. M., & Maton, K. I. (2000). A longitudinal study of stress-buffering effects for urban African-American male adolescent problem behaviors and mental health. *Journal of Community Psychology, 28*(1), 17–33.

Zimmerman, M. A., & Rappaport, J. (1988). Citizen participation, perceived control, and psychological empowerment. *American Journal of Community Psychology, 16*(5), 725–750. doi:10.1007/BF00930023

Zimmerman, M. A., & Zahniser, J. H. (1991). Refinements of sphere-specific measures of perceived control: Development of a sociopolitical control scale. *Journal of Community Psychology, 19*(2), 189–204. doi:10.1002/1520-6629(199104)19:2<189::AID-JCOP2290190210>3.0.CO;2-6

INDEX